Voice of the Soul

Learning to Work With and Talk About
Our Souls in a New Ways

By

Rev. Stephen Rodgers, MFT
Steve Bearden, PhD.

Dedications and Acknowledgements

From Steve Rodgers: I want to honor my family with this work. My mom and dad, Lynne and Walter, have always inspired me. My sister, Puddie, taught me in her life and still teaches me in her death, and my brother Bill has always been the best big brother I could hope for. My two sons, Luke and George are a constant source of joy and inspiration, even if they don't know it. My life is blessed. A special thanks to Dave Marshall who will never understand the depth of what our friendship has meant to me. His life is a witness to many.

I can't possibly list all those who have had an impact on my spiritual development and life but I would like to list a few; Rev. Alan Mack at the beginning of my more formal focus on ministry and spiritual development, Rev. Alan and Billie Houghton who taught me much about spiritual life in the real world, Rev. Dick Hunt, S.J. whose constant search for spirituality and openness to different traditions changed the direction and focus of my life in seminary and beyond, Lesley Sepetoski for her creative spirit, Don Riso whose work on the Enneagram from before the printing of his first book has inspired me, and all the people I have known in churches and schools I have served. Priscilla Young Rodgers and Jody and Chuck LaMonte who have always encouraged my journey, and of course to the spiritual forces of the cosmos. Also to the parishioners at Church of the Holy Spirit, Battle Ground, WA. who asked questions about the manuscript and encouraged the work.

Finally to my co-author Steve Bearden; professor, colleague, friend, and fellow traveler towards the One, I give great thanks for his creativity, grace, and belief.

TABLE OF CONTENTS

Preface   p.   5

1. Survey   7
2. Introduction and the Traits   9
3. The Continua—Intro   46
4. The Collaborative Unconscious   83
5. Niebuhr: Christ and Culture   89
6. Worship and Soul Types   90
7. Mark 2—How different types read scripture   97
8. Descriptions of the 32 Soul Types   99
9. Dreams   224
10. God and the Brain   243
11. Theory of growth (Steve Rodgers' overall theory)   252
12. Activities for Soul Growth   270
13. Glossary   330

PREFACE

People and faiths have different ideas about who and what we are, what this life is about and what happens upon our deaths. This book is based on the premise that we all have an eternal soul. A few assumptions we make are important to note up front although they will be discussed at greater length in the book.

1. We have no need or intention of proving the existence of the soul, we simply accept it exists. We believe there is ample anecdotal evidence, but acknowledge that is far from proof.
2. We do not concern ourselves as to when the soul was created, to do so from our perspective is not helpful.
3. We believe the soul will go on after our bodies die but do not discuss that aspect of the soul's existence. It is fully unknown and only conjecture and we won't truly know till we arrive--- contrary to what some may tell you.
4. We believe what is important is to actively work on developing our soul in the here and now. Having a mature soul matters to our lives and in the end matters to what we become in the next life. This is the premise of the book.
5. Finally, we believe we are in the world for a reason. We are to find a balance in the world between our spirituality and our worldliness. We are to be fully present to God and the transcendent as well as fully present to the world. This does not mean we do what the world says, but we are aware of it and understand that part of our existence is to serve the world, to be beacons of hope and light. This is not a call to isolationism, but a call to do what we are called to do and understand why.

This book started out of a discussion about the soul. We came to realize quickly that there is no consistent language with which to discuss our souls. We note that there are volumes to discuss the intricacies of the human psyche—our psychology—but little that specific about the soul. Often the two are confused and there are those who believe they are the same.

Our belief is they are different and yet intimately connected. Each has a place in our being and each has its sources of information it uses to grow and impact the other. Our belief and hope are that you will find this book helpful, that you will be able to see yourself and specifically your soul, in a new way. We hope this gives people some new ways of discussing their spiritual growth as well as some very practical ways of growing.

It is our intent to be value free. That is to say we do not intend to make one trait of the soul better than another or one type better than another.

We hope you find this work interesting, informative, and practical. We have tried our best to not get technical or complex, the book is meant for everyone. We appreciate any feedback you can give us. This is a work in progress. If new editions come forth down the road it will be because of input we have had from those letting us know what works and what doesn't.

The layout of the book is straightforward as you will see in the table of contents. We talk about the overall theory, then the various traits, and then each of the subtypes. The second part of the book is primarily work by Steve Rodgers. It shows how this work is connected to Neurobiology (the brain), the world of Chaos Theory, and finishes with a theory Steve R. has about life in general. Each of these sections can be read independently although they do discuss the traits. They are all non-technical and avoid the scientific jargon as much as possible. If you do not have these chapters in the book you have purchased you can find them at the website: voiceofthesoul.info.

It should be noted that when speaking of God we use both "he" and "she." We believe God is gender neutral and this is our way of helping foster that understanding.

Apologies from Steve Rodgers for any errors of formatting or typos.

We encourage you to take the survey first to find out what "type" you are before you start. You can take it for free and get instant results at : voiceofthesoul.info. The reason for this is that once you know the traits you may be more likely to pick certain answers to fit a way you want to perceive yourself rather than who you actually are. We understand that for many, identifying your soul as unique and different than your psyche is difficult. Our hope is that you will be more able to do this as you work with these concepts.

GLOSSARY: There is a glossary at the end that has brief working definitions for this book for terms used you may not know or that may have a variety of definitions.

ACTIVITIES: There is a lengthy list of activities at the end of the book that will give ideas of what you can do with each of the traits to move towards balance. We encourage you to send us other ideas you have found that we can add to the list.

THE SURVEY:

The survey can be found at voiceofthesoul.info. At this time it is about 60 questions and is in the process of being researched so we can consider it a valid and reliable instrument. We encourage you to take the survey at least once a year to see if what you are doing in your life is having an impact on your soul. In taking this survey we encourage you to go with what your initial response is. Don't put a lot of time into each question, you will probably out think yourself.

On all surveys, honestly is important. Sure, you can fake your way to being one way or another, but what good does that do you? The hope is that we all want to grow. We grow by starting from where we truly are, not where we'd like to be. There are no value judgments within the types, no one type is better or worse than the others. All of them have their strengths and weaknesses.

If you would like here are a few questions you can answer that will give you a very rough idea of where you might be in this type system. With each question you have to choose one or the other, the balancing and fine tuning comes later, right now you are just trying to see which way you lean on each trait. You will learn more about each trait as you move through the book and you may change your mind based on what you read---that's a good thing. Please note that there are no right or wrong answer, picking one over the other does not make you more or less "spiritual." There are three questions for each category. Whichever one has two or three of the same letter, that is what you should assume you are to start with.

Transcendence—Meaning

1.   When things happen to you do you think about them more from a spiritual perspective (S) or a more psycho-social one (I)?
2.   When you read the bible do you tend to focus more on the deeper spiritual truths (S) or on the more practical and social implications (I)?
3.   Do you remember your dreams (yes is an S, no is an I)and think about what they mean for you (yes is an S and no is an I) and seek spiritual guidance from God in understanding them (yes is an S, no is an I).

Holiness—Self-Identity

1.   Do you feel you are unique, special and sacred in God's eyes at all times (A) or do you not think a lot about how God sees you or perhaps not think about those ideas (T)?
2.   When you describe yourself to someone else, is a significant part of that identity dealing with the spiritual side of life (A) or is it more on the psycho-social end of life (T)?
3.   Is who you are as a spiritual being and as a child of God a significant part of your day to day idea of who you are (A) or is it more in the background (T)?

Connectedness—Relationships

1.   In most conversations with people do you tend to talk more about "spiritual" things (M) or more worldly things (E) ?

2. Is your relationship with God found more internally (M) or do you find God more through others and what you do in the world (E)?
3. Are you more of a concrete person in relationships, working more with what presents itself to you (E) or are you always looking for ways to deepen the relationship and perhaps bring the spiritual into it (M)?

Imagination—Creativity

1. Are you a more logical person (R) or intuitive (N)?
2. When you have creative ideas do they come more from within (N) or making connections to things outside of you (R)?
3. Do you find a lot of spiritual "coincidences" in your life (N)? Do you go through life and just take things as they come (R)?

Call—Purpose

1. Do you feel you have a direct Call from God (D) or do you feel God gives you principles and lets you figure out what the Call is (P)?
2. Is fulfilling your purpose in life something you spend more time thinking and praying about (D) or doing (P)
3. Do you find your Call more from God directly (D) or from God working in and through your natural talents, interests, and how you find God in the world (P)?

INTRODUCTION: SPIRITUAL IDENTITY

What do humans come into the world with? What do we leave the world with and are they different? We believe we enter this plane of life with a spiritual identity, a soul. As we grow as humans that soul has the potential to mature as does the rest of us. This book will not debate when or how that soul arrives in our bodies. We accept as fact that at birth every human being has a core spiritual identity that is unique.

9

Humans are complex beings whose identities are in formation over a lifetime. Each of us has an emotional, intellectual, physical, social, and cultural self at minimum. Personal human identity is a complex amalgam of genetics, environmental influences, and experiences which are all mined for personal idiosyncratic meaning. Our belief is one's spiritual identity is the most basic and fundamental of our natures and is the most overlooked and cared for. We enter this world primarily with a genetic and physical identity. We are predisposed towards certain ways of being, certain attitudes towards things. Science has yet to explain this, but we know it to be true. There is a predilection of the offspring of abusers to become abusers, of addicts to become addicted. This is certainly not a guarantee, but whether biological or emotional, there is that predisposition.

We know when we are born, attachment to a caring individual is important. The strain on the developing mind of not having attachments has profound consequences. For example, how we relate to others, how secure we feel in our own skin, how resilient we are when things happen to us, and how open we are to the spiritual realm of life, are all affected by how we were raised as children. Our upbringing does not write the script of our lives, but does set some rudimentary constructs within us. All of us have accepted and rebelled against parts of our childhood. Those who have children probably do some things you experienced as a child and avoid others. For most, our religion is what we were raised with. For example, we shouldn't be surprised the predominant religion of people in America is Christianity and in Egypt is Islam. Those have been the dominant religious traditions of those countries for many generations. The culture accepts them as the norm and most people fit into norms. Our tendency as humans is to move within comfort zones, to do what is comfortable and to conform to what the norms of any given society are. This is who we are, our identity. In and of itself, this is not right or wrong, it just is.

If one is a church-goer, how often is one's spiritual identity a conversation piece at fellowship hour? How often is even one's personal relationship with God a topic of discussion? We may tend to keep hidden or remain unaware of that which is at the very core of our being. Perhaps it's because we lack the tools to express our inner lives because we have not been taught how. Or it may be because we don't know that much about our faith, our beliefs, or our spiritual needs. In order to become a doctor, one spends 19 years in school and between 3 and 7 years in residency. Would you let someone perform surgery on you that had not made it through grade school? By and large doctors know about medicine and are constantly learning more. In the larger picture of what being human means, we believe our spiritual identities are the core of our existence and yet we seem to attend to them relatively little. This is an important question to ask ourselves: Why do we put so little time and effort into developing the spiritual and transcendent side of our being? Just as becoming good at a musical instrument or a non-native language takes conscious effort, so too does becoming spiritually mature.

Our belief is that our relationship to the Creator and with the created order engages more of our lives and takes more effort than any other relationship we have. In no small part, we think this is because we can't look God in the face (at least most of the time). We don't always experience our relationship with God as a two-way conversation. We experience this relationship as more one-way, us to God. Some may feel they have an adequate understanding and don't need more. Moses, Elijah, Jonah, and Jesus are all good examples of people that wanted God to change his mind, but in the end listened and responded to the one that created them. In the end, they listened with the core of their being, not only with their intellectual, social, and emotional selves, but with their souls. They all had to let go of some things in order to find those answers and to hear the still small voice of God. Even before the crucifixtion, Jesus asks God to take the cup from him, but in the end says, "Not my will but thine."

Their efforts were not measured by quantity as much as quality. We believe we are created by the Creator to listen, to be still and know; not to clutter the conversation with our own floatsum and jetsum that are irrelevant other than in our own minds. Our souls are the essential ear bringing the voice of God into our physical minds.

To some degree all persons are labeled. One may be a geek, jock, brainiac, bible-thumper, or a bully. Sometimes people rebel against those labels and at times they may wear them with pride. Ultimately, each of us needs to accept responsibility for who we are, we can't let others have undo influence in how we define ourselves. There are certainly times in one's life when others will be key players in shaping our identity. As our identities are formed in life, there are pressures from all sides. John Dunne in Meditation XVII said, "No man is an island unto himself." Hilary Clinton wrote a book called *It Takes A Village* (Simon and Schuster, 1996). We are all part of and impacted by the communities of which we are part. When growing up, we have very limited choices as to what community or communities we allow to influence our lives. When we are adults we usually have the freedom and authority (whether we use them or not) to make those choices on our own.

Physically, we know a person often judges them self and others by physical attributes or athletic accomplishments. This begins at a very early age. At times parents push or force their children into activities such as sports which have the potential to lay heavy baggage on them in relation to their identity. Our intentions may or may not be pure, moral, or righteous. Many of life's problems could be solved by understanding our personal intent.

Young children are judged by intelligence, even though we know for a fact many children do not develop their intellectual abilities early on and some early bloomers fade. We notice socially aggressive and passive behaviors, whether you stand with or against your cultural heritage, and of course, what religious tradition you are. Wars have been fought over these things and families have disintegrated over them.

The challenge is this; how does one sift through all of that "stuff" to find who they really are? What is at the core of my being? How is that essence in line with or counter to the identity I now accept as "me?" Is it possible to isolate parts of our identity? Is there a process to discover the difference or is all of this mental gymnastics seeking to explain things that in reality don't exist?

On a philosophical level, we realize we can never fully and truly know one's core because everything we think, do, and say, is filtered through the lens of who I am right now. It is not possible to wipe away all bias in our view. We do believe we can catch some glimpses of our essence, that we can see some uniquenesses our spiritual identities have in relation to our other identities. We feel giving spiritual identity its rightful place in the schema of who we are in order to most properly align ourselves with the created order and the intentions of the Creator is essential for a deep understanding of the self.

Just stop reading for a few minutes, get out a piece of paper and pencil and see if you can write down ten things about your spiritual identity that wouldn't fall under one of the other categories we have mentioned; emotions, intellect, physical, social, cultural.

Tick, tock, tick, tock.

Most people find this task difficult at best. We tend to blend and blur the distinctions between these categories. "My relationship with God," some people will write. But what does that relationship look like? "I feel his presence, I see him at work in the world, I meditate on God's word and find God there." But all of these fit into the categories above, they are not uniquely outside them. How is the presence of God different than the presence of one you love? How do you see God differently in the world than you do a person or a tree? Push yourself, can you verbalize an idea that is uniquely outside them?

Most cultures are not spiritually oriented, their attention is on survival and success in this realm. As a result, we do not have a language with which to discuss our spiritual identities. The Christian tradition talks about the eternal nature of the soul, but there is great conflict about what it is. When we die; do we maintain our bodies, do we grow wings, do we actually have the same identities we had on earth, do we become spirits outside of space and time, how do we communicate, and is there a pecking order in the next life? What do we know about our spiritual lives, identities, and souls?

Books have been written about seeing the light in near death experiences and about people passing over to other realms of existence. People tell us things they learned from someone who had passed away they shouldn't have known. Is the only explanation-- that they talked with a dead person? The world of Physics is constantly changing and continues to suggest new ways of understanding physical processes. Newton started the modern age of understanding how the physical universe worked. Einstein helped us understand that at the atomic and sub-atomic levels, Newton's laws didn't work. Recently we have come to learn there appears to be "dark energy and matter" that we can't see, but that weighs more than the physical universe we can see. The more we learn, the more our views of the universe have to adjust to the new reality.

In a similar vein of inquiry, can we learn more about the soul? Is what was known about the soul thousands of years ago the end? Have we learned anything about the soul in the past 2000 years? It seems reasonable that the Creator would want us to have deeper and deeper understandings as time moves on? Why let us comprehend the physical universe but not the spiritual?

So, you might be asking, how do you know this dimension of life and of personality exists? How do we open ourselves to something new, to deeper understandings that may go against what we have held to be true? As we said earlier, there is no proof of an eternal soul nor that we are born with an identity other than the gene pool and what our environment gives us. But we believe there are hints, tracks in the snow, evidence like the wind blowing in the trees or on your face.

First, there are the narratives of experience. Untold throngs of people have experienced something they understand to be outside this world, something holy other or transcendent. Those in A.A. acknowledge this as their second step, the acknowledgement that a higher power is needed to move to the next stage of recovery. We have people of all faiths connecting with God or something beyond the realm of this world or beyond the realm of our most immediate experience. Like the wind, we do not physically see the soul; but we see how it impacts our lives and the lives of others. We see it in miracles, bursts of creativity, our dreams, and through our own development of self.

Secondly there are the stories of synchronicity which we will go into more in depth later. Have you ever "known" something before it was known or had an experience of meaning or connection beyond all understanding? Modern physics can't explain it, but they know atoms know at some level what is happening across the universe. *The Unconscious Quantum: Metaphysics in Modern Physics and Cosmology* (Victor J. Stenger , Prometheus Books, 1995). If this is true, why is it such a far reach to believe humans have a connection to God or other humans through a transcendent force?

Thirdly and perhaps most importantly, people go through lives without a connection to the transcendent and it doesn't take long to see the hole in their lives. They may cover it up with busyness, money, and things, but talk with them and the void is obvious. We see the inability to talk about the spiritual realm or perhaps even denying its existence.

There are different levels of connection. We can know about something purely through our minds. Most have never been to the moon, but we can learn a lot about it from literature, television, seeing it through a telescope or reading on a computer. Those who have actually landed on the moon, speak from a different level of connection, one that joins the sensory to the intellectual. This does not place a value judgment on that connection or experience, but it does place them in a different realm. Our various levels of attachment to things speaks strongly of these connections.

One can't buy a relationship with the soul, one must work at it. All living things need nourishment. Plants send out roots, or trap insects. Primates learn strategies to crack open shells, attract insects to sticks or work as a team to overwhelm the prey or to protect themselves. Humans need to exert effort, some of it unconsciously, to exist. Why would the spiritual realm be different? One part of the Buddhist eightfold path is Right Effort. Jesus exhorts us to count the cost of discipleship. Muslims follow the five pillars of faith which are all about putting forth effort in order to deepen the relationship with Allah. This book does not make the claim your soul can only grow when in relationship with God. We do believe the soul can't mature as deeply without that relationship. We also believe the soul is eternally active, whether acknowledged or not. You may have an innate ability for music. Without practice, the ability will remain innate and inert, you will never play a beautiful piece of music.

One final thought before we delve into the traits of the soul. Throughout history, the soul has been seen as a metaphor of things in life. The soul is like a tree, a castle, works in ways not dissimilar to physics or chaos theory, or is a type of relationship. We always come at the soul from the world and imprint the world onto the soul. What if in reality we have that backwards? Why not seek to understand the soul, which after all is eternal, and see how it speaks to the world? Perhaps the world is a reflection of the soul. Maybe if we more deeply understand the ways of the soul we could speak more clearly to physicists, doctors, therapists, and teachers. There are some books that do this in a circuitous way, but in the end the ideas are behind the curve. The Tao Of Physics is a brilliant book. It's a book of hindsight, joining the world of spirit and physics together, demonstrating how each is a reflection of the other. But why not push that envelope? Why not use the soul as one of the core essences of the universe to understand the created order? Can the soul in and of itself give new insight into dark matter and energy, chaos theory, cultural ups and downs, healing, and how to make it work more often, and the basic cornerstone of everything that is human; relationships? We believe the soul can.

At the core of this endeavor is the understanding that the traits we are giving to the soul are in fact traits of the created order. Because science can't measure them, they are discounted. But if in reality the universe is both physical and spiritual, we avoid the spiritual to our peril. They feed one another, all things feed into the one thing---God.

One of the things we find interesting is how easy it seems to be for theists to say, "I don't know, perhaps it's just a mystery," and how difficult that same statement is for scientists. God gives us brains to think, to challenge and to discover. God does not expect us to stop thinking or finding new things out about the created order. God loves scientists. God gets frustrated when science is used to destroy rather than to create and when people fail to acknowledge that on the human level, mystery may be an ultimate answer.

So let's look at some of the characteristics of the soul as truly distinct.

Trait 1: TRANSCENDENCE : Meaning

Our souls are that aspect of our being that go beyond what the mental and physical parts of our being grasp. It is the soul that directly experiences the nature of God. Just as God is a spiritual being, so too our souls are wholly spiritual. They are in our bodies, but transcend them. Transcendence is at the essence of the soul. Souls are not bound by space and time, they transcend all earthly concepts and parameters. In this sense they are a mystery. They have not had a full voice because of the mystery. We can engage and converse with the mystery while not attempting to fully comprehend or define it. To do so would be to deny the very essence of its transcendence. One way of seeing this is in relation to culture. If you were to visit China never having learned anything about it, you would miss a great deal of what was going on. Were you to speak fluent Chinese and studied China, your experience would be different, but still not that of a native.

The most obvious characteristic of the soul, is that it has the potential to help people transcend normal ways of being and becoming human. It motivates depth and growth in many areas of our lives. The traits of the soul are uniquely different from earthly characteristics while at the same time infusing them. This is obvious because for those who acknowledge its existence, there is no proof and yet we admit to its influence in our lives. To transcend means to go beyond, to surpass the limits of what we normally know. Our souls are designed to help us maximize the potential and even go beyond the accepted limits of our genetic, social, intellectual, and psychological lives. Our souls affect and are affected by the other aspects of our lives, but also have independence, an independence based on their relationship with the transcendent.

We believe the transcendent aspect of our nature is connected to the eternal within the universe. As the scriptures say in I Corinthians 13:8, "Love never fails. But where there are prophecies, they will cease; where there are tongues, they will be stilled; where there is knowledge, it will pass away"----except that which is eternal, one's spiritual identity. This connection between the spiritual and the physical worlds, the eternal and the temporal, is what aligns people with the purpose for which they exist. Just as we know how critical it is for babies to attach to a caregiver in the first months of life, our souls need to re-connect with the eternal in order to grow, mature, and be in relationship with the rest of the transcendent universe and in communion with our immanent natures.

Some people talk about not being able to "feel" God, hear the voice of God or experience God's presence. We wonder if, at least in part, this is because they are neglectful or ignorant of their capacity of transcendence. How can a purely transcendent being communicate with a purely material being? One of the reasons God became Jesus, was so the transcendent could become more immanent, to call us to become more transcendent and to be aware of the transcendent embodied in the immanent.

Many religious traditions have this sense. Zen Buddhism tells us we can't find this nature unless we let go of all preconceptions about reality. In the end most Buddhist schools believe that journeying to have a connection to a personal transcendent reality is ignorance. On the other hand they claim that clinging to the world will only deepen that state of being. A person needs to let go of all that to find the truth. We agree, we just happen to believe the reality at the end of that process is different.

Jesus tells us we can't find ourselves until we die to ourselves (Matthew 16:24-25). Zen believes we find the transcendent by being transcendent, by being shocked out of our reality. The famous koan, "What is the sound of one hand clapping?" helps us see there is no logical answer, one must move beyond logic. Christ tells us if we have faith of a mustard seed we can move mountains-------how is that a rational concept? If we try to find, evaluate, and grow the soul only on rational grounds, we will lose. We negate the transcendent nature of our being as well as missing an opportunity to more fully understand the totality of who we are.

The Bhagvad Gita, a Hindu scripture tells us, "Shake off this fever of ignorance. Stop hoping for worldly rewards. Fix your mind on the Atman. Be free from the sense of ego," counsels Krishna (BG 48). "You dream you are the doer, you dream that action is done, you dream that action bears fruit. It is your ignorance, it is the world's delusion that gives you these dreams" (BG 5). "Seek this knowledge and comprehend clearly why you should seek it: such, it is said, are the roots of true wisdom: ignorance, merely, is all that denies them (BG 13)" "When men have thrown off their ignorance, they are free from pride and delusion. They have conquered the evil of worldly attachment. They live in constant union with the Atman. All craving has left them. They are no longer at the mercy of opposing sense-reactions. Thus they reach that state which is beyond all change." (BG 15)."

Islam says that in order to explain the complexity of unity of God and of the divine nature, the Qur'an uses 99 terms referred to as "Excellent Names of Allah" (Sura 77:180). Tawhid constitutes the foremost article of the Muslim profession. Tawhid is the core of monotheism, the idea of the Oneness of God's divinity. To attribute divinity to a created entity is the only unpardonable sin mentioned in the Qur'an.

These previous paragraphs give but a tiny view into how different the world's religions are in their description and understanding of the soul and the divine Creator.

This transcendent nature of our spiritual identity is like the wind. One doesn't actually see the wind, one can't catch it in a jar, one can only see its effect. Wind is created by high and low pressure masses of air colliding, along with the movement of the earth revolving. Forecasters have gotten much better at predicting where a hurricane or tornado might appear, but the full mechanics of them are still a mystery. We hope our writing is another step towards understanding the soul; how it matures or regresses and what drives those processes.

We can feel the soul within us. We can see how our spiritual identity impacts our lives and how it connects to the universe and to others. We know it is an emotional part of our being that is both sacred and profane. We are able to sense something in our minds and hearts that is larger than simply being human, we feel a connection to others above and beyond any earthly connection we may have. Our notions transcend this plane of existence and awareness. The bible speaks of the Holy Spirit giving people the gift of speaking in tongues. This non-comprehensible language is not unique to Christianity, but its purpose is fairly common to all traditions—to speak in the language of the transcendent because earthly languages fall short. Philipians 4:7 tells us, "And the peace of God, which transcends all understanding, will guard your hearts and your minds in Christ Jesus." A feeling that comes from God transcends our reality.

Carl Jung, a well-known figure in the field of psychology talks about a temenos, a sacred space that is safe and protected, where creative energies are kept in and interruptions and bad energies are kept out. This represents our goal and ideal; a temenos for our spiritual identities. Originally, a temenos was a piece of land reserved for kings and royalty. Temples were considered temenos' for the gods. Tibetan Buddhism uses construction of a mandala as a temenos. They are sacred "pictures," usually symmetrical that represent balance and wholeness. All of the outer layers are protecting the inner space, the temenos. The layers are reflective of our lives, of the world, of the universe. What do you do to protect the spiritual part of your life now? Do you have internal and external spaces that are truly sacred for you?

How do we engage this transcendent aspect of our nature? The easiest answer is to live according to the purposes for which you were created. How do we find that? How is it different than who I am? There are no definitive answers, but there are directional one's. We believe there are no absolutes other than a few and one is that you have a unique place and purpose in the universe and the Creator knows what it is. This purpose may change during your life, it may change many times in accordance with the needs of the world and your position within that network, but let's stop for a moment. When is the last time you sat still for 30 minutes, emptied your mind of all the junk you think about that really isn't that important, and just listened. Elijah experienced it as the still small voice of God (1 Kings 19:12-13). This focusing attention on that which lies beyond ourselves and at the deepest center of our being has also been called practicing the presence of God, the Sacrament of the present moment, and the cloud of unknowing. In order to truly listen, we must shut up, still the mind. Most people find it almost impossible. We have become so used to cluttering our minds, we cannot quiet them down. Some believe dreams are God's way of speaking to us because we're incapable of listening while we are awake. Many people don't remember their dreams, perhaps partly because they don't quiet their minds down, even in sleep, or perhaps they fear having a relationship with the transcendent. The center of transcendence is meaning. How do we find meaning in the world? How do we use our souls to discover that meaning, even when the world may be giving us different meanings?

What is it we are actually listening to when we pray and meditate, when we still our minds enough to hear the transcendent? When we are in a conversation with others, we hear through a series of mental lenses. We bring all of our biases, opinions, dreams, and thoughts to bear on what is said. Have you ever thought you fully understood something being said or asked, but in reality you misinterpreted? Look how many times Jesus challenges the Jewish leadership and their lack of understanding of the Old Testament scriptures. They say one level of meaning based on their transcendent system and Jesus saw another. Look at the current idea of global warming. You would think it is pure science, facts are facts. Even scientists view "facts" differently which is why there is a significant debate on the issue.

One of the differences between a good and a bad counselor or therapist is the good ones are able to hear what is truly being said in spite of the filters in their own minds. This is true of all listening behaviors; to fully hear, you do your best to put aside your filters---for the moment.

No one is capable of seeing the world or hearing without the influence of our internal filters. We can be cognizant of those filters and decrease their influence with effort. This is not the same as giving them up, changing, or surrendering. We simply make a conscious choice to enter the world of another for a period of time, to see the world through their lenses. Debaters are often called on to vehemently defend a view that is the exact opposite of what they believe. They learn to see the issue through another set of eyes. They learn to hold their own opinions and passions at bay for the sake of confidently trying to win the debate. Even if we are on the side of a debate with which we agree, we spend time researching what the other side believes because we know they will be attacking our side and knowing what they will throw at you is very helpful.

It is how Jesus so quickly and fully understood others. While being supremely confident of being right, he heard not only the words and arguments of others, but also their fears that kept them from truth. His concern was primarily getting people to let go of their false notions for true ones, of disintegrating boxes they had put themselves, others, and God into that kept them from a full life. To hear the transcendent means we need to be willing to hear the impossible, to listen to that which may blast our filters to bits. Think about it this way; do you honestly believe everything you think is actually true? Do you believe that if you were elected to be the president of a country or of the world and everyone did what you said, all would be well? If not, then can you point to which ideas are wrong? If you could, you would probably change them. If you really believe you could be a great and benevolent dictator, perhaps something else needs to be checked. God knows you better than you know yourself. God knows which of your ideas need to change, but you won't hear God's voice if you are full of filters. Elijah had filters. He wanted to see God in the wind, fire, and earthquakes, but God wasn't there (I Kings 19). Finally, he let go of those lenses and heard God as the still small voice within. God called him to something he didn't want. God persuaded him to change his beliefs and filters. That is the process of being in communion with the transcendent.

Try it, set a clock for 30 minutes, sit and see what happens. See if you get one minute of solid internal silence in that time. We are talking about mental silence, no thoughts. It takes great effort. Later on we will talk more about this process and how to find this inner stillness. Even those who have been working at emptying their minds for many years, many hours a day, still have trouble. In the end, sitting is one of the purest and easiest ways to the transcendent nature of our being. In those moments of silence, wisdom and clarity may arrive, you see things you haven't seen before, understand things that have been cloudy, and your heart is filled with a sense that comes through no earthly means. Every religious tradition has a variety of methods used for stilling the mind and sitting. At its simplest, sitting is habitual and habits are learned. We place ourselves in the presence of the transcendent. Our minds need to be in a space where they are not occupied with other things like walking or listening to music. This is not to say you can't see or hear the transcendent via any means, but simply sitting and clearing the mind is the most consistently direct way. Science has proven the benefits of meditation and clearing our minds. What they haven't and cannot show is the connection established with the transcendent universe and the power such a connection brings into our lives. Newberg and Waldman in **How God Changes your Brain** (Ballantine/Random House—2009) and others learn anecdotally what takes place. We are seeing how the brain is physically working during these times of insight and stillness, but science can't measure transcendency—their filters are far too structured and limited.

   We believe we all have the capacity to engage the transcendent. The mind is phenomenal. We can use this powerful tool to rationally isolate the more worldly parts of our lives, to separate that which is good and creative from that which is bad and destructive. To some degree we can isolate our social, psychological, biological, cultural, and anthropological selves. We can pigeonhole ourselves with all kinds of personality, genetic, and cultural tests. We could build a map of who we are on the wall and trace most of those "selves" back to someone or somewhere in our lives. We grow, we interact with the world, and are shaped by those experiences. We are all in the process of becoming, the past invests and imprints itself onto the present and into the future. We, to some degree, determine how these experiences are processed and used to make us who we become. Our active will can bridge the gap to the transcendent or blow it up.

Our will is one of the prime agents we use to change. Right effort in the end is an act of will. We consciously or unconsciously make choices to move toward the transcendent or away from it. By choosing to do nothing, we move away. People with very active minds enjoy this pathway to the soul, even though quite arduous and in the end not getting them to the more irrational nature of the soul. The mental constructs of the soul and the logical framework the Creator has instilled in the universe are available to us even though they are not an end in themselves. Let us be clear: The soul and transcendency are only irrational because of our limited knowledge and cognitive abilities. They are not irrational at all in their natural state of being. When we become fully transcendent beings, it will all make perfectly rational sense or maybe not (a bit of Zen). So we should not stop seeking answers to the questions that remain wrapped in mystery, the questions we feel are not without answers. However, don't count on them becoming clear. Enjoy the journey and the mystery.

Martin Buber talks about the "I- Thou" relationship with God. In this most intimate and holy of relationships, we come to understand who we are in light of the Creator (**I-Thou,** Martin Buber, Scribner, 1958.) . If we are wise, we do not deny our connectedness to the Creator; we fully embrace it, welcome it, and develop that intimacy, desiring to be at one. Rudolf Otto (**The Idea of the Holy,** Rudolph Otto, Oxford University Press, 1923) talks about the "holy other" who is beyond all things, yet is in a relationship with all things. We need to find and accept the holiness within ourselves even as we reach out to the holiness of God that is the transcendent journey of finding our spiritual identities.

Transcendence then is at the root of our soul. Our soul is able to venture where the mind, in and of itself, can't. This nature within us exists in all humans, whether acknowledged or not. We make a choice to seek our souls or to deny them.

Our souls act as centers of meaning. Spiritually oriented people see the world differently than those who are more worldly and temporally oriented. We all need meaning in our lives. We create meaning both from the world around us and what our senses give us as well as our internal lives and minds. Most of us, if we are honest, have some things we believe in that are not right. We live in delusion. At times delusion can actually keep us safe or can act as a defense mechanism that protects us from ourselves or an idea that may damage us in the short term. In the long run, truth is always better and the soul seeks truth, especially deep truths.

Many of us have had times in our lives where we think one thing but inside we feel or sense something different. Our transcendent souls have access to the infinitude of the transcendent realm, they are not limited by our small brains. Their meaning system has the potential to transpose the mind of God onto our own minds.

What does this all mean? Why am I here? Why do things happen the way they do? What is the meaning for you behind any given event? Take a few minutes, pick an event that has happened to you. Think about what that means to you and where that meaning comes from? Dig deep, go back, think about how your meaning system developed and what part of that, if any, comes directly from God and the transcendent as opposed to the world. God is not against gaining meaning from your senses and your brain, we believe he just doesn't want it to be the only source.

Trait 2: HOLINESS: SELF-IDENTITY

We just mentioned the idea of being holy. In scriptures this word is rich with meaning. Included in these are: clean, sacred, and set apart. We believe while all of creation is valuable and important, humanity has a unique spot on this planet. Humans are the most fully conscious of all life, we have more power to create and destroy than other creatures, and we believe we are more fully able to relate to the Creator out of will rather than out of instinct. God has set us apart. We are called to be different. We are called more than other creatures to bridge the gap between the sacred and the profane, the transcendent and the immanent. In the Genesis 1 creation story we are made last, the pinnacle of all that God created. In the second version, Genesis 2, God creates us and then builds the much of the world around us. We are called on to name things and naming was and is very important. In Genesis 1 God creates man and woman at the same time. In Genesis 2, God creates man, creatures and then woman out of man because animals aren't good enough for man, he is lonely. We are created with the capacity to co-create with the Divine. One symbol of that relationship is the creation naming command. The naming of something gives it an immediate place, meaning, and power in the world. There is a reason why some families name their children after themselves or ancestors (jr., III, IV). Why is the most popular name in Islam is Mohammed? Consider the time people spend naming their children or how many focus groups are created to name a new product or slogan. This is not to say the planet and all of creation are not important, they are. If the world's relationship with the Creator was strong, we wouldn't be where we are. There is only one creature on the planet that has the ability to fundamentally change the way of the world for better or for worse—Humanity.

A great deal has been written about being holy. We have listed a few in the bibliography. We'll touch on a few of the attributes that connects our more transcendent nature to our more temporal one. We believe holiness includes attributes that make it possible for us to nurture our souls.

Below you see a list of potential opposites. Rarely is a person purely on one end of the spectrum or the other, but two things are important as you move down the list and try to see where you are on each scale. First, let's understand the ways of the world tend to pull us to the left, our worldly selves are not uncomfortable moving towards or living with those attributes although it may not be politically correct to admit such. It's not that the world can't be altruistic, free or persuasive, it's just not human tendency. In order to fully live out the right hand side, our transcendent souls must at least be in balance if not dominant. Think about people who live lives that embrace those characteristics. Most of them, if not all, will be viewed as saints. They will be people in a religious tradition. They will claim their power to live that life comes not from them, but from a connection to a greater force or at least a deep understanding of the transcendent. We will only look at a few of these in depth, but we do encourage you to think about each of them; to discuss with someone else these concepts and ask what is keeping you from moving to the right (or left) more fully, why you are uncomfortable where you are, or why you feel the left hand side is a good thing—which they can be. They just aren't the whole thing. We understand that ruthless honest is necessary for this assessment which is one of many reasons why we encourage you to do it with others. We value ourselves by being courageous enough to speak openly about where we are and who we are. Others provide a checks and balance system for self-delusion which is rampant in the world. Finally, we find more wisdom in a community of seekers than on our own. Colliding filters and lenses provide insight, novelty, and creativity that can't be found in isolation.

Self-centered	Altruistic
Selfish	Selfless
Autocratic	Collaborative
Destructive	Creative
Resistant/Stubborn	Willing
Ego Driven	Spirit Driven
Fear	Courage
I-It or It-It	I-Thou
Isolated	Communal
Parasitic	Symbiotic
Coercive	Persuasive
Live more in the past	Live in the now and future
Shame/guilt	Grace/redemption
Enslaved	Free
Guarded	Open
Self-Doubt	Self-acceptance
Dominates	Empowers

We will discuss only a few of these continuums at this point.

Isolated/Communal-----We were created as social creatures. Many people grow up being taught to be independent, when in reality we are designed to be interdependent. We believe independence is an illusion. Some see a lack of independence as weakness. Part of this is our need to control, a fearful, destructive force that stifles the work of the transcendent.

Sometimes we think of ourselves as healthy social beings because, after all, I am surrounded by people. I may have a family, lots of friends, and coworkers. But how deep are these relationships? How emotionally close are we to our friends, even our families? How emotionally connected are we to ourselves? We may be more isolated than we like to admit. In part this is because some see relationships as a means to an end. Our transcendent and holy selves see them as ends in and of themselves. The notion of holiness lets us understand we are set apart by

God. Our unique natures, our unique purpose, are found only in and through our relationship with God, with others, and with the planet. How do relationships affect me? What do I give to my relationships? What is the deepest spiritual relationship I have with another person and how is that different from other relationships I have? What tends to make me a hermit, to flee the world and seek solitude? How many different masks do I wear? Would my close friends and family recognize me in all situations or do I change so much in certain settings that I am not really me? Am I comfortable being myself in relationships, or do I need to project a certain persona? **Who am I at the core of my being?**

We believe the vast majority of humans are somewhere in the middle. "No man is an island unto himself," says John Dunne. On the other hand, even the most gregarious, social person on the planet carries baggage that impacts relationships. Perhaps the most visible way of seeing this is to watch a politician. Their being changes depending on who they are talking to. Messages shift, body language loosens or tenses and tone, rhythm, structure, all adapt. Does this mean they are lying? Not necessarily. It means they understand we all view them through our own filters and they attempt to change their persona to open up filters that may be closed. The challenge for politicians—for all of us—is to be true to our core being as we adapt to different environments. Historically, Christians were persecuted and threatened with martyrdom. Not all were martyred because they adapted and did not go running down the street screaming they were followers of Christ. They showed they were disciples by the love they showed one another. Those called to be bold with their faith did so. The key is to understand when and why you are adapting and changing. It goes to understanding who and what you are in relation to the world, God, and yourself.

Our holiness comes through understanding who we are in God's eyes and being true to that. In Acts 4:18-19 Peter tells the Jewish leadership that they choose to be obedient to God rather than to humanity when the two are at odds. This is pure holiness. In order to become holy, we must accept our holiness as the root of our eternal being, knowing our time on this planet is but a blip on the screen. We are not called into being simply for ourselves, but for the sake of the world.

It is interesting to note that almost without exception in the world's religious traditions, people were called to isolation for a time, but always returned empowered by that time to serve others. Jesus in the desert, Mohammed receiving the Quaran while alone, Elijah in the cave, Moses and the burning bush and Siddartha under the Boddhi tree. Isolation from other humans is fine in order to spend some time with the transcendent, but we are in the world for a purpose. We should not be surprised that in each of those situations and countless others, people found new and deeper meaning from their "desert" experience. When one comes face to face with the transcendent and let it impact their lives, things change.

Past—present/future—Many of us live through our positive and negative memories of the past, and our visions of the future, uplifting or depressing as they may be. They give us anchors with which to ride the tides of life. We hold onto bad ones because they are too painful to face or we use them as ammunition against ourselves or others. People go to the extent of repressing memories so deep they are unable to acknowledge them on any level. This is to protect their current view of themselves and the world about them.

The past and future are ultimately mental constructs in our minds. Yes, they are based on pieces of reality, but in the end, they are not reality, they are fabrications, something we can change, editorialize. We control mental ideas much more than we control reality that looks us in the face. The beauty of the soul is that it transcends space and time by being inside and outside the space-time continuum. Our souls allow us to be fully present, not partially present, but fully present to the present as well as holding the potential to illuminate the past.

Part of our holy nature is we are set apart because of our transcendent souls. We are unique in that we can consciously be aware of being outside space and time, we can transcend all things. Most of us have a tendency to live more in the past, present, or future. Where do you live? Are you always talking about what happened? Are you a dreamer that constantly thinks about the future? Do you ignore the past because it is to threatening? Do you have dreams and goals for the future? How does one live fully in the present but be attentive to the past and move into a purposeful future?

We have limited amounts of energy. If our lives are focusing energy on the past, how can that energy be used to live in the present? If all we do is dream about the future, how are we engaging the present to get us there? Jesus seemed to know early on that his purpose on earth was in the end, to die. We know that because he told his disciples. His ministry was not dominated by the future, but by the present. He did what the transcendent called him to in the moment. He used the past to give him strength. He told the woman at the well to let go of the past, seek forgiveness, change, and move on. He empowered her.

To be holy includes understanding you are a sacred being, you have purpose and meaning within yourself. The Creator believes in you. To be truly holy we must act upon this understanding, not just think about it. This idea of being holy is present oriented. Whatever an individual has done in the past is history, for better or for worse. This does not mean the repercussions can't move into the future, but the act itself is done. Holiness is an experience lived, not a story told. Holiness is the power of understanding sacred things, including ourselves. If we do not experience ourselves as holy, we are missing an essential component of how we were created. God made us as good, as images of himself, holy. What we do with what we have been given can make life far less than holy, but the choice is ours. To be holy is to claim our place in the universe as sacred. Our holiness comes with a sense of Presence, knowing we are not alone, but are surrounded by Holiness.

Shame/guilt----Grace/Redemption---We live in a culture heavily influenced by shame. We are told we are nothing and we pass that belief and accompanying feeling on to others. Many live in such extreme poverty that dreaming of a different future is near impossible. When a person or culture is denied the means to exist, they feel shame. They are made to feel they are not worth the world's attention. In our own culture we climb the economic and social ladders as we overtly or covertly shame others. The ability to be free from that guilt or shame is a manifestation of the transcendent at work within us. We are lifted out of that cloud in our lives when we are in touch with the holiness of who we are. We are as unique and loved in the eyes of the divine as are all others. "As you treat the least of these, so you treat me." (Matt. 25:31-46). When we understand and feel the concept of holiness in our lives, there is no choice but to deal with all people with respect and the dignity they deserve. Guilt has not set us apart. God has not made us holy in order to feel shamed or guilty. This is not to say at times we should not feel ashamed or guilty, but it is not our created nature. In and through understanding and knowing our holiness of who we are in our weakness helps us respond appropriately to guilt and shame in ourselves and others. We talk more about shame later and give a specific way of dealing with it.

Grace and redemption are perhaps the clearest way God reveals our holiness to us. We are redeemed precisely because we are holy in our natural state. We have become separated from our holy nature through the interactions we have with the world and the choices we make with our free wills. God knows the potential of what we can become, he redeems us in order that we might seek that identity. Redemption is bringing us back to who we were created to be. Grace comes as a free gift in spite of the darkness that surrounds it. Our souls mirror that relationship. When we accept ourselves as holy, we give our souls an opportunity to receive grace and redemption and to pass that understanding down to our immanent natures. We then make decisions to enact that within our own lives or to negate it. What is it that blocks you from the power of grace and redemption? Are there things you find it hard to let go of? Do you make others feel bad, shamed, or guilty? Why? Do you feel better when you make people feel guilty or help relieve people of their guilt or shame? What is shame keeping you from doing?

Just so we are clear before we move on. Guilt is how you feel when you have done something wrong. It can be remedied and changed via actions. Shame is a core belief about who we are as a person, it is the opposite of being holy. Shame tells us we are not worthy, that we lack the dignity of being cared for or listened to. It is very destructive and against the very nature of transcendence.

Guarded---Open-----Many of us go through life with tunnel vision. We have created a limited worldview or allowed it to be created for us. Our defensiveness creates a vision of the world that both protects and distracts us from reality. All of us need defense mechanisms in our lives to help us survive and thrive. The fight/flight response is one such posture we take. We repress harmful memories, we feel shivers down our spines when around certain people, and we know what we fear, even if we don't know why. These in and of themselves are all good things. On the other hand, our defensiveness may keep us from seeing truth, taking risks that would be good for us, allowing our emotions to surface,

30

or working through a relationship that needs attention. As if we have all truth. We of course will never admit to believing this, but our actions show we do. We become very defensive of our perspectives. We protect them with our minds and culturally with our might. We as individuals guard our beliefs and we as a culture attempt to do the same, the essence of nationalism. If you're in touch with the transcendent, there is no need to guard your beliefs; what can someone else do to you by challenging them? We become open to see other perspectives, other ways of building relationships that are creative. This does not mean we believe everything and everybody. It simply says we are open to receive deeper truths if they become known to us. When I am internally confident I do not need to be defensive or aggressive with those who differ. Terrorists are the most insecure people on the planet. They have no self-identity, they merely believe what others tell them because for whatever reason they lack a sense of self. This holiness helps us understand how unique we are and yet how tied into everyone and everything else we are.

A sense of holiness enables us to let down our guard, to see things as they are—both good and evil. Jesus was about building strength on a spiritual level. He was well aware that those who simply relied on their humanness would struggle with faith. Those who relied on God through faith could endure all things. "If God is for us, who is against us?" (Romans 8:31) Part of the problem is that we raise our defenses even against the transcendent. Obstacles to grace are very real. We fear giving up our identity. We fear what God may call us to do. We exchange holiness for the falsely assumed state of self-preservation.

We become guarded because we believe we know what is best and anything that moves against that knowledge needs to be thwarted. There are certainly real attacks, spiritual and otherwise in our lives. The challenge is to discover which are real and which are fabrications that keep us from allowing the transcendent more deeply into our souls. Internally, what do you feel a need to protect? When do you find your defenses going up? What are some negative images that occur in your dreams? What is your attitude when someone has different ideas than you?

You can think about the rest of the scales and figure out the connection of each to our transcendent and holy natures.

Our souls are holy. Our spiritual identities have needs just as the rest of our being does. To claim that the soul has no needs would be peculiar at best. The deepest need of the soul is to be in relationship with its Creator—to be attached.

The attributes of the holy are seen on the right of the list above. Add to those some other manifestations of the holy such as humility, patience, gratitude, compassion, simplicity, trust, responsibility, and faith, and you have a good start as to what a life of holiness may look like. What this means is that our actions come from who we know we are at the core of our being. Our actions reflect our holy nature. Read the lives of the saints, they understood this. These traits are not just spiritual traits, they are found and used in the world as we work through our souls to strengthen them.

Here is the secret: at our core, all of us have the potential to be holy. We are born holy and become profane. Orthodox Christianity sees this as the effect of Original Sin. The idea is while we may have a core of holiness, we are brought into the world as already sinful, just by being human. We all need redemption, even from birth. While some may not believe we are born into sin, few if any, would claim that we have no sin within us. What is important for this discussion is to understand it is through our souls that the potential for holiness becomes actualized. As we allow our inner natures to be redeemed, we are drawn to the qualities of the soul we are discussing. As we are drawn to that world, we see the lenses through which we view the world, change.

Deep inside our being lies the entity that makes our relationship with the transcendent possible. Merely by being human we are in touch with that part of the universe. If that relationship is on the scale of one to a hundred, where are you? To be at 100, you need to be manifesting all the right qualities all the time and be a relationship with God where you are attuned to her voice and presence.

You might ask, "Well what about tough love, how does that fit in?" There are many manifestations of the right hand side characteristics. The key is to understand their purpose, their intent, and their source. Jesus was showing love as he cast out the money changers from the temple, challenged the Scribes and Pharisees, and spoke to the woman at the well. Let's understand that being fully present to the soul does not mean ignoring our immanent side. The Trinity is three in one; Father,

Son, and Holy Spirit, Creator, Redeemer, Sustainer, all in one being. We are called to die to ourselves to find ourselves. We must stay connected to our souls in order to fully embrace our immanent natures. They are tied together more profoundly than most of us know.

The exciting news is we become more holy from both the outside in and the inside out. We can actively work on exhibiting more traits of holiness which will in turn help our souls mature into their holy natures. We can also do our internal work and strengthen the soul which will in turn persuade us to act more holy. When we are not holy, we build walls around the soul that make it more and more difficult to find and easier to avoid. We have two choices in life; to become more holy or to become less holy. To refuse holiness is to refuse to nurture the soul. This results in a lack of connectedness with the transcendent and all it brings and damages the bridge between our transcendent and immanent natures. We are called to accept our holiness and build on it.

This sense of holiness is different than a sense of self we create from what we glean in our material and psychological selves. It sees a larger picture, attaches to something greater than ourselves, and gives us a sense of perspective the world in and of itself does not understand. At times this sense of holiness will be at odds with the world, maybe even at odds internally with our own ideas. It calls us to believe in things the world may say are wrong and yet we know are right.

God knows us better than we know ourselves. God believes in us more than we believe in ourselves. God works directly with your soul and works in and through others to affect change in you.

Trait 3: CONNECTEDNESS

If we were to ask you how you are connected to other people and to things, you might give us a variety of responses. "I'm very close to my siblings and my parents." "I have many close friends." "I love my piano." "I feel very attached to my house and my cabin on the beach." These relationships and the connections they represent are critical for life on Earth. We could not exist as sane human beings without them. But in the end, this is not all there is to life or to our connectedness. There is a transcendent web that interlocks all creation. Our spiritual identities are what bring us into contact with that realm. When we're in touch with the spiritual dimension, we link up to that which is not bound by the past or present and offers much hope for the future.

We hear words about connectedness like synchronicity, coincidence, déjà vu, or the collective unconscious. In the right context these are some of the languages of the soul, some of the fruits of their existence. Not all coincidences are the working of our spiritual identities connecting with the web of life. Some are merely coincidences. Does it really matter which is which? Do we really need to identify one from the other? We think not. It is enough to understand that part of who we are is attached to all that transcends the world we perceive and that perceives us. But the universe that is invisible to our own minds and senses is fully available to our spirit or soul. Think of it this way. We are surrounded by millions of sounds we can't hear. When you walk down the street, every phone conversation on a cell phone, every wireless computer connection, every radio and TV station are around you. Because you are not sensitive to those frequencies, you don't hear them. What would life be like if you did? How long would you last if you were receiving all that information all the time? Not long. Now, multiply that amount of information by many thousand fold and you have some idea of what the soul has access to.

Have you known something was going to happen before it did? Have you arrived at a place and known it, even though you've never been there before, seen pictures of it or heard it described? Have you known someone at a different location was ill or hurt before you found out about it? These are all occurrences in people's lives. They tend to happen more often for some people than for others, but they are available to everyone. God has created the world in such a way that the potential for synchronicity is hard wired into our being. God wants the world to see these events as normal, not as supernormal. Were Christ alive today, many would say what an amazing intuition he had. We think he'd laugh at that and claim he was just connected like we should all be. The depth of his soul connects the wisdom and knowledge of the universe to his immanent and communally oriented nature.

Every thought, every event, every movement of humanity is recorded and noticed by this web of life. Within this web there is no space or time, so we shouldn't be surprised when we listen to the spiritual side of our identities that we come into contact with that world.

It makes sense that we connect more fully with those things and people that have direct meaning to us and the world we know.

Visually it may be helpful to see your thoughts and actions as forms of energy. We know energy doesn't disappear, it merely changes form and seeks entropy (chaos). So part of our energy enters a transcendent world. That energy is the movement of the Spiritual Web, the memory of all that has existed and exists for the purpose of helping us to fill our purposes. This ability to connect is part of what makes us holy. This is part of what we are calling the Collaborative Unconscious. You can read more about it in a later chapter.

We can choose to believe we are alone. We can choose to believe in coincidences and in a rational view of miraculous healings and events, or we can be open to the movement of transcendent energy that leaves no scientific trail. At times, choosing to not believe does not mean something isn't true, simply that it can't be proven in a modern scientific sense. Science has a word for things scientists think may be right but can't prove, and that word is theory. Theories abound in science. Much of what people claim to be science is in reality, theory. As evidence is gathered, some theories become fact. Facts are discovered, theories are created to speak to the facts and project them forward. Then new facts are obtained to slowly prove the theory—which in turn leads to more theories. An example may help. For a long time most humans viewed the earth as flat. That was an accepted fact by most. Then someone came up with a theory that perhaps it wasn't so flat—really only one way to find out. Upon going around the earth they discovered it was round. Now a new problem arose, how does water stay on the earth if it is round? Gravity and theories around it came to be. Facts were garnered to support various ideas. Today we have a firm understanding of basic gravitational forces---science, not theory.

Spirituality does not play by the same rules. The spiritual realm is one of stories, anecdotes, experiences, ideas, and faith. It's a catch 22. The only proof of the soul is an individual's experience of it and you can't experience the soul unless you believe it exists. And there are certainly times when we have deep spiritual experiences but don't understand them. As spiritual beings we are called to enter this spiritual world, to use it to move the world and ourselves forward.

If we were created to be social creatures and to be in relationship, then it only makes sense that our growth, both physically and spiritually, would be tied to those relationships, our connectedness. We are not talking about networking in the post-modern sense of the word; such as how many people you know, how many business cards you hold, or how many phone calls you can make. We are suggesting a networking that comprehends how the ultimate network works. We are asserting that we should be part of it for the sake of the world—not only for our selfish desires. Humanity is capable of infinitely more than we think. We are trapped by our limited vision. We are imprisoned by our lack of connectedness to one another and to the spiritual world. Let's look at it on a very material and pragmatic level. How much time a week do you take to see the big picture, to intentionally and compassionately feel the pain of others? Do you take time to see yourself as part of the means rather than an end and to be spiritually sensitive to God?

We are not saying this to induce guilt, but to give us perspective. Being connected takes effort and time. We need to be diligent and deliberate as well as patient and gracious with ourselves and with those around us. Mutual support, accountability, and grace are vital components to building our sense of soulful connectedness.

Much of our world lacks this connectedness. All of the "isms" are evidence. On an intellectual level, most of us know that racism, sexism, ageism, and others are simply signs of ignorance. We are amazed how often one person's biases disappear when they build a relationship with the one they are biased against. We imprison ourselves with our biases and prejudices. We keep the Spirit from allowing us to be connected to all God's creation. Perhaps this is the biggest sin of the world. The Bible tells us that in God's eyes there is no male or female, slave or free, black, Hispanic, white, asian or other race---there is simply his created order and a stunning array of God's glory revealed in humanity.

Chaos theory teaches about a principle called the butterfly effect. This says very small events can have massive impacts, that a butterfly flapping its wings can be the start of a hurricane. Fractals are built upon this premise. Fractals are a mathematical way of seeing the world. They are found throughout nature. In essence they are created by creating a mathematical formula. You put in numbers and when you get an answer you stick that back in. You do this millions of times and come up with a picture---a simplistic view of fractals. For more, see the chapter on Chaos Theory. The idea is that very small changes in numbers can lead to an infinite array of pictures.

Many of us can point to a teacher or person that had a huge influence on our lives, even though they would be shocked to hear about it. We all know that polluting oceans, killing rain forests, taking too many antibiotics, eating all foods with additives, and other such things impact our lives. If you follow the thread of any one of these, we can see how it impacts a much larger system. You and I do not know how decisions we make will impact ourselves, others, and perhaps the world down the road. It is incumbent upon us to make the best decisions we can. If this is true on the earthly plane, would it not also be true on the spiritual one? Our souls make conscious decisions whether to connect to that which make us whole or that which tears us apart---integration or disintegration. We need to choose to be connected on all levels.

So look at your life and your relationships. See what those relationships are based on. How many have an active and conscious spiritual dimension? How many are based on material gain? How many touch you in a deep way? What does your relationship to God look like? Do you feel an attachment to that transcendental realm of existence?

Trait 4: IMAGINATION

Human imagination is yet another attribute that sets us apart from the rest of the animal kingdom. There is no doubt creativity is part of the evolutionary process. You can't help but see animals and know that at some point they were being creative and imaginative. How conscious they were of that ability we may never know. We may never fully understand the subtle differences in consciousness between various creatures. No one can deny the phenomenal creative imagination of humans. It is our imagination that created the concepts of the pyramids, of art and architecture, of flight, the table of elements, of electricity and of travel off our planet. What is at the root of this imagination? What is it we bring to our plight of being and where does that come from? Is there an imagination gene? Are there common elements that all people with great imaginations have?

It is important to note imagination does not necessitate novelty. We can take ideas that have already been known and form them in new ways mentally. Nothing that Dr. Martin Luther King Jr. said was unique or unheard of. His command of the English language, his ability to speak in ways that spoke to the hearts of people, and his ability to use tact and timing showed the uniqueness of his imagination and creativity. He was also at the right place at the right time. He was a man of deep passion and vision.

Our deepest imaginations do not come completely from ourselves. They come from an attachment and connection to the spiritual realm, the transcendent. As you can see, the different aspects of our souls (Transcendence, Holiness, Call, Connectedness) themselves are interconnected. Our souls, minds, and bodies, working together form our deepest imaginations, the source of our most illustrious of creative ideas.

Congress is deeply embedded in the world, there is little opportunity for redemptive imagination there because that side of their being is minimized. Often, churches having little imagination tend to be underdeveloped in terms of spiritual growth. Let's look at this another way. Take a product that has not changed for decades, like Coke or Pepsi. There is little new in the product itself. They have not changed, other than perhaps an additional flavor now and then which don't sell nearly as well as the original one. What changes is how the product is perceived through advertising. If they still ran the commercials they did in the 50's, would they still be so successful?

This brings up an important point: Can you develop your imagination and creativity without a healthy soul? Again, we all have souls whether we accept them, or not. We all have access to the Collaborative Unconscious merely by being conscious, sentient beings. The question is how deep and broad is our access to the wellsprings of these two things? Knowing the "spirit" of a culture is different than knowing the Spirit of God. You can have focus groups to let you know if an idea has traction in the advertising or entertainment industry. You can feed the economic side of life with very little imagination, but can you change the planet? Can you get people to change their lives?

There are very few Americans who will deny we eat too much junk, watch too much TV, get enough exercise, and are fairly selfish. We all know these things to be true. We hear about them constantly in the media and yet over all, nothing is done to change them. Our spiritual natures have taken such a back seat, we fail to even acknowledge how out of touch with the transcendent we really are. The other possibility is that we conform the spiritual to the material, we convince ourselves that what we are doing is spiritual. We come to believe that God wants us to be materialistic, eat junk food and not care for our neighbor. **We rationalize our behavior to make it look good rather than to open ourselves up to the wisdom and imagination of the transcendent**.

We lack a cultural imagination sufficient enough to motivate us to change. We lack a deep connection to the transcendent. We lack the will, political or social, to even engage the process on a significant level. Barely half the population of America even votes (54% in 2008). Think about it this way. In virtually every election of the past 40 years, if someone could register 7% of the non-voting public and get them to vote one way, they could swing every national election. That is an average of 100,000 per state. It's actually pretty stunning in what it says about our apathy. Our souls know the power of the individual. Our souls know that it is my responsibility as an individual to get connected, use my imagination, and spread the message of holiness.

Our imaginations are not, for the most part, rational parts of our being. We tend to find this deeper side of ourselves in "Eureka!" moments; through dreams or daydreams, or through experiences that get us out of our overly rational modes. Because the plane of transcendence and that of immanence are not the same, we have to shift our way of seeing the world in order to come into contact with that which is not worldly. Imagination is on one level a transcendent idea. We must move beyond what we know to imagine what we don't know.

Sometimes, the imagination is so far off the map we talk about someone going off the deep end, losing their minds, becoming psychotic. We would contend that at times the issue is more of perception and perspective. Many mystics have gone off the deep end, but that is where they found God. It's interesting that we read in the Bible that Peter, James, and John, went with Jesus onto a mountain top and there saw him talking with Moses and Elijah. They wanted to build houses there for them all to keep the experience alive. Jesus told them to go back to the world with the understanding that came from that experience. If I preached a sermon today where I claimed to have actually met and talked with Jesus, Moses, and Elijah, there is a good chance I'd lose my job, and be locked up. It's interesting we accept the validity of a story but not of a reality we are faced with. This is not to say all visions reveal truth. Certainly there are indeed people with severe mental problems who hallucinate. But how do we know the difference? Are we afraid to accept the possibility that people may in fact have experiences of the transcendent and the Collaborative Unconscious that far surpass anything we have experienced?

The soulful imagination does several things. First, it is creative. The imagination brings people together, makes connections, and furthers the innate purpose of creation---to support and maintain the web of life. A holy imagination does not put ourselves at the top of the food chain, but seeks the betterment of the world for others. Imagination comes with emotion---positive emotion that raises our spirits and encourages us and others. Imaginations may warn us of impending doom like that of the prophets, but they always come with hope and a solution attached. Those who only speak of the end of the world are hardly imaginative.

Imagination can be as destructive as it can be creative. There are times in our lives when we must destroy something in order for the creative to be born. Christ tells us to die to ourselves in order to find ourselves. In this case however we know (albeit through faith) the end. We can see examples of others who have done it and how it has impacted their lives. There is no true destruction but rather a peeling of the onion to find the center.

Here are a few questions for you to think about in light of your own imagination and creativity.

Do you dream? Do you remember them?
Do you daydream? How far off reality do you get?
Have you had a direct experience of the transcendent? The Collaborative Unconscious? Of God?
When does your imagination come most alive?
Do you ever find yourself taming your imagination? Why?
Do you know someone with a very active imagination? What traits do they have that foster that sensibility?
Why do you think children have more active imaginations than adults?
If God gave us the ability to imagine, why did he do that?

Where do you see the imagination of Jesus coming into play?
Do you consider your church imaginative?
Are you more a person of intuition or of reason?
Do you enjoy flights of fancy?
What are some of your favorite examples of God's creativity? Do you just see it in nature?

Trait 5: CALL

When we are children, we all want to grow up to be something. Some want to be a fireman or a doctor, an astronaut or a movie star. Those ideas and ideals change many times as we grow into adulthood. The average college student changes their career ideas at least three times during college. Most people have more than one career during their lifetime, sometimes out of necessity and other times because they feel unfulfilled in their current job.

In the best of all worlds we become what feels right and what brings us hope, meaning, and financial reward. We do what we are able to do physically and intellectually while often hoping for more. Steve R. thinks it would be great to be a brain surgeon, but trust us, you wouldn't want him operating on you. He doesn't have the hands for it and we are not sure he has the brains, but he does love reading and learning about the brain.

The universe is a funny place. We tend to see it as this massive amorphous blob expanding, creating space and time in its expansion, motivated by a series of natural laws, and we wouldn't disagree with that. But to deny there is more is to really miss our point. Many of us that believe in a God or know there is more, have experienced and witnessed the grandeur of the universe. We may believe there is a being that knows us, who also knows everything that is taking place in the cosmos, for whom time and space are meaningless constructs. Even that notion is, in the end, impossible for us to truly grasp—there is no space or time? Humans were created to be in contact with that Being. How amazing is that!!??

What is the purpose of this contact? God does not expect us to change the universe, that's not our job. He has given us a planet and one another with the job of loving each other and keeping this planet going—

to be good stewards of what we have been given. Just as in any family or in any business, each person has a job to do, so it is with planet Earth. When we all perform our jobs or roles well, things run smoothly, when we don't, things get messed up, they impact other systems, the domino effect. We have seen this boldly in the world economies of 2008-20011. Bad loans and other poor decisions years ago are now collapsing the entire system. Every aspect of the system is hurt, except perhaps those who leveraged and bet against the system they are part of. Each of us has the potential for many purposes. Certainly the book by Rick Warren, **The Purpose Driven Life** (Zondervan, 2003), points to the fact that all humans are endowed with purpose and part of our spiritual responsibility is to discover that purpose. It not only brings meaning to our material lives, but builds on the very relationship that makes that purpose known. How one lives with that purpose in their lives can be quite varied.

The aspect of trying to discover our purpose at any given time is what we are naming: the Call. You will hear pastors often speak of being called. How often do you hear a lawyer, engineer, homemaker, grocery clerk, or others talk of being called? They should.

How do we know when we responding to God's call? We feel connected to the work, our imaginations soar, creativity abounds, we feel alive and enthused, our work has meaning beyond the work itself, our inner selves are at peace, and there is a sense of peace and presence deep within us that passes human explanation. This is the fundamental problem when we talk about the transcendent. By its very nature it surpasses human comprehension or the ability to describe it. We can use metaphors, poetry, stories, and the like, but in the end, there is no human language to describe transcendence in us. The origin and essence of the Call sometimes seems beyond comprehension. There are points in our lives when we need to accept mystery. This is not to say we shouldn't think about things, ask hard questions, perhaps even have some doubts or trepidations. If we had to fully understand something before acting, most of us would do very little with our lives. The difference with the call of the soul is that we are trying to hear the voice of the One who knows everything and how best to use the gifts we have.

Some of us are called to that which comes naturally. Musical prodigies often become and are called to a musical career. But we should not make the assumption that just because one is musical they should only be a musician. David was a shepherd and became the best king Israel ever had. Peter was a fisherman and became the leader of the church. Paul murdered Christians and yet opened Christianity to Gentiles—and that is true for many of us. If we are to heed the call of God, we need to be willing to be used by God, rather than to use God to suit our purpose as many of us do in our spiritual lives. We can use God in our lives to help us, to seek wisdom, to comfort us in our suffering, and to give us eyes to see the world through His eyes. We can be used for God for a myriad of reasons; as angels unaware, to exhort the world, to spread love and grace. We can also use God as an excuse as countries often do in time of war. When in doubt, blame God or Satan rather than taking personal or cultural responsibility. God calls us to be responsible, to listen and to love.

Like most things, the call is part of a continuum. On the one hand is God's pure call to the soul and on the other are our internal drives that propel us into the world. Are we called to wear certain clothes or eat a certain thing in the morning? Probably not very often. Are you called to say specific things to specific people at specific times? Perhaps. Are you ever called to be anything less than a caring and loving human being? Probably not. Are we called to a certain path in life in relation to our careers? Perhaps, but this does not necessitate that if you choose a path other than what God would desire at any given moment, that God can't use you on that other path, it's just not the best path.

Let's say for example you are in God's call and you follow that will and become a teacher. God wants you to teach in the inner city. In order for that to happen, a lot of people also must be in God's will. What if those others aren't and they choose someone else for the job and the only one you are able to get hired for is in the suburbs. Are you finished? Did you disobey God because some other people thwarted God's plan? Obviously not. The dynamic of what God wanted has changed, but the overall use of you and your gifts has not. Those people in the suburbs have needs as well, your gifts can be used there. Let's push this a bit further. What if there were no teaching jobs, that everywhere you turned, God's will for you to teach met a roadblock? In order to pay the bills and feed your family, you had to paint houses—nothing wrong with that career. This is not on your personal top ten list of what you wanted to do or what you felt God had in mind. It was not on God's top ten list of how to use you in his plan, but it does pay the bills and the la st time I checked, God doesn't write personal checks. So now you are a long way from what God's intentions were for you, sidetracked by a lot of people not listening to God. God is bigger than we think. God is connected to all things and if you are willing, God can use you anywhere at anytime---- we are called 24/7 to be present to God's use of us. That is the ultimate call.

Being responsible in the midst of seeking a call is important. We should never sacrifice our responsibilities just to heed God's call. Does God want you to be unemployed for 10 years while you look for a teaching job? Probably not. On the other hand we need to ask questions like, "Am I willing to look outside a 5 mile radius from my house for that position?" "What if God is calling me to teach overseas or as a missionary?" "Am I being called to teach at a private school or perhaps even to start a school?" "Is there anything I am doing that is getting in the way of my being hired?" Dressing like John the Baptist may seem good in your mind, but as an ex-principal Steve R. can tell you he wouldn't hire you—no offense.

Every second of every day, God attempts to communicate with our souls to call us to how we can live out his message, of love, and grace, to the world about us. The problem is not God. The problem is us. We ignore the call. We put God on hold. We tell God we aren't really interested in his ideas. Ours are better. Our pride is the root of our sin and of our lack of presence in the midst of God's overwhelming universe and love for us. Be honest, where does your pride show itself, in positive and perhaps negative ways?

The call is part of our soul experience, because it is that aspect which relates to the transcendent part of God's connection to the universe. It is that aspect of our lives that reaches beyond the ego, beyond our selfishness, that reaches out in faith and trust to the one who knows, to God.

We need to learn how to be sensitive to God's call to us and to be bold in living it, whether or not others acknowledge the fact. I have no doubt there are clergy who felt called that were not and people who were called to be clerics who were told by others they were not called.. We create hoops people must jump through in order to prove their worthiness. But these are often human hoops based on human egos and worldly ways of being. God doesn't function on that level. Think about it. What criteria did God use when he chose leaders? I don't think many of us, having seen the resumes of some of the greatest biblical leaders, would have hired them. David, an adulterer, liar, and murderer; Moses, a murder; Solomon a philanderer, tyrant, and brutal leader of his people; Peter, a corporate guy who denied he even knew his boss three times, and Paul, a murderer of the people he eventually joined. When a replacement was needed for Judas, did they form a committee, collect resumes, check references, and do five interviews? They drew straws. We have lost a complete sense of intuition and spiritual connectivity. God is in the workplace. We may choose not to see or feel his presence. We have relegated the call of God to a bunch of forms rather than to practicing the presence of God.

   We all know there are more ways to an end point than just one. There are thousands of good teachers and even though God may have desired that Tom get the job and they chose Mary, life does not end. It merely changes the plan. Some changes have more significant consequences down the road that we might not see---but God sees. Anyone who has hired someone has had the thought in their mind a month or two after hiring someone; "Shoot, wish I'd hired someone else instead of the one I did."

   The soul is that part of our being that is designed to be actively seeking the presence of God. Through the soul we connect to God, to our fundamental purpose of being, and to what God needs us to do. That's right, in order for God to bring this part of creation to fruition, he uses us. That is how he set it up. We are not robots. We have free will and we can certainly choose against the created order. Below are some basic questions around call as part of the soul.

What do you believe you are called to do? Called to be?
How do you feel when you think you are doing God's will?
How do you know when you are out of God's will?
How do you determine when someone else is out of God's will? Who gave you that right?
When you blow it, how do you react?

How do you share your sense of call with a community larger than yourself? If I were to ask a family member or friend what your call is, would they know?

How do you deal with a situation where you feel called, but it is thwarted by others?

Can you sense and do you take the time regularly to sense when you are attuning to God versus attuning to yourself and your own egocentric desires?

This spiritual web we connect to is one of many resources available to our spiritual identities to bring hope, grace, love, and power to our lives. You will see these themes of transcendence, holiness, and connectedness, the call, and imagination repeated often in this book, they are the core principles of what our spiritual identity is based upon. Take time to reflect and see them at work in your lives and to understand they are part of the totality of who we are.

THE CONTINUA

Each trait is an umbrella that covers a wide range of possibilities, each a continuum and all of us fall somewhere along that line. The next several chapters will focus on those continua and aspects of them. In the end, there are 32 core types. What we find is that your type changes over time.

There is the transcendent end and the immanent end. Relative to a healthy life, both are essential. The transcendent connects us with "spiritual" things in a direct way. The immanent side is how we work with and find the spiritual on a more worldly plane. God put here for a reason. God could have chosen to create us as purely spiritual beings, she chose not to. Balance is finding both in our lives. The hope is that we become more balanced, but each person moves along any given trait continuum. What follows is a fairly brief description of each trait and its continuum.

TRANSCENDENCE --- Center of Meaning

Supernal (S)---Immanent (I)

Transcendence has to do with our search for and relationship to the transcendent and where we find meaning in our lives. Victor Frankl in his brilliant book, **Man's Search for Meaning** (Beacon Press, 1959) talks about our innate need to make sense of the world, even in the midst of chaos. We all seek answers to the difficult questions in life. Why do some suffer and some don't? What is the nature of evil? Why am I here? There are essentially three core places we find these and other answers. The first is in our minds. We create answers that fit with the world as we see it. We rationalize everything and have blind spots with those things that don't fit. Because there is still mystery in the world, everyone has blind spots. Claiming you don't have one is a blind spot in and of itself. We start this mental process at a very young age, before we are aware we are even doing so. We make excuses for why mom, dad, siblings, or others behave the way they do. We justify our reasons for doing something wrong. President Nixon was an extreme of this ability to mentally create blind spots that others see so clearly.

The second method is to use the world around us. We look and see what the world says about things. We adapt to the culture around us and glean meaning from it. We do things because that is the way it has always been done. We avoid conflict with those ideas because they challenge the foundation upon which our worldview is based. Part of using the world is using its history and interpretations of it. Books and literature, the media, and relationships we have developed all feed this method of bringing meaning to our lives.

The third way of finding answers is spiritually, developing a relationship with that which is greater than the world, with God. Most of us would admit that God probably sees the world differently than we do. Just by the very nature of God's capacity to be aware of all things at all times, God has a fundamentally different perspective. As we attune ourselves to that perspective, our own changes.

In reality, few if any of us only use one of these methods, we are an amalgamation of at least two if not all three. Our search for meaning in our lives gathers and filters information from the world through the use of our minds and sometimes in conjunction with the transcendent. We are placed in the world to be part of the world and we are given brains to use. As is true in virtually all things, balance is imperative. We might want to say that just being transcendent would be the best, then we'd see the world as God wants us to. We would be more Christ like. Let's remember that the incarnation of Jesus was done precisely so God would become human, to see the world and to suffer as we do. Jesus was the perfect balance. He fully understood the world around him, used his mental capacities to reflect on various worldviews and put them into a perspective that worked for him and in the midst of that, attuned to the voice of his soul, the Spirit of God living within, to add another dimension. It's a type of checks and balance system and yes, all of them have the potential to be out of balance or misused. There are certainly people who do things they know are wrong even though they will look you in the eye and claim that God told them to do it, culture says it's ok or needed, and they have no guilty conscience. This is perhaps the most important reason why we need to be in relationship with others, to challenge our assumptions, to help us find balance.

Let's look for a moment at the different types of meaning we find through these avenues. The world gives an amazingly wide variety of meanings. Look at the vast number of worldviews on the planet. Pick any given issue and you will find a continuum from one extreme to the other. Now put all those different issues together, each feeding and impacting the other and you see the myriad of views possible. Here is the important piece to think about; 1) all of them are accurate for the person with that worldview, or they'd change and 2) they are only wrong from your perspective because it is your perspective. Who makes the rules? Who gives anyone the right to "truth?" Cultures in and of themselves have a worldview. In dictatorships that worldview comes from the mind of one person and culture is "forced" to accept it. We do not believe people are born racist, they are taught those ideas by the culture they are raised in and by the experiences they have (often negative) with a subculture.

Some people choose not to think. They let the world or some part of the world do all their thinking for them. They listen to a particular preacher or radio personality and glean all truth from them without questioning. Their worldview is in fact the worldview of someone else.

You can tell this because as soon as you start to ask questions, they shut down. They become defensive or avoidant, they clearly have no answers and because they can't face that reality, their defense mechanisms pop up to protect them. It's so easy to let someone else do all the work, especially when you have no responsibility for the woes of the world, it's someone else's fault and problem. Sure, you'll get on the band wagon, as long as you are told what to do. Many religious groups do this; they have a doctrine that is very specific and speaks to all issues. Yours is not to challenge, but to just accept. The question becomes, who made up the doctrine and why do you give them that authority? Let's remember that nowhere in the Bible does Jesus call for the writing of what he said, the putting together of a collection of books and letters. He could have hired a scribe to take notes, he didn't. This is not to deny the importance of the Bible, but to point out that it has authority because we choose to give it authority. All religions do this. We must accept responsibility for giving someone or something the power to determine how we find meaning in the world.

The world however is where we live. Avoiding the world denies its reality and impact on our lives. We have our five senses with which to pick up cues to build and challenge our worldview. The amount of sensory input we take in every second is staggering. Most of it is filtered out. On one level we become numb to the world, only letting in significant input from our senses. Seeing two cars collide is hard to avoid. But walk down a busy sidewalk, get to the end of the block having seen a hundred people and then have someone ask you about what you remember seeing---in detail. Our minds can't handle all the input and there is nothing wrong with that.

We are bombarded with information from the media. We tend to take in and respond to those things that fit into our worldview with a "yea, you got that right." The other extreme is when something is said that is diametrically opposed to our beliefs. Then we feel the hair stand up on the back of our necks and our blood pressure rise. Rarely do we take the time to actually listen to them to see if what they are saying has any merit---why bother, I'm right?

True meaning in the world is found when we are open to what the world has to offer, when we don't just accept things at face value, but ask questions and seek answers and are open to the notion that our worldview could be wrong.

The second way we see reality is through our minds. Yes, we do use our minds even when our perspectives come from the world. However, the use of filters in our minds is turned off. At some point, those people who accept at face value what someone else tells them, have shut down part of their brains. They fail to ask questions, bowing to the idol of "the other." It's an idol because no person or entity can have all truth. In the end, we have given that person or entity a power they have not earned or deserved.

Our brains are amazing things. There is nothing like the human brain on the planet. While it may not be able to do computations as quickly as a computer, it does things a computer can't and never will do to the same extent; think and have a conscience. Computers are only as powerful as the information they are given and the processing speed they carry. Chess programs can out think people because they carry within their memory thousands of chess matches and can access all of them almost instantaneously. They play by sheer brute force rather than by finesse or intuition. They are, like Spock, logical. They are linear. Most of us know that life is not linear by any stretch of the imagination. Humans see webs of information, coming up with creative ideas to very complex problems. Watch the movie Apollo 11, a remarkable look at what the human mind can do.

Our brains love being used, they grow as they are challenged. This is especially true during the early years of life. Adults need to help children learn to use their brains as they were designed to be used. The only reason to not use our brains is because we fear the truth. If we have no fear of truth, we should be free to ask questions and to wrestle with issues. Freedoms can be taken away from us, but no one has ultimate control of your mind, only we do.

When we actively use our brains, several things happen. First, we activate the filter that assesses the sensory input. Obviously this can be a plus or minus. If our brains analyze data incorrectly then the brain simply becomes an agent of justification. Learning to internally challenge even strongly held opinions and beliefs is difficult—but possible. We can become aware of the filters we use and discover where they came from. Simply being aware is a step towards deeper understanding.

Secondly, we use all the components of our brains. The brain is not a single seamless organ, it has parts and each of those parts has a function. We can increase or decrease part of our brain's activity by what we do. There is no guarantee that simply by increasing brain usage we will be right in our worldview. But it's a good start. The brain at its best is curious. It is creating a worldview from the day of its creation. Synapses are being formed in the womb. A person's infancy has deep and profound impact on their lives. Before a person even knows they have a brain and what the word "think" means, they are doing it. Before we know what the word "worldview" means, we have formed one. We have to exert energy and effort to change our views and opinions and most of us do. Let's be clear, this has little to do with education. If it did, people with advanced degrees would all agree and speak the truth. We are all aware of how false that is. In point of fact, sometimes the brain gets in the way. It certainly has the potential of interfering with our spiritual lives which are not completely rational or linear. In order to function in the world, our brains need to have a world that makes sense to it. Our minds treat the world like a jigsaw puzzle, moving pieces around so as many pieces fit into the view we have created as possible. We all have pieces that just don't seem to fit, that appear to come from another puzzle. Most of us put them aside and ignore them. The brain is frustrated with this, our brains were created to know, to seek understanding, to comprehend the world of which it is a part. Finally, when we use our brains, we are enlisting one of the three key ingredients in creating a balanced worldview. Our mind brings with it our conscience and psyche as unique and different from our purely spiritual self, and the world in which we live, the other two ingredients.

The third part of this continuum is that part of our being that connects to and gathers meaning from the transcendent world. The world of transcendence exists on a plane without linear thinking, without physical substance, without human language. So how is it even possible to know and talk about this level of reality? We can only talk about it in and through what we know; our language, senses, and the world around us. Even those who have mystical experiences or out of body experiences discuss them in terms of more immanent or worldly ideas, how else could they. Biblically, part of the reason the gift of tongues is one of the gifts of the Holy Spirit is because it is a language that surpasses human languages, a language that more fully expresses the speakers deepest feelings towards God. So as we talk about the transcendent we need to accept the fact that at some level, it can't be described, perhaps not even fully experienced in this life. We can only approximate levels of understanding.

The Episcopal Church has for centuries used the idea of Scripture, Reason, and Tradition as the threefold way of finding God's will. Sadly they tend to ignore experience which is the only pure spiritual reality. Their methodology, while good, misses the core of our access to God. Our experience of the transcendent and what it brings to us may in fact supersede the others. Did scripture, reason, or tradition line up for any of the leaders of the bible? Did it make sense for Peter to start the church? Was there a tradition of fishermen doing that? It was Peter and others spiritual experience of God that led them to move forward with this.

The transcendent world views our life and world differently than we do. It sees the whole rather than just the sum of the parts. The Sufis tell a story about a group of blindfolded men who are told to express the creature they believe they are touching. Each is given a different part of an elephant. One touches the trunk, the other the tail, another the leg. Just by knowing that one piece, they are to describe the entire beast. It's not possible. Our spiritual selves see significantly more of the whole because it is not attached to space. The dimension of the transcendent does precisely that; transcends space.

The realm of the transcendent is more experiential than thought filled. Brother Lawerence in his profound book, ***Practicing the Presence of God*** (Paraclete Books, 2010), says it right there; the presence. It's not that the transcendent world has no thought, only that our finite minds can only catch glimpses of the breadth and depth of those thoughts. Mystics of all religions speak more to the experience than to the thought behind it. You can feel them struggle with trying to linguistically identify what those experiences mean. You can see them attempt to use metaphor after metaphor and consistently come up short from the full nature of the experience. Martin Buber talks about the pure relationship with God being an I-Thou relationship rather than an I-It. In our earthly existence, that I-Thou relationship will probably never fully be complete.

The transcendent in and of itself has no need to dominate who we are. There is no need or desire to have a human become fully transcendent in this life. The transcendent within us exists to help give meaning and purpose to our lives, to connect us to the universe, to one another, and to God.

The person existing near the transcendent end of the spectrum is rare indeed. They are perhaps the most existential of human beings, living fully present to the experience of the moment. They have let go of any need to explain to them self or others what they are experiencing. Their connection to the world is as minimal as it can be. When we think of who these people are, two main types come to mind; hermetic mystics and psychotics. We certainly do not want to put these two in the same group, but it is interesting that on an experiential level they are often similar. Visions and hallucinations are common to both. An inability to express what is happening is another. Sometimes they will try, if only to appease others, but they always fail. For them, most of us are missing the point of life; to find the higher spiritual plane on earth. They feel most of us are well below that level that they have reached. This is not a judgment on their part, just an observance based on their current experience.

Few can maintain this level of existence for long. We were created to be in the world, to be connected to it and to build relationships. Many talk of "peak" experiences. Peter, James, and John had the mountain top experience of the transfiguration. The writers of the books of Revelation and Ezekiel clearly had experiences of transcendence. Many people talk of moments in their lives where they felt amazingly close to God in a way that was different from others, in a way they could not find words to describe.

This part of our being is critical because it is where we are going. When we die, we enter the transcendent world. We have a piece of it now, we get glimpses of what will and can be. The transcendent pulls us to something greater than the world. It lures us to the divine. It puts our lives into the context that is the totality of existence. The meaning the transcendent potentially instills within us is the true meaning of what it means to be me. This is different than what the world tells us, or even perhaps what our minds tell us. There is a deep significance to who I am as an individual and that purpose can only be accessed by using our understanding of the world, our minds, and our souls.

We should work to find balance in our lives. By being in the world and sensitive to it we maintain our grounding. By using the brains we were given, we build a view of the world that makes sense to us, into which we find our purpose. The effort we put into our spiritual lives connects us to the whole and to God. All three are important. At any point in our lives, one is probably stronger than the other, more dominant. There is nothing wrong with this, just something to be aware of.

The person at the Immanent end of the spectrum finds meaning and through what the world offers them about God, be it truth or not. They rely on others for their faith. Through books, parents, friends, the Church and other institutions, they give significant authority to something other than them self.

It should be noted that humans are brilliant delusionists. We are remarkably good at convincing ourselves of just about anything if we want or have the need. We need to have a check and balance system outside ourselves, to call us when we stray too far off track, to give us a kick. How many times have you heard someone claim they know exactly what God wants or thinks and you thought there were out of their minds? Who is right? Are both wrong? How do you know? We may never know for certain, but by using what has been discussed above and by building a group of people to bounce ideas off of that don't all think like we do and who are willing to challenge us, we save ourselves a lot of frustration in the long run.

The Supernal/Immanent continuum is a gauge of where we find meaning in our lives. It's important for us to know not only what gives our lives meaning, but where that comes from, how we enhance it, and what we do with it. There are no value judgments about one being better than the other, all are valuable and imperative in our lives. The Supernal end is the purely transcendent and the Immanent is the more world-based end. Supernal means heavenly or divine.

HOLINESS –Center of Self-Identity

Sacred (A)---Terrene (T)

"Without holiness no man shall see the Lord" (Heb. 12:14).

Holy cow! Holy Toledo! Holy mackerel! We hear these often and don't really think about it. Take a moment and consider what the word holy means to you. It is a word packed with history and like many words, it comes with unique inputs received in our personal lives that can subtly change its meaning. Our souls know the true meaning of the word and try to live out that meaning within us.

If there were no soul and this life was it, anything holy or sacred would have to come from our perception, not from the created order itself. We make things holy or unholy in relation to the lenses we wear. Nothing is holy in and of itself from a human perspective. Our souls are what bring an intrinsic and inherent holiness to creation. The stamp of God is what makes the universe a holy place. This notion of holiness has to do with our perception of ourselves and our place in the cosmos. It is not about relating to the transcendent, it is about how we see ourselves. When we look in the mirror what do we see and how does that impact our lives? One way of looking at this is thinking about our egos; that is a measure of self-perception. We talk about self-esteem and confidence. We all know people who are full of themselves and those who have feelings of worthlessness. But there are people who the world says are worthless who know they are a treasure and special. This does not come from the ego, it comes from the soul. Our souls can rise above the world and stand in contrast to it within us. Our souls can counter, if need be, the barrage of criticism and contempt the world may shower on us. Our souls can also humble us and give balance to a life that perhaps takes too much ego stroking from the world. Our souls know our place in the cosmos and try to help us see it and believe it.

On one hand it is a difficult concept to believe that in the expanse of the universe, you matter. Even in the solar system, let alone the galaxy or universe we are small potatoes. Six billion people on earth for somewhere between 0 and 110 years. Even those who make significant dents on the landscape of humanity are either unknown or forgotten by the masses of the world. This is not said to depress you, just to be honest. Relative to the world's view, we are not that special. Sure, now and then a few individuals may make an impact, but even then how many know or care? In light of the history of the universe even human's existence on earth is minimal. Yet here we are, and God considers us holy and wants us to know of our holiness.

On one end of the spectrum lies the Terrene. Here, our identity comes from the world. We are our family of origin, our culture, the choices we make, the religion we choose. If I see something special in myself, it was my doing. If there is something unique about me, that exists because I created that view, certainly with the help of others. Our identity comes from the things and people around us. I am a lawyer, clerk, doctor, teacher, mechanic, or homemaker. Our identities are also formed by how we perceive our physical selves. Think about the impact of how you perceive yourself physically and how that helps form your identity. There are times when our physical nature dominates our identity and can be psychologically problematic. This is often true of people with eating disorders or with obese people. It is an interesting exercise to keep a piece of paper with you for a week. On that paper, write down anything you think of, either specifically or generally, that impacts who you are as a person. The start of a list might look like this:

General	Specific
Church	Wearing a suit, putting on a good face
Family	Playing with and having children Not providing as much as I would like Seeing myself in my children Bearing witness to what love can be
Job	Relationship with others Fulfilling a purpose I was called to Job satisfaction and meaningfulness
Nature	Seeing the mountains A walk on the beach
Appearance	Going bald, keeping in shape, not worrying about what I dress like to please others
God	Going on a retreat, meditation

While our core identities do not change that much in adulthood outside of significant experiences or lots of effort, we are all chameleons, changing a little bit in every situation and in relation to every relationship. It's natural, fine, and good. But who are you at the core of your being? What do you know about yourself? When all the facades are taken away what is left? At the root of who we are is our core identity and our soul. Our souls are not mere reflections of the rest of us. There is a connection, but they are different as we have talked about. Our persona has an impact on our soul and visa versa, but one does not rule the other. Each makes a choice to listen to and heed or run from the other.

Because this is a book about the soul, we will not spend time on the psyche or persona. The important thing to remember is that while they are intimately connected, they are separate and at times in conflict. Another way of looking at it is to think of the two worlds, material and spiritual. You have a material identity and a spiritual one. In the best of all worlds, they reflect one another. In the worst of situations they are at war. We see both around us.

When we are at the extreme end of the continuum that finds our material selves dominating, we don't listen to our spiritual side. We look to the world for answers to questions. While we are profound believers in the world of science, it will never have all the answers. The more we learn, the more questions there seem to be. Terrene people don't like mystery and in the end, accept science as a god. We see this in the political landscape as well. People want a Messiah, be it a dictator or a democratically elected leader, some people believe the political state can solve all their problems. Their identities are completely tied to science, being taken care of by the state, or a variety of other non-spiritual parts of their lives. Their hope is dependent on earthly wealth and power, leaving a legacy of some kind, and more often than not, leaving offspring to hopefully carry on the legacy. Think about how many truly saintly people you know or have read about that do not have a significant spiritual side, probably not many. People on this end of the continuum, the Terrene, build their identity around the world. They know they are here for a short time and it's over. That mentality breeds identities that seek material things and a more self-centered approach to life—and they

57

aren't ashamed of it, nor should they be, it is a choice they have made. We need to make sure we don't confuse this end of the spectrum with wealthy people. There are many deeply spiritual people of power and wealth. The key is to discover where their identity comes from; the wealth or something else.

Let's understand that God is fully present in the world, but God is different than the world. God's view of things is different than the worlds. Jesus tried to point this out time and time again. The Beatitudes are an exercise in showing the differences between how the world views things such as meekness, mourning, righteousness, and poverty. Take a minute and look at Matthew 5. Stop after each "Blessed are the......." Ask yourself how the world would finish that statement and then see how Christ does.

We need to mention here that being and doing are two different things. Our identity is reflected in our actions, but not completely. Most of us are hypocrites to some degree. We have had presidents and civic leaders we thought were good and righteous people turn out to have significant flaws. Some will spend the rest of their lives in jail. They did things that looked good but were a masque of their true self-identity which came from a world view of "me first."

The Bible tells us over and over that worship in and of itself does not lead to a deep relationship with God. Neither does Bible study, doing good deeds, bringing 2000 people to Christ, or a host of other actions we think we can do to buy our way into that relationship. God does not want to be in relationship with hypocrisy, but with honesty and integrity. God knows us better than we know ourselves, if we think we are going to pull the wool over God's eyes, guess again.

At the Terrene end of the continuum, we find people who may believe they are unique and special, but because they have created them self that way, not because they are inherently holy.

When Jesus was before Pilate he said that his kingdom was not of this world. There are two kingdoms, a worldly and a spiritual, Jesus lived in one and rules the other. There are two parts of our identities, the worldly and the spiritual. We are told time and again in the Gospels that we need to make a choice and that choice comes with a cost and a consequence. Are we children of God or children of the world? Remember, God put us here, we are in the world for a reason, but that reason is not to succumb, accommodate or assimilate completely to what the world tells us.

We will talk more about balance in a bit. Suffice to say at this point that our view is that living fully in this world is not the best option, nor is, while having a physical body, living in the spiritual world. Both have their dangers. God chose to put our souls into a physical body, there is a connection for a reason; the spiritual nature living with and in the midst of the material. So we should learn to be in the world but not of the world. We need to learn to see how God works in the world and how God views the world, to wear the lenses of Christ.

On the other extreme is the end of the Sacred. One might ask, "How is it possible to be too holy, too spiritual?" Let's understand that people truly at either end of the spectrum are very rare. The people at the Sacred end have essentially disowned the world---completely, they have forsaken their bodies as temples of God and the planet God put us on. They live only to move on to the spiritual plane of existence. They believe their identities come purely from the soul and from God, the world has no impact on them. As we hope you can see already, this isn't possible, only a fabrication of someone's mind. It sounds good. My identity comes purely from God, the world does not affect me, and I see everything through God's eyes, but it isn't a realistic view.

Not even Jesus as a human made that claim. His humanness got him driven to the desert to be tempted. is humanity had him cry out on the cross, "My God, my God, why have you forsaken me?" He cried, he got angry and drove people out of the temple, he was filled with sorrow at people's lack of insight and faith. The depth of his love for his mother, even to the extent he would change water to wine for her, showed his humanity. Jesus was a human, affected by the world around him.

As we move more towards balance and the center we come more into the range where most of us exist. Some people live and breathe spirituality. They use spiritual language, their every move is sought through contact with God. Often, the older they get, the more like this they become. In India, Sanyassins are Hindu men who leave their homes and wander, letting go of the world, having done what they were supposed to in this life. They want to use the end of their lives to rid themselves of attachments to the world. Hermetic monks are not unlike this. They remove themselves from the world in order to not be affected by it, to find their identities in God alone. These people tend to be more introverted. They may be quite humble about their self-identity. They have created an intricate notion of God and of themselves and that intricacy can be quite simple or vastly complex. But a calling to this form of life is rare.

Most of us are called to be in the world, but not of it, to have our identities come from the understanding of who we are as God's holy children and yet fully alive and identifying with the struggles of the human race. Our sense of holiness is founded on our knowledge that we are created with purpose, that God knows our names, loves us and believes in us more than we can imagine, and desires to have us be the vessels of his grace in the world. Our sense of holiness also comes from our relationships to and with the world. In this life we can't fully separate our souls and bodies, they function as one.

Balance allows both ends to feed off one another. Our bodies, minds, and psyches, are nourished by the soul and the spiritual realm. They glean wisdom and insight from the perspective the soul offers. In return, the soul has a conduit for the work it is called to do in the world. The soul receives input and does its best to transform us and our view of the world.

Transformation is at the heart of what the spiritual world is about, but God's desire is that we are transformed here and now, not in some distant future. The kingdom of God, in essence, is the fullness of God's presence. Through a mature soul that is in congruence with a person who is acting in the world through that maturity, we can have that full presence now. Why wait?

This sense of balance comes from having a conversation within ourselves and with those around us who have a sense of the journey. We look honestly at how we are acting and being in the world and reflect on that through the lens of our spiritual side. Yes, we can be delusional and convince ourselves that something is just when in reality it isn't. We overcome this to some degree by being part of a "holy" community. We allow others into our lives to both encourage and challenge us. We do not surround ourselves with only those who agree with us, but with people who truly want to deepen the life and work of their souls. People who have all the answers are not open to change and when you are closed to change, you are closed to God. If we are true to our faith and our journey, we have no fear of listening to the ideas and opinions of others. We relish anyone or any idea that can bring us closer to our true natures.

How am I out of balance, which side of the spectrum needs more attention and what should that attention look like? How can I use both my soul and the other parts of me to work together more fully? What am I willing to do to deepen the maturity of my soul and to act out of that maturity? Do I understand the depth of my own holiness in God's eyes? Why or why not?

This idea of holiness defines who we are in relation to God and to others. One impacts the other. Think about who you are and who you want to become. Do you feel that how you describe yourself is how others would or do describe you?

Connectedness—Center of Relationship

Mystical (M)-Temporal (E)

One of the buzz words of the past 20 years is networks. We hear about neural networks, computer networks, and social networks. We know that those who have a vast social network seem to get jobs more easily. Facebook, LinkedIn and Myspace are immense computer social networks that are making the world seem like a very small place. We are connected in ways we are unaware of. Identity theft shows us how much of our lives are interconnected. Some of us seek to build networks while others tend to shun them, preferring a greater degree of autonomy. At the core of networks, no matter what kind, is the notion of relationships.

Neural networks describe how the various facets of our brain communicate with each other and how the brain communicates with and directs the rest of the body. Thanks to Neurobiology, we have good ideas about the function of each part of the brain. We know where language is centered, that the amygdala is at the core of our emotional being, and that the cerebral cortex determines intelligence and personality to a large degree. The human brain does all of this without our having any conscious understanding. The functioning of the human brain is not predicated upon our understanding of it. Knowing about the neural networks can give us deep insights into why some people are depressed or struggle with language. We can see parts of the brain are not functioning or are triggered in certain situations. We can learn how our brain may be deficient with types of neuro-transmitters and need medicines to help overcome those deficiencies.

The brain was created and has evolved with many different components that are in relationship with each other. The depth of those relationships determine how we function. How does one neuron have a relationship with another? How does the frontal lobe relate to the anterior cingulate, two important parts of the brain? It's not a relationship of consciousness, but of chemicals. Chemistry is perhaps the arena on earth where relationships are most clearly defined. There are unique and very subtle bonds within the network of the brain. When these are out of balance, so too are we. There are times when these imbalances are corrected easily by surgery or through the use of medicines. There are times when brains are damaged or an imbalance is so severe that nothing will repair the network. One of the beauties of the neural network is that we often see where some brain damage is done and the brain figures out a way around it---delegating the now defunct function of the brain to another area. Systemically, we see this in the work place all the time. Someone is sick, on vacation, or quits and the rest of the office picks up the slack, creating a new network. However, networks that are built upon only one core central piece live on the edge. One can see even the fallacy of calling it a network if the central piece runs it all. The relationships of the people in the office will determine the strength of the network and what it can accomplish.

Our souls are part of several networks. One is with the transcendental realm; God and the Collaborative Unconscious. The other network is with the brain, which the soul uses to pass information from the spiritual to the material world. Our souls are the mediators of these worlds. The two ends of this continuum speak to how we relate to these different worlds. On the one extreme, the Mystical, we see all things as interconnected and feast on the plethora of relationships, almost incapacitating us with its overwhelming nature. On the other end of the continuum we see things simply with our senses. Connections are limited to what is before us or in our mind and the focus is on the material task at hand. The given task is paramount and ripple effects from that task are not considered to a deep degree. Neither of these is completely bad or wrong, they are just very narrow.

We are surrounded by linear thinking. People get tunnel vision and surround themselves with others who have the same view of the world. Group think is a consequence of linear thinking. The oil spill in the Gulf of Mexico is another. In these cases we either don't ask questions that will interfere with the desired end, or we shun minority viewpoints. History has shown us time and again that often times the minority turns out to be right, but how do we know at this time?

We think of linear people as being more left brain. The more logical part of the brain is dominant. We shouldn't be surprised that with this tendency, the soul is impacted. Our souls relate to our brains in ways the brain is comfortable with, to do otherwise would be to set up tension before the process of communicating even starts. When our souls become oriented and directed in a linear fashion it sets a goal or purpose in front of itself and receives guidance from that goal. Finding and serving God are perhaps two of the biggest over all goals the soul and brain are created for even when they won't admit it. A linear soul follows a normative progression of linear thinking which includes getting input and resources, doing activities and processing, having outputs and outcomes, seeing the impact of the activities, the context in which they were done and seeing what assumptions are being made. It's not that you can't find God with linear thinking, it's just limited.

This may all sound very broad, but in reality this type of person is very narrow in their focus. Everything revolves around the goal and the narrowness of its focus. If the goal is to understand a dream, this type person will focus on the one dream and will tend towards being very concrete in their assumptions rather than metaphorical or symbolic. They will do some research on dreams and will usually pick a model that is brain driven rather than transcendent driven. They are very evidenced based people and prefer tried and true methodologies and theories rather than novel approaches or more ethereal ones. They process things going from A to B to C to D. There is an order to the world, to their mind and to the spiritual world. They like the ten commandments, the order of the beatitudes, and Paul's lists. They love the order that God gives to the world and feel it is important to replicate that order in their lives.

The prayer lives of linear people tend to be, you guessed it, linear. They like acronyms like ACTS (adoration, confession, thanksgiving, and supplication). The belief is if they do the ritual in the right way, they will get the right effect. "Ask and it shall be given, seek and ye shall find, knock and the door will be open." How linear can you get? The end goal for all spiritually oriented people is the same, the means to that end is what shifts.

The danger for purely linear people is what they miss. Their perspective becomes so narrow and focused they miss lots of things around them. One of the best examples of this is the story of Elijah on the mountain in 1 Kings 19. He keeps expecting to find God speaking in and through nature. Fire, thunder, and earthquakes all bring him out to the front of the cave expecting to hear God, but God wasn't there. He had to let go of those ideas to hear the still small voice of God in his heart. Peter was a very linear thinker until he received the Holy Spirit, then he opened up. These people fail to see the larger picture. When they create contexts, it's a like entering a tiny village when in reality they have just entered New York City. The spiritual dimension vastly expands all contexts. This group of people certainly make connections with the world around them and even with the spiritual world to some degree, but the connections are on their terms, on their timing, and in reference to the goals they have set. It's not that they are self-centered, they may be quite altruistic, they are linear. They rationalize their behaviors in seeing that things get done, often with great efficiency. The problem is they forget to ask who asked to get those things done and what are the greater and systemic impacts of those actions. Again, this end of the continuum is called the Temporal.

At the other end of the spectrum are those who see connections everywhere, sometimes where they may not exist. They are Mystical, creating a language of their own. Their time is spent simply making connections for no reason other than to make connections. It's like the neurons in the brain simply connecting. When neurons connect, there are specific reasons that part of the network is being created at that time. Some people have vast social networks, for what? Some people have huge stacks of other people's business cards. Do they actually have relationships with these people? Are all those people connected in some way that matters? The mind of the connected person believes they are.

Connected people see life as a giant system, there really is no direct cause and effect of anything, it is a vast series of causes and effects. They will get bogged down in the system and miss the point. There is no denying we all live in a variety of systems, but again, the system is a means to an end, not the end itself. These people see everything through the lens of inter-relationships. They take Paul's letter to the church at Corinth in the twelfth chapter to heart. There he discusses how everybody is a part of the body (metaphorically) and all parts are important. One part can't say to another, "I have no need of you." It is the interworking of all parts that makes the body seek and find its potential. The reality is each part has a specific role to play. The eye can't be a foot, nor the brain a heart. Our eyes see and the rest of our body adapts to the messages it receives from the eye. Just seeing isn't enough, we need to respond or react to what we see. We feel cold and respond to it. We sense the presence of God and respond to it. We have dreams and hopefully react and respond to them. All actions call for a response, often an unconscious one. Connectors will get so consumed by the connections they miss the response. They see things many of us do not see, but seeing isn't enough.

Seeing the connections between things and between people is overwhelming. To be so in touch and see how people and things are entwined is a powerful gift. The challenge is using this gift for the benefit of others. Their minds rarely stop seeking and finding new ways of seeing the world.

Now, take this fascination with and ability to make connections and add to it the dimension of the transcendent. We are not simply talking about being connected to God, although spiritually they feel deeply connected to God, often at the expense of how they are called to serve the world. They are also connected more than most to the Collaborative Unconscious; to the totality of all experiences. They see history unfold in different ways, they find God in the world in ways most of us would never dream of.

Some of us have moments in our lives when we sense this level of relationship and that is what it is about, relationships. The issue here is that the relationship is with the system itself, not with parts of the system. You may be a member of a large company, you may understand all the departments and how they function, but if you are to hang onto your job, you need to do what you are asked to do. If all you do is sit around and tell people how the company works, you will be quickly unemployed. Our souls are bound up in deciphering the spiritual domain when at this end of the continuum. They are asked to go outside their normative parameters.

The prayer lives of this group are quite varied. Some will have lengthy prayer lists because of all the relationships they feel they have and all the prayer chains they are part of. Some will meditate, trying through the silence to connect more dots and receive more ideas. Internally, the rationalization is to connect more and more dots, more and more people, because it is in and through the connections that things get done. They believe that seeing the system is the answer. In reality understanding the system helps get us to the answer and connecting the dots in order to build relationships that matter, but note how the idea becomes pragmatic.

The other way the Mystical end of the spectrum sees things is to completely let go of the world. Rather than seeing the system, they let go of it. They become like a drop of rain falling into the ocean, disappearing as a unique part of the whole. Both of these styles are good as part of a larger picture, but when they become the norm, we are avoiding the world in which we exist.

Our souls love making connections; both to the divine and mondane. Our souls should be at the heart of all relationships. It is their nature. Our souls connect to God in order to build that fundamental relationship. Our souls connect to the Collaborative Unconscious precisely because it wants to use that information to guide and help us know ourselves and the world better. Our souls want to develop connections with our psyches so the two can become one, so we more fully understand who we are and what we are to become. All of this comes with a sense of balance.

In the middle we find balance. Most of us do not live at the extremes, except from time to time. Our tendency is to either be a bit more linear or a bit more systemic. The connections we make in life, the networks we build, need to have a purpose and need to be based on solid relationships, not just business cards. This isn't to say that for a particular reason you may just need someone's business card, but having a card is not the same as having a relationship. Our souls deepen based on the relationships they develop.

In the middle the soul takes what we glean from our perspective of the world, hopefully a systemic and holistic one. The soul combines that with what the Collaborative Unconscious gives it and then offers the person an idea of what to do with that information, a pragmatic response. The soul knows one without the other is less than complete. We are called to be people who build relationships. "Love your neighbor as yourself." "A new commandment I give to you, love one another as I have loved you." (Mark 12:30-31) Love necessitates relationship. We believe most would claim those we most love are those with whom we have the deepest relationship and connection—it makes sense.

We tend to think of relationships as being between personas or psyches from a psychological perspective. When was the last time you heard anyone talk about a soul to soul relationship? If our souls are unique entities within us and are connected to the transcendent, then why couldn't they relate to other souls independent of the rest of us and certainly in concert with us? We tend to leave out the authority and substance of the soul in conversations with others. Just think about how often one talks about the specific topics in this book with others in relation to the soul. This notion of soul to soul direct communication may be at the core of an explanation of déjà vu, synchronicity, and other phenomena we can't explain. Our souls are not as bound by space and time as we are, they connect to a dimension of the universe our physical natures can't.

Our connectivity plays a large role in how we relate to the world and to God. We need to be open to the idea of seeing more connections in both the mundane and spiritual worlds. We need to spend time and effort seeking them out and understanding why they are important and how we can use those connections to deepen relationships.

How would you see your connections in life?
What are your relationships based on?
Do you have spiritual relationships?
How often do you share your spiritual journey with others?
Do you feel connected to the transcendent?
What do you do with your dreams?

How does God speak to you?

Do you tend to look at the big picture or at a smaller piece most of the time?

Do you feel you seek deep relationships or are more comfortable keeping things on the surface?

What is the purpose of having relationships?

IMAGINATION CONTINUUM—Center of Creativity

Inspiration (N)—Reason (R)

All of us have imaginations. We daydream, dream, and fantasize. Many enjoy reading stories and books that show us the active imaginations of others. We are surrounded by creativity in our lives. Food, cars, architecture, technology, and the arts all speak to the human ability to imagine and create. Think where the world would be without an imagination, it's a bit frightening.

Science, with all its good intent, has bound us into a way of seeing the universe. While it seems to broaden our horizons, in reality it is constricting us. The more "laws" they discover, the less freedom we have. Isaac Asimov in his wonderful Foundation trilogy, talked of predicting social history. That while individuals may do odd things, societies act in specific ways under specific conditions that are predictable, very predictable. It is the science of anthropological prediction. We don't disagree with science, although we highly doubt Isaac Asimov's imagination in this respect is accurate. Much creativity is based on what went before. A PBS television series called Connections, showed how modern day inventions were linked to very ancient discoveries. He traced how one thing led to another and finally to the present. There is a reason computers were not invented in 500 AD or even in 1900 AD. Our minds and the capacity to create such machines didn't exist. If you read science fiction you find that people's imaginations are often well ahead of the technological curve to create their visions. This is only one part of our imagination and creativity. This is what we would designate as worldly imagination. There is also a spiritual imagination whose seat is the soul and whose power comes from the Collaborative Unconscious and God.

Jesus tells us we will do greater things than he has done and with God at work in us, we can do things unimaginable to our purely human mind. Paul tells us Christ desires to do in us infinitely more than we can ask or imagine---infinitely more!!!! Christ's imagination knows no boundaries. The depth of what God knows about the human condition and the physical laws of the universe are a bit larger than what we know. After all , God created them all.

Few of us doubt the reality of true miracles. Things happen in the world we can't explain and yet we believe. Healings, remarkable changes in a person's life, coincidences that make no sense, physical occurrences that defy understanding and others. We visualize them in our mind's eye easily, we love seeing them on the silver screen; but there is nothing quite like witnessing a true miracle, when natural law appears to be somehow suspended. And this is small in comparison to the miracles that surround us at all times in the spiritual world. For those who understand and appreciate the mysteries of science, our planet is a miracle and humanity's existence is a phenomenal miracle. It's a matter of perception like so many things in life. If we but look at a person walking down the street we don't think twice. If we take time to understand the immense complexity that enables that person to even be alive we start to understand the miracle of living. The position of the earth that allows us to exist, the connectedness of our cells, trillions of them that let us move, think, and breathe. We are all walking miracles. Perception.

The Imagination continuum speaks to the depth and breadth of our imagination and creativity. As has been true with the others, one end of the spectrum receives everything from the world, the other from the spiritual domain. Let's take a look at world based imagination first.

We call this end of the continuum Reason. All ideas, inventions, models, or living things came from somewhere. All can be traced back to often humble beginnings. Every philosophy has a root in another philosophy going back to before there was writing. Hume did not come up with Empiricism out of thin air. The artificial heart didn't pop into Dr. Barnard's brain having been a school teacher. Even Jesus came after a long list of prophets and John the Baptist. There is a time and place for every earthly thing. Our planet offers an immense array of materials with which to feed and nurture the living things on it. Our consciousness gives us the brainpower to use those materials as good or bad stewards. Humanity has always had a drive to be creative at all levels. We seem to go through periods of history where that drive is greater than others, but there are always people pushing the envelope and there always will be. Our psychological and cultural minds rarely keep pace with technology. We invent things before we have a clue how they will impact our lives, for better or for worse. We don't take time to count the cost, we just push forward. There is an inherent stewardship of creativity. The idea that our creativity is for the world, to help build relationships and a planet where seeking balance is easier and a common goal is a sound one.

All of us have imaginations. Some have more specific ideas and are more internally driven to bring our dreams and visions to reality than others, but we all have them. We want better lives for our children, we envision a better and more peaceful world, we dream about a world without crime or hunger and where children are cared for and not abused. Some do their best to create that world. Some have more resources and can do creative things that change the lives of millions while others of us try to help change the life of one here and one there. All are important.

The more world oriented person understands the resources that exist and focusses on them to build their dreams. Their goal is to create a better world, first for them self, then for those they care about, then for others. At some level, the world is a game with pieces and someone needs to move those pieces, why not me? They can be very altruistic, although this is rare. Their vision may be to save the planet, to be better stewards of the resources the world offers. They push the edges of science and experiment to make the world a better place and we desperately need that creativity. They believe that part of the reason they are alive is to creatively serve the world. God is more distant to them but is clear about what she wants and expects.

The economic and political engines of the world run this machine. Are we surprised that if you look at the major inventions of the last 150 years, most come from America? Why is that? It's not because Americans are smarter or have better imaginations, but because the political and economic engine allowed those to flourish rather than to be squashed or squandered as in many other countries. The geography, climate, culture, resources, and size of a country along with their political structure and economic structure all have an impact on how those imaginations are fostered and allowed to bloom. The reverse is also true. There is no question that the explosion of ideas and inventions in America has come with a price. It may be a price worth paying, but it does come with a price. The collapse of the family, increased violent crimes, an epidemic of obesity and juvenile diabetes, the list goes on. Our planet was created within amazingly narrow parameters. If we were 2% closer to the sun or further away, we would probably not exist. If the moon were 3% closer or further away we would probably not exist. Social dynamics are no different. There is a narrow range of parameters that when we go outside them, things go wrong. Our imaginations have a very hard time believing this and containing themselves. They believe they have the world's best interests at heart.

This view of creativity finds the answers to all questions in things and people. Many politicians are like this. They truly believe they can solve the problems of a country, that they are the hope of that country. Policies can truly bring about consistent and persistent peace and economic bliss. Do you really believe this?

Take a minute and think about creative things you do or creative ideas you have. Where do they come from? Can you trace them back to a source? Where do you think that source got them from? How far back can you go? How many generations can you trace your personality characteristics too?

This end of the spectrum is rational, it is based on the sense experiences we have. Our creativity comes from what has been and what is. Novelty is rarely seen in this vein although it does happen. Finding the transcendent in the midst of the world is a wonderful thing. Knowing that the Creator created your brain and expects us to use them is another miraculous and wonderful thing—although at times we may wish we were just given orders and followed them like robots. There is nothing wrong with reason and there is nothing wrong with world oriented creativity, they are both fabulous. But like all the other spectrums, when you ignore an entire domain, you miss out on the possibilities about what can happen.

The other end of the spectrum is the spiritual which we are calling Inspiration. Here we live in a different world. We care for God's

71

children, but not about the world. We hear Jesus say that his kingdom is not of this world. We see Jesus tell the rich man to give everything away if he wants eternal life. We hear money is the root of all evil. The purely spiritual person does not care. After all, in heaven we probably won't need money or food, everything will be covered, if we even have bodies. For these people, we are wasting our time focusing on taking care of the planet, "leave the dead to bury their own dead." What we need to be doing is focusing solely on God's kingdom---they kind of forget the rest of the sentence. We are to seek first the kingdom of God, it didn't say seek only the kingdom of God. Like the other traits on this extreme end, these folks fail to see that we are in the world for a purpose, that God gave us this planet and its resources, not to be avoided and ignored, but to be utilized.

The imagination and creativity at this end are at times mystical and magical. The very language of those who are this end of the spectrum is difficult to understand. Because the spiritual world is spiritual, there is no language, so attempting to express the spiritual life in worldly language is hard at best. When we read Ezekiel or St. John of the Cross some of the images are wild and clearly symbolic. Jacob Boehme uses words that one can really only comprehend if you are at the same place he is. In the end, the spiritual life is an experience and the deeper the experience the more difficult it is to describe. Poets, artists, dancers, preachers, and writers all try, but most will claim they fall far short of what they truly want to express.

This end of the continuum usually has significant contact with the Collaborative Unconscious. They have remarkable vision, but lack any sense of what to do with it in the real world. And they don't really care. They feel lost in the world because their ideas are not at all based on worldly premises. We all know reading about a culture in a travel book is different than actually visiting that culture and that is different than living there and that is different than having been born there. When most of us travel, we buy a guidebook as a starter and we learn from that. We may hitch up with a tour guide to give us some better understanding of the lay of the land and where the hot spots are, usually the hot tourist spots. If we are lucky we know someone there that can show us the more "local" things, seeing the world from their perspective, but we are still foreigners, we can never fully enter their culture. Spiritual and worldly cultures are fundamentally different creatures, different countries. They speak different languages and have different purposes for existing, yet they exist in the here and now, side by side.

Spiritual imagination is necessary because it connects us to the most creative mind in the universe, to the mind of God. It connects us to the Collaborative Unconscious that in turn connects us to every creative thought and idea that has ever existed. We need this connection because the world can't solve all the world's problems. We are not completely worldly people, we have souls and those souls have a home in the spiritual dimension of reality. Both are imperative to our well-being. Spiritual creativity gives us a fresh perspective on the world, it allows us to envision miracles, to supercede science and grab hold of powers science has yet to or may never find. When there is a true balance between the soul and the psyche, between the spiritual and worldly realms, humanity will soar. If one dominates the other, individually or culturally, in the end, we perish.

There are always times in our lives when we are pulled more by one side than the other. In prayer and meditation we are trying to consciously connect with the world of the Spirit. The religious heart yearns for a deeper relationship with the divine. We want to understand the signature of all beings as Jacob Boehme puts it in his book of the same title. When someone is doing math homework, their focus is not on the Collaborative Unconscious, but on the mathematical laws of the world---we don't believe you'll need math classes in heaven. So our lives move back and forth along this continuum, but where do you spend most of your time?

Our souls connect us to the infinite imagination and creativity of God and the Collaborative Unconscious. We are able to see and do things outside what the world says is possible, what you believe is possible even for yourself. This connection also gives us deeper understanding of the other traits of the soul; our transcendent natures, holiness, connectedness, and call. There are times we need to break free from the parameters the world has put around us. St. Francis was not raised to be what he ended up as; it took deep spiritual imagination and openness to God's voice and call. In order to let go of ideas, thoughts, habits, and opinions we have in order to be what God desires us to be, we need internal and spiritual creativity. The core purpose of this aspect of our soul is to open us to the kingdom of God internally, at the level of our heart, not just as a mental and intellectual construct. Within us, the kingdom and God and the world can become one.

One of the ways God works with our souls via the imagination is through our dreams. Many people remember very vivid dreams with remarkably imaginative symbolic images in them. This is your creative side working with God to teach you about yourself; pay attention. There are patterns in dreams, recurring themes that are pointing us to something. Why wouldn't God just be direct and spell out for us what he wants in a dream? Dreams are usually after truths we either don't want to see or are incapable of
seeing. By using symbolic language, God eases us into deep truths and realities. We are made to think about what is occurring on the creative level of our minds and souls, to look at things as metaphors or symbols. It makes us look at our worldly lives in a different way and hopefully not only discover what God is trying to show us, but also how to creatively deal with it. God's deepest desire is to be in full relationship with everyone. Our dreams are but one of the ways God tries to build those bridges.

Our lives in the world connect us to one another, to the air we breathe, the food we eat, and the ground on which we walk. We have purpose and that purpose is to join together our soulfulness and our worldliness in order to be good stewards of the planet and God's children. How those purposes are worked out is where our imaginations come in. Our souls can give us new ways of looking at the world, new avenues for science to investigate, and new ways to express God's kingdom. God is the greatest scientist in the universe, does it not make sense to learn from Him?

We should have one foot in each world, working together to make us whole. We should caution ourselves to not be overly dominated by one or the other, save for brief moments in time. Remember when Jesus took Peter, James, and John onto the mountain and he was transfigured with Moses. They wanted to stay there, to build tents, they'd reached the peak of spirituality in their minds. They'd arrived at the gates of the kingdom of God. What did Jesus say? He told them to go back to the world, that was where the work was to be done. Yes, we need spiritual experiences, yes we need that deep and ongoing relationship with God, and yes feeling the presence of God in our lives 24/7 is the goal, but this all needs to happen while we are in the world, not on a mountain top.

Are you pulled more by the world or the spirit? Make a list of what each one does for you and to you.
How do you see your creative side expressed in each realm?
How can you empower your imagination?
What keeps you from having a more active imagination and expressing it in creative ways?
Do you trust your intuition or your mind more? In what situations do you trust one more than the other and why?
How do you see creativity in your relationships?
Would you say you have a creative and imaginative relationship with God?

THE CALL CONTINUUM—Center of Purpose

Idealist (D)—Pragmatist (P)

Our transcendence gives meaning to our lives. Our deepest meaning comes when we are within the purposes for which we were created. Those purposes are our callings. This brings us to a very important piece of theology; does God need us? Our belief is that God does indeed need us, he built the earth with that end in mind. Does God need us to exist, of course not. God gave us free will. This allows for the possibility that we could all choose to ignore God. Even Jesus had the ability to ignore God, "not my will but thine." This is not to insist that we have power over God, that we can look to the heavens and say, "hah, do what I want or I won't do what you want." In the big picture let's be honest, each of us is nothing, "from dust you came and to dust you shall return."(Gen 3:19) God is fully aware that many will not listen or choose to heed his ways. God also knows many will and he relies on those to spread his message. God may assume the worst and accept the worst. He gives everyone the potential to fully realize their humanity, without exception. Those who do not, do so by choice. This means that in the end, all of us have chosen to not follow God to some degree, since no one has reached their full humanity. God created us, believes in us, loves us unconditionally, and knows us better than we know ourselves.

If God is fully present to the world, fully conscious of what is going on, past and present, then God is in a good place to let us know what would be in our and the world's best interest for us to do. That is our Call. God calls us.

In the letter to the church at Ephesus, chapter 4, the writer tells us that we were giving gifts in order to a) build up the body of Christ and b) serve the world. Those are at the core of our callings, to build up the faith of those who believe and to serve those through love that are around us. Our calling has nothing to do with selfish and egocentric needs or desires. We can't become fully human if we only serve ourselves. This brings us to the two ends of the continuum we are calling the Call. On one end is the purely God given call, fed by our souls and understood through our connections to the world and the transcendent. We call this end Idealist. It's focus is on the spiritual, the lens through which the call is perceived is based on what can happen through hope and God. The other end is our more egocentric drives, the "me" focused call. We call this end the Pragmatist. They are more task and goal oriented and rationalize that it is for God, but their motives are different. "Not all who call me Lord will enter the kingdom of my Father, but those who do the will of my Father." (Matt. 7:21)The goal is to have both, to have one feed the other in a symbiotic relationship that nurtures the psyche and the soul.

We all have drives. We aren't talking here about sexual and survival drives, although they certainly come into play. People with decent self-esteem want to do something with their lives. They want to become something. They want to provide for their families if they have them and leave a mark on the world. Some are more driven than others. We all know of severe type A people who are workaholics and seem to exist solely to make more money, gain more power, or create more fame. There are those that are driven to create, not for the purposes of helping the world, but for the sake of their own ego-gratification. They will stop at little for self -gratification, even if they try to hide it behind a false sense of humility.

There is nothing wrong with being driven. Much of the technology we have on the planet would not exist if it wasn't for driven people. If people were not driven by certain values, many countries and cultures would not exist, certainly not the United States. Many saints were driven. Paul was driven. If you read biographies of driven people you will find there is no common thread amongst them as to how they got that way. Many entered the world driven, it was part of their nature from birth, even though there was no drive gene that could be found in their ancestry. For others it was how they were raised. Type A parents tend to raise Type A children. Taking Tiger Woods out every day to golf from a very early age may have had something to do with his drive. This is not a value statement, just a fact. Others are bitten by a passion sometime during their lives and are driven by it. Perhaps a bad experience. Someone has a child killed by a drunk driver and becomes driven to do their best to make sure it doesn't happen to others. Someone sees pictures or travels to a third world country and sees suffering and puts their energies into stopping it. We would contend all presidents are driven by a need for power. There is nothing wrong with this, we need leaders and most of us do not have the fortitude or drive to do what is necessary to reach that point. As you can see already, drives and calls can be connected. People on the drive end of the continuum have something in common, their drive is centered on them self. They may rationalize that what they are doing isn't for them self, but it is obvious that it is. Ask most driven people if they could have everything they have without needing others and sharing what they have with others, would they do it and many would say yes. They want more fame, power, money, and health. Others are merely pawns in their game. You need to make the pawns feel important, but you believe in the end they aren't nearly as important as you. Driven people change the world. You can feel a deep calling by God, but if you have no drive, you may not make it out the door, you will simply talk about your calling rather than becoming your calling.

Most of us wish we were more driven than we are. There are a few that wish they had less drive, although they seem to be rare. Again, let's remember the amount of drive in and of itself is not a bad thing. St Francis, Mother Teresa, and Jane Goodall were or are driven people. It's the attitude we bring with our drive that matters. There are those who need to increase their drive and those that may need to lessen it. Our drives and what we do with them can be controlled to some degree. We will see more about this in the sections about the specific types.

A few of the questions we should ask ourselves are; what is my drive doing for me and to me? What is it doing for and to others? Drives can ruin families and potentially destroy nations. Even drives we may feel are for positive things can destroy relationships. When a drive becomes the core focus of who we are, red flags should arise for us and for those around us. A drive can be an addiction.

There is a theory in psychology called drive theory. It claims that drives and motivation increase as we have needs, especially physiological needs, that aren't met. They are reduced as needs are met. We all know people whose drives are immense even though all needs have been more than met. In fact, those with the greatest drive seem to have the most and don't stop, they want more. Some consider the types of things we are discussing as secondary drives, which is fine. Primary drives would be for thirst, hunger, and sex. These are more instinctual and are survival skills. The drives we are talking about are well beyond the need to survive.

Some other drives psychologists have mentioned are the curiosity, activity, and the need for affection. Some people want to know everything about everything, others can't stop being active, they tend to be high physical risk takers and adventure seekers, while others seem to have an unquenchable thirst for affection, often in the form of sexual activity. The question again is to look at where the drive is coming from and where the focus is. When it is on the individual, something is out of balance.

The Pragmatist is exactly that, pragmatic. They are calculating and goal oriented. They see something that needs doing and they do it and marshal the necessary forces to do so. They tend to have high energy and a need to be with other people, usually giving orders or discussing their accomplishments. As we have said, they convince them self and often others that this is all about God and indeed, depending on how extreme they are, some of it may be. You can help people and still have a selfish motive. An interesting discussion would be to think about motives and actions. If you do something good out of a bad motive, how does that affect your relationship with God? The soul is engaged in this work, but from a distance because the worldly drive is too much.

Our drives while based in the world are assumed into the realm of the spiritual and the spiritual is adapted to fit the drive. God wants us to be doers, to act in and for the world. We are all called on to feed the hungry, clothe the naked and visit the lonely. You can do all these things without any sense of being spiritual or having a soul. The idea is to figure out where the Call is coming from; are you creating it out of some personal reason, because of conformity, doing what the world tells you to do, or because spiritually you feel called by God?

The other extreme we are calling the Idealist. This call comes from the transcendent realm and tends to avoid the world. Its sole purpose is to guide us on how best to serve the world and attain full transcendence. The Idealist in this context looks at all the pieces of the pie that are the world and sees at any given moment with what we have at our disposal, how we fit in. The soul will never ask someone without any musical talent to become a professional musician. Our souls know our internal abilities and drives better than we do. While drives are world based, the call is spiritually based.

Our call is not based on rational thought even though it may make rational sense. Because we can't make all connections, we can't connect all dots. Sometimes things don't seem to make a lot of sense. A person who follows their calling when it goes against rationality is a person of very deep faith. At times many of us might think they are off their rocker. At times it will be difficult to tell one way or the other. There is no guarantee that if you are following God's call you will be successful. All people have free will, not just you. Others can choose to not believe you and go against you, even when you are in God's will, heeding God's call.

One of the key differences between being called and being driven lies in the notion of where they originate and how they are carried out. Drives originate within ourselves and the world around us. We carry them out with the skills we have learned or been given genetically. Our calling comes from the transcendent and is carried out only through the help of and access to that transcendent.

St. Francis received a calling from God to serve the poor, and to start an order. He didn't have a clue how to do that or even what it meant. Through prayer and sharing with others he followed a path. That path led him to do some things that made no rational sense. His humility and submissiveness to God are what paved the way, not his drive, which clearly he also had.

This calling has to do with the purpose for which we were created, through which we find the deepest meaning in the world. It is a purpose created for us rather than a drive that creates its own purpose.

We find this calling by listening and being attentive to the transcendent. There are times when the calling is crystal clear and others when the calling comes out of a haze. Our callings need to be tested in the world, they need to be communicated to others on the spiritual journey who can pray with and for us, who can ask questions and challenge us.

These callings are not normally the magnitude of the ones we hear about like St. Francis, Mother Teresa or many missionaries. You may be walking down a grocery aisle and God may call you to talk with someone you don't know. Will you be sensitive enough to hear that voice? Your calling in life may be to be a good listener or a teacher. If we feel called to something then we need to discover the meaning behind the calling and its purpose. There is a reason God calls us to things, it's not simply a whim. What is it about you at this time and place that God is calling you to something?

We do not see calling as only in reference to a job. You may be called to be a doctor, missionary, teacher, business person or anything else---and then again, you may not. The calls of the soul can range from a life focus to making a phone call. Calls can be short term or life-long, they can change at any time and for unknown reasons. The only thing we know for certain about receiving a call is that they are directly from the transcendent realm and tie us into the purposes of creation and its coming to fruition.

So what is the danger of having all call and no drive? Drive is what moves and motivates the calling. If all you have is a voice telling you to do something, then you have a message but no means to pass on that message and the meaning of it. We believe in the power of medicine. We also believe in the power of prayer. The two combined are remarkable. Try relying simply on prayer for a few months. Take all human activity out of the world, just sit and pray. We would all die. God needs and uses us to carry his purposes, will, love, and grace into the world. Listening without action does little. Most therapeutic theories say listening is critical, but if all the therapist does is listen and never says anything, the person will not change as quickly as when the therapist reflects, asks questions, and shares insights with that client.

If we are honest with ourselves, most of us know our calling. We may lack the motivation and drive to follow through and carry the thought to action. We need a nudge or a kick from others.

We believe life should be lived as much as possible in the middle. We receive the calling and feed it with our drives. Any drives we have should be balanced with the questions of the soul as to purpose, motivation, and meaning. Our drives working in concert with our calling make for an amazing combination of the supernal and the immanent. They feed one another.

As we look at the continuum we need to be honest with ourselves.

What motivates us?
What are the motives behind where I spend most of my time?
What do I derive meaning from and what is the purpose of that meaning?
Do I feel my life has a larger purpose and connection to the world than just my actions themselves?
Does God give me purpose?
How do I discover that?
How do I know if I am doing what I am called to do?
Are my drives a means to an end or an end in and of themselves?
What do I need to do in order to achieve a greater sense of balance on this continuum?
Have I shared my thoughts and ideas on any of these questions with others?
Who would I be comfortable sharing them with?

Summary of the terms on the Continua

This is just a brief section describing each of the ends of the spectra and what they mean. Some of the terms may be new to the reader. We tried to find words that were not heavily laden with value because we believe strongly that to be whole we need a balance of both ends. There is a tendency to think of spiritual things as positive and worldly as negative. We could not disagree more, it's a matter of perspective. There are things of the world that are amazingly creative and there are spiritual things that are remarkably destructive. All of these terms are value free from where we sit or perhaps more accurately, we see them as value neutral. They are what we make of them in the context of who and what we are.

Transcendent—center of meaning
S Supernal—heavenly or divine, of being above and beyond human experience and understanding, of a spiritual and transcendent nature
I Immanent---having to do with the inherent nature of our physical nature. Attached to and from the world, a more physically oriented presence, including the mind. Grounded in the senses.

Holiness—center of self-identity
A Sacred--- sense of identity founded in the idea we are created by the Creator as a special and unique child of that Creator. A spiritual foundation that is not reliant on the world to sustain it.
T Terrene—a rare word for earth that carries with a significance of the wholeness of the world, its sense of symbiosis, inter-relatedness. A holistic view of the world but grounded in the sensorial.

Connectedness—center of relationships
M Mystical—Connected to things spiritual, especially the Collaborative Unconscious and more abstract and intuitive ways of connecting. Relationship based more on intuition and an understanding of deeper things that we all have in common, known or unknown.
T Temporal— Connected to things of the senses and in the world. Relationships based more on what you see and can directly act upon.
Imagination—center of creativity

N Inspiration—While all creativity is from God, this end finds creativity more from within, coming up with novel ideas that come from nowhere and are not founded upon anything in particular. There is often an absence of seeing how the connected dots got them there. Intuition is a significant force at this end.

R   Reason--- Their minds help them see how to connect dots in the world to come up with new and wonderful ideas. Their creativity stems from using what is available to them in the world in new ways.

Call—center of purpose

D   Idealist—This end of the spectrum feels the gravity that is the call of God. God calling them to do something in particular that may be out of their comfort zone. They may or may not have an explanation that makes sense to them or others as to why they are doing what they are doing. This call always builds up and is creative. Their purpose is more about who they are and their vision of what God wants for them and the world than what they do.

P   Pragmatist—This end finds its way in the world. This person knows their personal gifts and talents and seeks normative ways to use them in the world. They find purpose by serving God in the world through what they do.

Finally, before we look at the types, there are four concepts we will be looking at within each of the types: The Collaborative Unconscious, Richard Niebuhr's notion of Christ and Culture, Worship, and the Gospel of Mark, chapter 2, verses 1-12. A brief intro as to how they fit in will be helpful to understand before you read about your type.

COLLABORATIVE UNCONSCIOUS

There are three central domains of our psychological being; the conscious, the subconscious and the unconscious. This book accepts the premise that the soul is a fourth domain in that make up. The unconscious includes all those things of which we are not conscious. Many believe this could be as much as 80% of who we are. To be conscious of something means to be aware of it, to mentally acknowledge it. At some level, all involuntary actions are unconscious or at least subconscious. We do not think about every breath we take, every step we walk or run, every bite of food we eat. Unless we write a speech and read from it, our speech is not a fully conscious action. To some degree we are aware of what we will say, but exactly how the words come out is not a fully conscious action. Consciousness means to be aware of what is happening or perhaps about to happen. It involves either receiving input from our senses or engaging a mental idea, processing it or them, acknowledging them, and creating a feedback loop. Our brains are very fast, but they are not instantaneous. Have you ever said something you wished you hadn't? Wished you'd rephrased something? Have you done things you wished you'd thought through more or gathered more information before making a decision? Have you felt a tenseness in your body or been afraid of something where there is no overt rationale for it? These are all examples of how our unconscious intercedes with our conscious selves. There is nothing wrong with this, it's just a fact of life. There is no way around this fact. We will always have a significant amount of unconsciousness in our lives.

Our unconscious and sub-conscious exist to protect us from the onslaught of what the conscious world brings. As in all things, we need a balance. The challenge is to push ourselves to learn more about and from the unconscious, to build a healthy relationship with it so that we know more about ourselves.

Many of the existentialist writers such as Camus and Sartre, discuss what life would be like if we were fully conscious of everything. We would have a break down very quickly just with respect to the sensory overload. Consider everything that you hear, think, smell, touch, taste, and see at any given moment. How much of that is just background, not present to what you need to be aware of with your senses?. Can you be fully present to everything going on around and within you? In the *Great Divorce* by C.S. Lewis he talks about a person getting off the bus in heaven, to check it out. Everything there is more real than on earth. The grass hurts it is so real, the fragrances are overwhelming. It is all too much. Thank God for the buffering effect of the unconscious.

We can, to some degree, make parts of the unconscious more conscious. By making efforts to be more aware, to unpack who we are and how we came to be, and by challenging ourselves, much is revealed. We can do this by using projective exercises such as sand tray or play therapy, painting, journaling, sculpture, free association, music, and dream work.

There is a psychological tool called the Johari Window (Luft, J.; Ingham, H. (1950). **The Johari window, a graphic model of**

interpersonal awareness. *Proceedings of the western training laboratory in group development* (Los Angeles: UCLA). It is a square that is cut into four parts whose sizes change. In one square are things that I know about myself and that others know about me, my public self. In another are things I know that others don't; my secret self. The third section are those things others know about me that I do not know about myself, the illusive or ignorant self. Perhaps the best known of these is addiction. Most people know a person is addicted before that person knows. Different people have different views of us because we put on different personas in different situations. Most of us do not act the same in front of our bosses as we do in front of our five year old child. The last section contains those things we do not now about ourselves and that others do not know about us; the unknown self.

	Known to Self	Unknown to Self
Known to Others	Public Self	Blind Spots
Known to Others	Hidden Self	Unconscious Self

These four sections overlap at times. People may be aware that someone is an addict, but they don't know the underlying causes or history. The addicts themselves may be unaware of what and why things happened. These sections are fluid. They change size and are different for every person. Usually the last section is the largest. We like to think we know ourselves and make ourselves known to others. We can't really even write down what others know about me that I don't know about myself because then it would move to a different category. Additionally, we can't write down what is unknown to me and the world because again, it would move to a different category once I know it. In reality, this last section which includes the complete scope of who and what we are as persons is the largest. If we accept the fact that most of our being is unconscious and we are unconsciously aware, then it is only natural that this would follow. This means that at the core of our being we know, we just don't understand on a verbal and conscious level. We believe our souls also fit into this window. There are things we know about our spiritual lives and there are things of which we are completely unaware. The greatest example to us is those who deny a soul, for them awareness is non-existent. They will claim we are ignorant. The challenge with the soul is to make it known and for the most part, public.

Our souls add a fourth dimension to our existence. They are a bridge and repository between the transcendent and immanent realms. They are a filter that adds depth and breadth to our understandings of the world and of our selves. The soul, in and of itself, is conscious and unconscious. We can be in touch with our souls but much of the work of the soul is done behind the scenes, sub or unconsciously. How much of your waking day are you focused and aware of what is going on around you on a spiritual level? Many of us are so engaged with the world we have little time for the transcendent. Our souls act as that bridge, being ready to meld the two when we are ready. It is interesting that we seem to be able to turn spirituality on and off like a light switch. We go to church or a bible study and "get spiritual." What would the world be like if everyone was spiritual by nature and had to turn the world off and on? This is what the world of the mystics is like to a large degree. The Collaborative Unconscious is fed through the soul on behalf of our entire being and helps with the fluidity and consistency of this switching.

Analytic or Depth Psychology has and will continue to study how the unconscious works and plays itself out to our conscious selves. Many complex theories exist and to be honest, we do not believe "the truth" about ourselves will ever be completely known. Like the wind and the Holy Spirit, we do see the impact and effects of things we do not consciously know. We will not spend time explaining the unconscious here other than how it relates to the soul. As we have said already, we believe dreams, visions, and deep insights often come from the soul, via the unconscious to the conscious.

This raises the question of where and how the soul gets all that information. If the soul is an entity that lives within us and is self-contained, how does it acquire novel constructs? Why couldn't our unconscious selves do that on their own? This is where the

Collaborative Unconscious comes into play. For example, we have learned that when you delete emails, they aren't really deleted. They exist out there in the electronic universe somewhere for an indefinite amount of time. Somewhere, someone had to tell a computer to save a copy, but after that, they just sit somewhere until accessed. Someone has to know where to look and have a reason to look. There are untold trillions of emails and conversations saved. No "big brother" is looking at all of them. There isn't enough time even if they wanted to. But they still exist.

Your thoughts, dreams, and actions are the same way. On the level of the unconscious, they exist for eternity in the transcendent realm. We do not know where they go or what "hard drive" they are stored on, they simply exist. This pool of information we are calling the Collaborative Unconscious and it is potentially available to everyone. Not only this, but this pool is collaborative, it knows about itself and about you. The Collaborative Unconscious is fully conscious to itself through God, but unconscious to you. It is distinct from God and other parts of the transcendent realm in that it is merely pieces of information that are completely interconnected; a giant jigsaw puzzle that grows immensely every day. The Collaborative Unconscious has one reason for existing, to help us. It is the prime connection between all humans and between space and time, because it is outside of space and time.

Just as the DNA of all humans is essentially the same except for extraordinarily small pieces, so too we all have the potential to access and use the Collaborative Unconscious. You may well ask, how is this different than God? We will explain with some examples. We could discuss our children for hours, but I am not my child. We can look at things our children create, listen to them sing or talk. We do our best as parents to guide them, to love them, to give them access to increase the options they will have in their lives. But attempting to force a child to become something they don't want to, rarely works. Persuasion and collaboration are better than coercion. If we knew absolutely everything about our children and everything the universe had to offer, perhaps we would be better parents. God fits into this analogy well. Because God has given us free will, God must work through persuasion and collaboration. God uses the ideas, language, culture, and thoughts we have to move us forward, when we are open to it. The real question is why wouldn't we? Why wouldn't we want to be moved by the totality of creation? Why would we want to be so self-centered to think we can do it on our own? In point of fact, the majority of the time that is what the human race believes and how is that working out for humanity?

Think for a minute what would happen if we actually learned from history? What would happen if we actually felt the suffering of others? What would happen if we all woke up and had a common dream or vision? Wow. What if we all woke up tomorrow and deeply respected and tolerated our differences? What if we woke up and acted on the belief that all people are equal and it was wrong to either have too large of an ego (and all that goes with it) or to diminish other people? What if we woke up and acted upon the belief that it was wrong to burden the next generation with our issues? Life and lives would change.

There is no proof the Collaborative Unconscious exists. There is just evidence. How else do we explain déjà vu, being in the midst of something and knowing you've been there before? How do we explain being at the right place at the right time? How do we explain synchronicity, that we have a common dream with others, common thoughts, that one thing after another just seem to line up? How do we explain when we know something is wrong somewhere or with someone? How is it we feel a pain inside and can't explain it, only to discover it was at that exact minute someone close to us died or was in an accident? How was it that prophets spoke so accurately of the future? In the future we hope to put together a book of stories of experiences of the Collaborative Unconscious breaking into the world. If you have one, send it to us. Skeptics may have all kinds of criticisms. Some will claim people are just making up the stories. After all there is no proof they had a specific dream or knew something was happening unless they told others before it actually happened. They will grant that coincidences happen. With the trillions of things that happen every day on earth, some coincidences are destined to occur. We agree, but the number and type are too overwhelming to avoid. In the end we all believe what works for us. For us, acknowledging the Collaborative Unconscious as an active part of our soul's ability to connect us to the transcendent is well worth it and it makes sense. This part of the unconscious explains a great deal and affords immense hope for the world.

We all access this reality to different degrees and in different ways. Some do so more directly while others are more passive. The Collaborative Unconscious is working on us 24/7. The choice we have is to listen to it or ignore it. Dreams, sudden insight, and being open to being at the right place all the time are three central ways it works.

Finally, we must understand that the Collaborative Unconscious includes and needs us. We are the fuel that feeds it. Who and what you are, what you do, what you think and feel are all there. We make the decision to a large degree of what gets there. Are we sending creative or destructive pieces into that world? The more creatively conscious we are as beings, the more creative information we impart to the future.

So how is God different than the Collaborative Unconscious? The CU does not think or act and have no sense of novelty. That is God's domain. The Holy Spirit working with the CU gives us the breadth and depth of insight and creativity needed to act on God's behalf in and for the world. Why do they need it? God has designed the earth and humanity in such a way that things build on one another, even spiritually. Certainly God could have created us in such a way that in 200 B. C. they could have landed on the moon with the known technology of the day. He chose to have us build upon human understanding with spiritual insight and novelty.

Note on Niebuhr's Christ and Culture

You will find in each of the types described below a few lines in reference to Richard Niebuhr's classic book, **Christ and Culture** (Harper Collins,1951) where he describes the different ways that Christ (and us) can be seen in relation to culture. We have described each of the 5 types below.

CHRIST AGAINST CULTURE—In this scenario we find the height of the two kingdoms (transcendent and immanent) at war. These are the absolutists that believe Christians are here to point out to culture their sinfulness and to call them back to God's world. Culture is human and what humans do is by and large evil or contrary to God. We are here to live in the midst of culture, but to be different. Classic examples of this are the Amish. They certainly deserve respect for their dedication to their vision in spite of amazing pressures to adapt. To their credit they do not judge culture, they simply live outside and against it. These are the people who openly oppose the evils within culture. At times they also speak against the religious culture. They and their views are correct. Those who disagree with them are wrong.

CHRIST OF CULTURE—This is perhaps the other extreme. They see Christ in the world and being part of the world. We are to assimilate into culture as opposed to standing out from culture. They see the best of culture and find God in the midst of culture. They believe that because they are a part of culture they can bring Christ to culture, adapting the message to the culture. They find common ground between the Christian message and values and that of the best in the world. This group tends to attach themselves to the ways of culture without really challenging them or themselves in light of Christ. Many of us are much more this way than we like to admit. We are very pious on Sundays but during the week it's hard to see a difference between believers and non-believers.

CHRIST ABOVE CULTURE—Christ looks down on culture, sometimes holding it in contempt but acknowledging it. This is often the Christ of the church, the institutionalized Christ that stands as a supposed beacon in the midst of culture, judging it from lofty towers. The problem is that Christ lived with sinners and if anything judged the religious institutional leaders, something rarely seen in our institutional churches today. While trying to find the balance between Christ in the midst of culture, they prefer setting them self as a bit better than culture---even though the people in the buildings for the most part, create the culture they ridicule.

CHRIST IN PARADOX WITH CULTURE--- This is the Christ of the two kingdoms: of the world and of God. At times he seems to be in culture and at times against. Sometimes he calls us to speak against culture, at other times he calls us to give to culture. His world is not of this world and yet here he is in the midst of it, living within its tenets. The problem here is that we are left wondering what we have to offer culture. If we are to be in God's kingdom and forsake this one, then why bother? If we are to be part of this culture, what does that say about the kingdom of God. It's a paradox. These people understand the world is here and we are in it. At times they will blame creation itself for their sinfulness. They struggle with the tension of being a spiritual being (in part) in a material world.

CHRIST as TRANSFORMER OF CULTURE—Here, Christ is about living the kingdom of God in the world to change the world. God created the possibility of culture, therefore God can transform that culture to be made in the image God desires. There is an acceptance of culture, but an understanding that culture in and of itself neither mirrors God's ideas nor rejects them. Hope is a key word for this view. Through God's grace, hope abounds in the midst of despair. Sin is not overcome by guilt or shame or judgment, but rather through faith, hope, and love.

Niebuhr did not believe any of these was the perfect answer. Each has plusses and minuses. He probably leaned towards the more transformative view but even that had its problems. He knows that our decisions and views of the world are colored by the very culture we are challenging. He understood that we live in cultures of relativism, different degrees of being relative, but far from absolutist. As believers we are not acting and in the world solely for ourselves, but for the world and for God. The way out of this conundrum is our faith. We freely choose how to live our lives and hopefully do so in such a way as to reflect God's creative nature, his love of his creation and his creatures and his desire that we would all be whole.

The traits of our soul are tied to these ideas of culture. Some of us avoid either the world or the spiritual. Some of us are overly attached to one of the two while being called to be in both while we are alive. We think of culture as being worldly and yet we create and are created by a spiritual culture that we need to pay attention to as well. By viewing how we relate to culture and the people in it, we can see how our soul relates to God.

WORSHIP

We will discuss worship on many fronts in this book and feel it is an important enough topic to discuss in more depth. Worship here is seen as more ritualistic ways we show reverence and pay homage to

God. This can be done individually or corporately. Scripturally there certainly is no "right" way to worship God. Each of us has styles we are comfortable with. For many, the style we grew up with is the most comfortable. For others it may be the style you experienced when you had a conversion experience. Some are pulled by lots of ritual, others by lack of ritual. Some are touched by music and communion, others by powerful sermons or hearing stories bearing witness to the power of God.

PRIVATE WORSHIP—When a person does something to show God how much they love him and want to serve him, that is worship. Jesus tells the woman at the well that someday people will not say you need to come to this temple or that to worship, but all will worship God in Spirit and in Truth (John 4). This is what personal worship is about; coming to God, adoring God with who you know yourself to be. Where our soul is in the continua makes a difference and impacts our worship tendencies because worship is one of the places our souls can rise to the surface. When Christ calls us to worship in Spirit, he is calling us to worship with our souls, with our spiritual natures. Some people go to corporate worship services and yet are worshipping in private, they are alone in the midst of a crowd and there is nothing wrong with this.

CORPORATE WORSHIP—People come together to worship in part because that is how it has always been done and in part because we are called to be social creatures. This notion of corporate worship does not insinuate a church or temple. When two or more are gathered and showing reverence or homage to God explicitly, that is worship. Corporate worship pulls us in to a common way of revering God. Episcopalians, Lutherans, Orthodox, and Catholics are more ritualistically inclined. Pentecostals, Baptists, Presbyterians and Free Methodists are less liturgically inclined and focus more on the Word of God and preaching. Again, the nature of our soul pulls us one direction or the other. We may try one style out and just not feel it nourishes us. That's fine, our souls need to be nourished and how we worship God pleases God and nourishes us.

So how do these worship styles show up in the traits we are discussing?

Transcendence

The key question here is where does one find meaning? If we find more meaning in the spoken word, in hearing how to live my life out in the world or in just talking about social justice issues, then a more immanent style of worship will pull us. We will be attracted to places with less ritual, mystery, and the potential for solitude in the service. We will enjoy places where we feel we are an active part of the community, that it is more a "we" worshipping God than an "I" in the midst of the we. Longer sermons, more abbreviated communion services and singing, less silent prayer and more congregational talking in prayer are hallmarks of a more immanent form of worship.

For those who find more meaning on a personal and mysterious level, the more liturgical forms of worship hold sway. Here, communion is often the center and everything points to that deeply symbolic moment. While people are worshipping together, the communion is between them and God, there is little sense that we are all doing this together as one. Prayers are more formal and the sermons fairly brief. There tends to be less clapping and hand-raising in these services and ritualistic mannerisms are more prevalent such as bowing or kneeling. Of course some of that is cultural as well.

Holiness

Holiness is about our self-identity. We find the spiritual nature of our being either through our relationship with the transcendent or with the world. In terms of worship, we are pulled to those styles where our identity comes from. There is no value judgment here. Many churches feel called to do more contemporary forms of worship, speak to social issues of the day, and externalize the church. This is fantastic and is certainly godly. The context and style of worship is just more grounded in contemporary understandings of culture and of how God works with and in the world. Those who find their identity on a more spiritual plane are more attracted by the more mysterious and individualistic styles. Tradition looms larger for this type and again, so does the lure of mystery and ritual.

Our identities are wrapped up in our worship. We are drawn to styles of worship that reflect who and what we think we are, in both kingdoms, spiritual and worldly. We feel uncomfortable in some houses of worship not just because it's different, but because the worship does not feed who we are, it grates on our notion of how to revere God. The bible tells us to be of one mind, not of one worship style. There are many ways to worship in Spirit and Truth.

It should be noted that some people have no real preference. They love a good contemporary service, high mass, or traditional service. They are comfortable in many styles of worship. These types have more of a balance within the soul and understand that different forms of worship feed different needs within their soul. This is not to say you can't be a devout Catholic or some other denomination and not be balanced. Generally speaking, worship is reflective of where our soul is at the time if it is a meaningful experience.. Most denominations are becoming more broad in their worship styles. You can find a very traditional Episcopal service or a very contemporary one. You can also go and sit in on a Taize service which is more on the mystical end of the spectrum. If you go to a worship service and feel nothing you either need to find a new service or check and see what is going on in your soul.

Connection

Connection is about relationships; their breadth and depth. Those on the more mystical end of the connection continuum tend towards the more mysterious and liturgical formats of worship. Those on the more temporal end move in the direction of the less formal and more social end. Again, both are important ways of relating. There is nothing wrong with being with a group of people and yet finding the mystery deep within. There is also nothing wrong with gathering with a group of people, clapping, praising God together, and openly bearing witness to God's power in our lives.

Does God call us to worship Him because He needs it? Probably not. We are called to worship because God knows we need it, we need to praise the one who created us and with whom our lives are made complete. There are an infinite number of ways to do this.

When we view worship as a means of building and deepening a relationship, things change. We look for God in the midst of our worship, we find the transcendent in the midst of those who have gathered if it is corporate worship. We find a degree of safety that allows us to let go of things that bind us and we are set free. Worship brings us into a more ritualized part of relationship. Baptism, marriage, communion, and other rituals in the church are all ways of transforming the relationship with one another and with God and that is what is at the core of God's world, building relationships.

We often feel better after a time of worship because our relationship with God and perhaps with others has changed, if only slightly. In the perfect world, life itself will become a form of worship.

Imagination

Imagination speaks to how we find and use God's creativity in our lives. Because God's creativity is in and through all things, it doesn't matter which end of the spectrum you are on, if we open our eyes, creativity is found. We find it in the architecture of churches, the artwork of icons, paintings, frescoes, and the wonder of art that comes through children. We see creativity in our songs and prayers, in how churches function, in how the Word is presented, in the clothing people wear, the food we eat, and the words we speak.

We are inspired by the Spirit to find ways of showing our appreciation for what God has given us. The Spirit knows God and is God so what we receive is from the Creator. Creation itself was perhaps the most amazing imaginative event. Our creativity is limited by our humanness and yet our souls are not limited in the same ways. Worship is an opportunity to let go of the world and more fully enter the spiritual end of life so that God's creativity may pour through us.

Many have either worked with young children or had them. At times we need to help them with a project they will eventually give to us. They do not have all the tools necessary to complete the project. We give them a sense of fulfillment in what they have done. God does the same with us. God helps us even as we are using what God gives us to praise and worship Him.

When we look at worship services through the lens of creativity we need to understand it shows up in odd and mysterious ways. A Quaker service of mostly silence can be as creative as a liturgy filled with music, liturgical dance, and art. Imagination need not only be externalized, but can live within our minds, hearts, and souls. Some people feed off a varied service routine while others prefer one that is more standard from week to week. Each gives that person a space that is comfortable to them in which to praise and worship God.

The question we need to be asking ourselves is what does our individual and our corporate worship do to us and for us? Do we feel our worship is pleasing to God? Does our worship touch something deep within that deepens the bond with God and with others? Do we feel our worship in a way that is meaningful to us?

Creativity is boundless and abundant. God has no limits on the imagination; spiritually or in the realm of humanity. We are the binders of the imagination.

Call

Call is about our purpose in life. Part of the reason we go to houses of worship or worship on our own, is to listen to God's Word and to attune our souls to the voice of God. We put ourselves directly into God's path and pray we hear her voice. Part of the purpose of worship is to help us separate from the world for a bit and rest in God. It's a time to recharge our batteries, to receive wisdom, to seek discernment, and to ask forgiveness. Worship is a time to be nourished in body, mind, and spirit.

We hear people talk about why they go to church. "To hear God's Word preached." "I go to receive the sacraments." "I go to confess and be forgiven." "I go to be in fellowship with others." "I go because that is what God wants me to do." These are all good answers for why we worship. Somewhere in there, we want to know what God wants of us. We want to get rid of those things that keep us from hearing God's voice clearly and openly. We know we are not fully mature people and have a desire to move forward and know we can't do it alone. Worship is a context where we believe those things can happen.

Part of having a purpose in life is sharing that purpose with others. Corporate worship is a place to do that when done right. It's interesting that in many houses of worship we have the more formal time of worship, then break for fellowship or social hour. How often in that setting do you talk about your purpose in life, your relationship to God, or the obstacles you have that keep you from God? It would seem the obvious time for those conversations. We have worshipped together, praised God, prayed, heard the Word, broken bread, confessed, and blessed. What better time to converse about the most important questions and ideas in our lives? If you don't, why not? This is not to say God doesn't want us to be social, we are created as social creatures. It's a matter of priorities and looking our fears in the face.

Part of worship should be seeking and acknowledging God's call to us. There is no better place to do that than with the fellowship of believers of which we are a part. Christ gave the great commission; "Go forth and make disciples of all nations." He gave each of us a special gift to use for the purpose of building up the body and manifesting his call to us. Worship is a wonderful time to expose that call and those gifts or to hear the voice of God and the voice of others help us discover what we are called to do, especially when we have no clue. God knows and God wants you to know. As we put ourselves into the path of God, things happen.

In the author's experiences, there are few churches that use worship as a focal point of looking at the call. Songs, prayers, confession, hearing God's Word, and breaking bread can all lead us into that part of our lives, but attention needs to be pointed there. Some churches have commissioning services which highlight particular people or "jobs" in the church, but what about the rest? ALL are called by God to some form of ministry, we all need to be commissioned.

So think about your worship, corporate and individual. How is it feeding you and deepening your relationship with God and others? Where do you find meaning in your worship? How does your worship work with each of the traits we have been discussing? What other forms of worship might you try for a period of time to move you more to the center? This is not a call to move from church to church, although trying a different one out now and then can be good on many levels. The challenge is to worship the Lord our God with ALL our heart, mind and soul, not just part of them.

MARK

Mark 2:1-12 is a wonderful story on many levels. Here it is:

[1] And when he returned to Caper'na-um after some days, it was reported that he was at home. [2] And many were gathered together, so that there was no longer room for them, not even about the door; and he was preaching the word to them. [3] And they came, bringing to him a paralytic carried by four men. [4] And when they could not get near him because of the crowd, they removed the roof above him; and when they

had made an opening, they let down the pallet on which the paralytic lay. [5] And when Jesus saw their faith, he said to the paralytic, "My son, your sins are forgiven." [6] Now some of the scribes were sitting there, questioning in their hearts, [7] "Why does this man speak thus? It is blasphemy! Who can forgive sins but God alone?" [8] And immediately Jesus, perceiving in his spirit that they thus questioned within themselves, said to them, "Why do you question thus in your hearts? [9] Which is easier, to say to the paralytic, `Your sins are forgiven,' or to say, `Rise, take up your pallet and walk'? [10] But that you may know that the Son of man has authority on earth to forgive sins" -- he said to the paralytic -- [11] "I say to you, rise, take up your pallet and go home." [12] And he rose, and immediately took up the pallet and went out before them all; so that they were all amazed and glorified God, saying, "We never saw anything like this!" (Revised Standard Version)

First it involves a wide cast of characters; some on the surface and some behind the scenes. The disciples for example are not mentioned, but are certainly present. Each player in the drama has a different role, a different way of seeing reality, a different need, and a different response to Jesus. Each player has a different perspective from the level of maturity of their soul. By looking at this passage through the lens of each type, we can get yet another idea of how they are differentiated.

One way you might do this is to read the verses yourself first. See with whom you most identify and why. What questions come to your mind? Which of the characters annoy you? What are the key elements for you in the story?

The cast of characters to make sure you think about are: Jesus, the paralyzed man, the men who took him to Jesus, the Scribes, the crowd, the owner of the house, and the disciples. We have put the passage in below and at the end of book for easy reference for those who have a printed version of the book. For those with an electronic version the passage is given with each type. For those reading this in print you will need to get your bible out or return to this section.

THE 32 TYPES

You will notice that the word "tend" is used quite a bit. Every person, every soul is different and unique. These types reflect people at the ends of the spectrums and their tendencies. We hope it gives insight to your personal situation.

We will naturally gravitate to look at our own type. Take time to look at all the types, you will learn things about the different traits that have not been mentioned and you will get a sense of how these traits work together in all the combinations. Very few people will be exactly like these because we are only speaking to traits as they are seen at or near their extremes. Most of us are not extreme but are a bit more balanced. Our hope is that this will give you a guideline on which to move your own spiritual dynamics to the center.

Here is a list of the types and their pages.

IAEND	100
IAENP	
IAERD	
IAERP	
IAMND	116
IAMNP	
IAMRD	
IAMRP	
ITEND	
ITENP	
ITERD	138
ITERP	
ITMND	
ITMNP	
ITMRD	
ITMRP	159
SAEND	
SAENP	
SAERD	

SAERP
SAMND   178
SAMNP
SAMRD
SAMRP
STEND
STENP
STERD
STERP   204
STMND
STMNP
STMRD
STMRP

IAEND

Immanent, Sacred, Temporal, Inspiration, Idealist

The IAEND is polarized. Their soul finds its identity which impacts their psyche through the sacred. Their imagination is also tied to the transcendent which builds relationships that support those ideas and ideals. Our self-identity is closely linked with our Call. How can you believe God is calling you to something if you don't see and believe that about yourself? We tend to move towards things we feel most confident and comfortable with. Steve R. entered ministry because he felt God calling him to it, but also because he believes he can be of use there and has been told that by others. If he didn't believe in the church, didn't have any pastoral skills or inclinations, or his ministry was not being supported, how would he hear God calling him to that, and why would God?

Certainly we have seen throughout history that God calls people to amazing things far beyond their self-concept. We believe God is revealing our deeper nature to us. Moses and Peter had leadership within them. At first they chose not to see it. Paul had leadership but had it focused in the wrong direction. So this type deeply feels the call of God and finds it linked to how they perceive themselves. This is a good thing.

Their self-identity however only relates to part of the spiritual world. By finding their connectedness in and through the world, they miss out on the Collaborative Unconscious and its use in their lives. They may fail to remember many dreams or seek solitude when God calls them. The world gives them their primary source of spiritual meaning and relationship. This sounds a bit odd doesn't it. How can the world give spiritual meaning? God created the world and embedded it with meaning. God's spiritual essence is in and through all things for those with eyes to see and feel. The person who is more on the Supernal end sees the world through a spiritual lens. They see what can be and often miss what is. At the other end, the Immanent soul finds God in the world, in the midst of suffering and yet lacks the depth of hope the other end brings. When balance is found, each feeds the other. Hope is brought into the midst of suffering, our meaning comes from the union of those two. Why do you need hope if all is well? What good is sharing hope if we do not see the need for it?

The IAEND uses their connections in the world to bring about change in the world and in their lives. They are idealists in the best sense of the word. They want a world that works, that functions under high moral standards based on the principles and life of Christ in the world. They love the work of saints, living and dead. Their call is to bring about that change in whatever capacity they find meaningful to them and to others. The IED (Immanent, Temporal, Idealist) combination is an interesting one. They are acting out their spiritual call through relationships in and of the world in a way that brings meaning to their lives externally rather than internally. In so doing, they feed the Supernal part of their identity.

For Niebuhr, this type is probably Christ in Paradox with culture. They are tied to culture for meaning and relationships and to the transcendent for their self-identity, call, and imagination. They move back and forth and are caught in the tension between the two. Interestingly enough we believe we are called to be in the middle, to be balanced. But that balance is within each trait. When this balance is found it is clear how the two can work together and how one is not complete without the other in this life. Our being out of balance in any given trait affects the others and throws the totality out of balance.

This type is comfortable with a variety of worship styles because their soul has a variety of needs. The Immanent-Temporal aspect enjoys more contemporary forms of worship while the Sacred-Inspiration-

Idealist prefers the more traditional and liturgical. They are comfortable with themselves and with others wherever they are in worship.

What the IAEND is attracted to

What they are attracted to depends on the situation more so than most other types. These types that are split 3-2 are very dependent on the situation. They enjoy activity and being on the journey with others. On the other hand, they enjoy a good time alone. Their inspiration tends to come from these quiet times with God. Depending on the struggles in their lives at the moment they may or may not remember their dreams. They can be highly avoidant because of the tension between the traits. Their relationships tend to be middle of the road; not too deep and not too spiritual, but very practical. They know who they are and do enjoy the presence of others who know they are God's special creation.

Growth areas for the IAEND

This type needs to learn to listen to itself. The balance is primarily found by having one trait acknowledge and respect the others. Each trait pulls the others to the center and in so doing moves to the center itself. This process is difficult because while any given trait or set of traits is being used, the others are being ignored and diminished. Learning to calm down any given trait is imperative for this type. On a practical level, the IAEND needs to push relationships to a deeper level, bring hope to everything they do, act out of grace and abundance, and become more practical and realistic in what they do.

Activities

1. Learn to meditate and listen to the still small voice of God.
2. Keep a journal of hope. Look for hope, be an ambassador of hope in your family and community.
3. Find an STMRP. Build a relationship and learn from one another.
4. Listen to what the world is telling you about yourself. Ask others what they think.
5. Try to get into conversations with people about more spiritual issues. Ask yourself what the Bible is telling you spiritually, not just practically.

MARK 2: 1-12

[1] And when he returned to Caper'na-um after some days, it was reported that he was at home. [2] And many were gathered together, so that there was no longer room for them, not even about the door; and he was preaching the word to them. [3] And they came, bringing to him a paralytic carried by four men. [4] And when they could not get near him because of the crowd, they removed the roof above him; and when they had made an opening, they let down the pallet on which the paralytic lay. [5] And when Jesus saw their faith, he said to the paralytic, "My son, your sins are forgiven." [6] Now some of the scribes were sitting there, questioning in their hearts, [7] "Why does this man speak thus? It is blasphemy! Who can forgive sins but God alone?" [8] And immediately Jesus, perceiving in his spirit that they thus questioned within themselves, said to them, "Why do you question thus in your hearts? [9] Which is easier, to say to the paralytic, `Your sins are forgiven,' or to say, `Rise, take up your pallet and walk'? [10] But that you may know that the Son of man has authority on earth to forgive sins" -- he said to the paralytic -- [11] "I say to you, rise, take up your pallet and go home." [12] And he rose, and immediately took up the pallet and went out before them all; so that they were all amazed and glorified God, saying, "We never saw anything like this!" (Revised Standard Version)

Depending on the day, the IAEND could relate to just about anyone in the story on many levels. They live in this paradox being pulled back and forth. For them, the meaning of the story comes through the value and integrity of friendship, the people hauling the paralytic to the roof.

Their connections and relationships are important to them and they are extremely loyal. One might ask how they knew this man and what had they done for him before? It feels obvious the friends are indeed that, a close group of people who share common beliefs. On the other hand their ties to the world call them to question who and what Jesus is and is doing.

The scribes found meaning through scripture, not through a direct relationship with God. Connecting the dots for them means interpreting scripture in their way. This type identifies with the man in that the root of his issues are spiritual. He knows his identity is founded in God. Note that he says nothing during the entire episode. When God is present, words are not necessary, and God was present in the person of Jesus. Jesus forgave his sins, healing the deeper nature.

Everyone is inspired by the event. Jesus creatively finds ways of meeting each person there at a place that is helpful to them. He challenges, cajoles, encourages, forgives, and blesses. On one level one might say people who came there were responding to the call of God; to listen, to take a person and put him before Christ, even to challenge and ask Jesus questions. This type finds God on many levels in this story.

IAENP

Immanent, Sacred, Temporal, Inspiration, Pragmatist
Like many types, the IAENP is torn between two worlds and they can enhance and complement one another or they can be in conflict and create chaos. This type is grounded in the world and their connections come primarily through their senses. Because of that, they are more motivated by what the world calls forth and in serving the world. Their connection to the world inhibits the relationship with the Collaborative Unconscious and yet because of their N (Inspiration), they are inspired by the transcendent sense of creativity. This creativity shows up in how they work with the world, but tends not to in relationships, especially with God. Perhaps the largest conflict comes in their self-identity. Because they find their identity comes from the sacred sphere of life, they are internally solid and understand their holiness in relation to God. Because they are so grounded in the world there is often a tension between what they do in life and a feeling they should be doing something else. They don't respond to that "holy other" because of their lack of connectedness to the transcendent.

In worship they are comfortable with many forms. The more liturgical services bring forth the AN (Sacred, Inspiration) part of them and more contemporary free flowing worship brings out the IEP (Immanent, Temporal, Pragmatic). The very pace of contemporary worship calls to the connectedness on the temporal plane of existence as well as their feelings of groundedness on this planet.

When these types are not at war with them self, amazing things can happen. The more rooted earthly aspects act as a feedback loop with the transcendent aspects, each accepting of the other, acknowledging the other. There is an awareness that this is how it is and a profound respect ensues. When push comes to shove, the more earth bound nature tends to take over. There is a distrust of their intuition and their foundations are based on practicalities. The inspirational side may try to break through the logic, but is often overwhelmed. Their dreams will try to pull them more to hear the still small voice of God and their souls, but they are often ignored. Because of the overwhelming presence of the world in our lives and how little attention and time we give to the spiritual, we should not be surprised that people tend towards the more world oriented dynamics of the soul in general.

The IAENP has a fear of letting go of what they get from the world and yet knows to some degree they must. This is their holiness yearning to bring a different kind of wisdom and understanding to their lives. Their purpose in life is more geared towards being than becoming. They are action oriented people who shy from solitude and mysticism. They ground their purpose in the underlying principles of the spiritual world as they perceive them.

Their meaning system comes from the world. Politics and psychology tend to be more interesting than theology and cosmology. They tend to be spiritual joiners and follow what others do that they respect. They can make connections with those around them but struggle at times to make connections to God in a direct way.

Because their identities are more internal, they are comfortable with decisions they make on both a worldly and spiritual level. They tend not to question themselves.

What the IAENP is attracted to

The IAENP thrives in the world. They enjoy being in and of the world, seeing its creativity exploding. They do not need to be that creative in order to appreciate the creativity of the world. There is a tendency towards environmentalism since they love the world around them and the creativity of God as shown in creation itself. Because their identity comes from God they know how humanity can't live without the planet, we are bound together, our mutual destinies entwined. Their connection to the world and their pragmatic nature beckon them to enjoy nature and preserve it. They are entranced by the imagination of God and relish seeing it. Part of their purpose comes from the belief they are serving God in the world for the world.

This group is more inclined towards Niebuhr's Christ and Culture in Paradox. They see two worlds and are torn. While they side with the earth, they are drawn to the spirit and want to find a way of bringing them together. They do want to transform culture, but not necessarily in a spiritual way. They want the principles of the transcendent without the interference. They believe we can run things fine ourselves.

Growth areas for the IAENP

The IAENP is torn between the world and the transcendent. Their conflict areas of the soul and where they are grounded causes internal and spiritual stress and confusion. They want to do what is right and overall believe they are. The challenge is always to seek balance. They need to find ways of connecting to God and the transcendent; through meditation, dreams, retreats, and sharing in a spiritually oriented fellowship.

The key challenge for this type is to find a way of letting the mix within their soul accept and trust the others. All of the traits are intertwined. As their spiritually creative side begins to trust the pragmatic side, a wonderful balance is found. The Immanent part needs to be reaching out to the Sacred side and visa versa so their identities are a joining of the transcendent and the immanent. There is a tendency when working on our souls to fixate on one particular trait. We do just what is necessary to move to the middle on holiness. When the soul moves to the middle on one trait, all others shift and are impacted and as the soul is impacted, so too the psyche and yes, the Collaborative Unconscious. By becoming aware of the traits and how they are working within us, we can more finely attune to how they are shifting and act accordingly, moving every closer to God and living for God in the world.

Another key for the IAENP is to move towards transforming the world to find God rather than living in the paradox. Jesus talks of two worlds and proclaims you can't have two masters. On the other hand, we do live in the world and are called by God to love those in the world and to be servants. This is a transformative vision that calls us to be in the world but not wholly of it. It's a matter of seeing God and the transcendent intricately involved with the world and yet pulling those in the world to something deeper and more profound.

Teilhard de Chardin talked about the Omega Point, (**The Future of Man,** William Collins and Sons, 1959) that we are evolving toward. Teilhard believed movement in the long run to God was inevitable, that the gravitational pull of Christ could not be avoided by creation. He believed our souls grow and evolve just as the more temporal world does. As our souls mature we are more in tune with what needs to happen and what our roles are in that movement.

The practical nature of the IAENP along with their internal compass and identity serves them well in helping find ways of spreading this message. They need to ensure they don't get caught up in the content and forget the process and the One who is actually doing the leading.

Trusting their intuition, becoming deeper people of prayer, and listening to what others tell them about them self are all important ingredients as they move to the center.

Activities

1. Start looking for consciously for God at work in the day to day world. Push yourself to find God. Write things down.
2. As you read scripture, look for more spiritual meanings. What is God trying to tell your soul?
3. Listen to your dreams and ideas that seem to come from nowhere.
4. Find out what others think about you. Ask them to describe you, look for common threads.
5. Build a relationship with an STMRD. Learn from one another.
6. Learn to meditate and listen to the voice of God inside more. Trust your intuition and use your mind to engage it.

MARK 2: 1-12 (see page 102)

The IAENP is a very practical person. They will ask all kinds of practical questions. How did people find out about Jesus? How many were there? Who were these people that carried the paralyzed man? Where is the owner of the house as they dig a hole through it? Why were the scribes there? Why did Jesus forgive his sins first? Were others healed? It said he was at home, did Jesus have a house? Why didn't the man say anything? These are all fair and great questions to which we do not have concrete answers. Their IEP (Immanent, Temporal, Pragmatic) natures pull them to ask questions of a practical nature.

Their creative side is enthralled by the story and all its components. They enjoy seeing all the different roles people play even if they don't get their lack of response. Their A (Supernal) aspect understands the need to forgive the man's sins first, but the rest of their nature doesn't, so they ask the question. They wonder what is going on in other's minds. How is this impacting them, how genuine is their glorifying God? Their E (temporal) nature helps them relate to everyone there in some way. They can identify with the scribes but yearn for them to get it. They share the passion of the crowd and their wonder and the brilliance of Jesus's working with everyone.

IAERD

Immanent, Sacred, Temporal, Reason, Idealist
The IAERD is usually dominated through the mind. They tend to be very rational people which of course causes conflict with that part of them which identifies with God and feels called by God in less than rational ways. They attempt to make rational sense of the world around them in spiritual terms. At some point this process breaks down because God transcends logic as do many spiritual things. This is one of the central issues between science and religion. Most religions accept science and feel there are explanations for many things. Science believes there are explanations for all things that are logical. The IAERD is caught in this tension within their own souls. Their IER (Immanent, Temporal, Reason) side struggles to make sense of the world while the AD (Sacred, Idealist) side accepts mystery. Because the world is what we know and experience best and most, these three dominate and at times overwhelm the spiritual side. Taking time to be in God's presence is not easy for this type. They find God more in the world than in them self.

While their call comes from God and in the end their identity is found in God, the more temporal and rational nature explains all of that to the mind in human terms. They will mouth the words that they are unique and special in God's eyes, but may not believe it because their brains tell them differently. Their idealism clashes with the realism of how they perceive the world. Their sacred nature is at odds with what they know from experience and experience often wins out. Depending on which traits are most prevalent at any given time they struggle with what to trust; mind or spirit. They tend to be more a Christ OF culture but can be Christ in Paradox. While they do see the evil in society they focus more on the good that humanity does, how humanity rises to the occasion in a disaster, surrounds people in crisis and the generosity of their hearts. This is both their sacredness and their idealism showing forth. They are pulled back into the world by the IER aspects. Let's remember there is nothing wrong with Christ of culture as long as they realize what being in culture means from a transcendent perspective. It is when we lose sight of that perspective and become immersed in the world for the world that things go awry on many levels. We contend that the major issue with the world is that we are losing touch with the spiritual side of life and the world in and of itself does not hold the answers.

Metaphors and stories that are grounded in the real world are more beneficial to this type. They enjoy the prodigal son and the practical writings of Paul. More theological and spiritual parables or writings of Paul (such as seen in most of Romans) are often difficult and not wrestled with. The IE (Immanent, Temporal) type would see the father welcoming the son home as an act of reconciliation and the grace of the father and the depths of depravity the son had sunk to. An SM (Supernal, Mystical) would look at redemption and mercy as the core values. They would see them se;f in the place of the son and understand that spiritually they are not that far removed from that son.

This type enjoys hearing about the lives of others and meshing them with their own lives. While their vision may not be as grand as God would like, they can be expansive and see systems in their entirety rather than just piece by piece. As long as the vision makes sense to them and is in line with what they know and feel, they are fine. Getting well out of the box is difficult for the IAERD. Leaps of faith and intuition are a struggle. Why would you try something on a hunch or feeling? Why wouldn't you wait till all the ducks are in a row?

This type like most 3-2 splits are attracted to many types of worship. They may find them self in one kind and be happy one day and bored the next, depending on which side of their soul is being dominant at that time. Jumping around to different forms of worship on a regular basis is probably not the best. There is a lot to be said for being a committed member of a community of faith. These types should let the worship service pull them to the center. When you are bored or uncomfortable in a particular service ask why?

What the IAERD is attracted to

The IER (Immanent, Temporal, Reason) part of this person is attracted to the world and how it works. They like connecting the dots and bringing others into that world. They are comfortable around others who enjoy what the world has to offer, not necessarily in a materialistic way, but as part of God's created order. Their spiritual idealism is sometimes mistaken for human idealism and they look to change the order of things in the world to a more idealistic paradigm. They enjoy people for whom justice is important and who work to achieve justice for all. They tend to be very tolerant people in relation to spiritual issues and can get frustrated with those less tolerant. They do well with various traditions and exposing them self to new ways of finding God, especially in the world. The AD (Supernal, Idealist) enjoys helping others find hope and God in their lives. They are optimists who identify with the things in life that pull people down. They see the world is in trouble and have an answer.

Growth areas for the IAERD

The IAERD needs to find more grounding in the transcendent. They need to find more connections with God, a deeper way of finding meaning in the world through God's eyes, and a way of tapping into the Collaborative Unconscious in order to deeper their intuition and creative side. Their identities have been subsumed by the immanent so they need to find the sacredness that exists within and allow it to bloom. The odd part of this is that they already have this, they usually just don't accept it. When they do, then they can move this trait to the center. Their idealism can be tempered and made more practical by the ER part of their soul. They need to accept that what they feel is their call from God is indeed just that and not try to rationalize it all. As they tune into their spiritual call, that will pull the IER aspects more to the center.

Activities

1. Go on a retreat. Probably the best thing this person can do is to get away from the world and be fully in the presence of God.
2. Find a STMNP and learn from each other. Push each other and listen closely to how each perceives the world.
3. Try to read the bible at a level different than simply the story line, find those deeper meanings.
4. Write in your journal about what you are doing in your life is serving God's kingdom.
5. Push yourself to trust and discover your intuition.

MARK 2: 1-12 (see page 102)

Being grounded in the world and very rational people, the IAERD looks at things through those lenses. They can certainly identify with the man's need for release from his sins which are perhaps an obstacle to his health. Clearly in Jesus's eyes that is more important than walking. Being more temporal in their relationships, this type will look at those relationships in the story. What about the man and those who took him up on the roof? What about the scribes, the crowd, the owners of the home? How do all these people relate to each other and to Jesus? There is a tension between the world and the spirit in this story. He is paralyzed, a roof is being destroyed and the needs of many are there.

The scribes are more interested in the version of scripture they have accepted through the generations rather than hearing a more spiritual side. Christ is interested in both. The IAERD will read this story with their idealized lenses on. They already know the outcome is in Jesus's favor. They want everything to be well and want to know how the scribes respond and are left wanting. Perhaps they believe optimistically they will see the light.

Being supernal in how they view identity, they are thrilled the paralyzed man has come to a deeper understanding of who he is as God's child. They want the same for everyone. The ending where the crowd is in awe and is glorifying God will lead them to believe many lives have been changed and opened. It is a sign of what they can do in the lives of others, that the call of God is to heal from the inside out and to bring hope to the world.

This story makes sense to them mentally. All the pieces fit in the puzzle. With their view of God and the world, this is all rational, they don't have to trick their minds into believing things that don't fit.

IAERP

Immanent, Sacred, Temporal, Reason, Pragmatist

The IAERP is very grounded in the world. They find meaning by seeing God's activity in the world; a world God created. Their core relationships are in the world and they view spirituality through that lens of the Temporal. Their networking and connections are in and through the world even though at their essence they are for God and the kingdom of God. They are very rational types and use the brain, a tool of God, to better the world. This type is also very practical and hands on. While faith is important, getting things done is the bottom line.

The self-identity of the IAERP is often lost in the activity. They find it difficult to settle down their internal soul enough to hear God telling them how special and unique they are outside their activity. God loves them in spite of their activity, not because of it. When they are able to slow down enough, they experience this, but that part of the journey is hard for them.

This type can be very visionary, but their vision is a down-to-earth one. When one discovers the soul and pays attention to it, even on the more immanent plane, the potential for vision is found. They are often very involved with God's creation. They have a high regard for the environment and believe that our being called to be stewards of creation is of primary importance. Failing creation is failing God. More than most types, they find God in the intricacies of the created order. They enjoy thinking about the merging of science and God, of the odds of the earth existing solely on scientific terms. The IAERP understands more than most that there are ample resources for all humanity to live a blessed life. The issue is not of resources but of distribution and greed. That is at the core of their internal struggle and of their activity in the world.

They are a mix of Niebuhr's Christ Against and Christ Of culture. They are against it because they understand the world without God will self-destruct. Greed and self-centeredness are a major part of what the world offers. God has a different vision and the IAERP sees part of their job to enlighten the world as to an alternative way of living in sync with the planet. Theirs is not a call to obsessive environmentalism, but a call to realism. They are spiritually-based environmentalists.

They are of culture because they believe in working within the system to get things done. They understand that talk is cheap and that one of the prime movers of change is the world of politics. Obviously this causes conflict. Leading a life of deep integrity while working with the systems of the world is difficult at best. When this type is true to their spiritual nature they can pull it off because while they are grounded in the world, it is through God that the grounding occurs. They know God is in and of the world, they just need the rest of us to see it.

They love the vision of the early church where everyone held all things in common. Each according to his need, each according to his ability was a common theme. While the world has not done so well with this mantra, the theological essence of it is pure. What a worthy goal to have. Those who feel they are entitled to more than they need should probably spend more time with God.

Their minds wrestle with questions for which the world has no answer. How can we overcome hunger? Is there an end to disease? How do you bring hope top the world? How do you help people end ethnocentric conflicts? They long to find a spiritual depth but rarely do because they can't let go of rationality and God is not a purely rational being. Their Sacred nature, while key to their self-identity is so overwhelmed by the others as to have a small chance. God's pragmatism is also not always in with the worlds.

The IAERP: uses their minds to work with their soul to bring the spiritual and the worldly together. It is a spiritual world that makes rational sense. Part of them has the desire to break through and experience the intuitive aspect of creation, but that process is difficult because of the strength of their mind and the pragmatism.

What the IAERP is attracted to

Naturally, they are attracted to nature and those who love it. They thrive with activity and are restless when not active. They prefer worship that is active with lots of singing. Sitting for long sermons does not bring them joy. They prefer churches that have large outreach programs and a vision of how to impact the community. They become frustrated with a lack of faith in action.

They are acutely aware of God's gifts to them that they use for the betterment of those around them and the world. They are not so attuned to deeper reasons God may have given them the gifts they have. Planning, strategizing, and doing are at the core of what they enjoy. Creativity comes through a well-conceived plan that is carried to fruition. While they like talking about the big picture, they are realists and want to start at "A" not at "M." They move through the alphabet logically rather than making leaps that don't work. Networking and relationships are key to them, but they keep these at a pretty superficial level. This is because the answer is in the world and not in the transcendent. Seeking the transcendent takes effort of a different kind and degree. Their goal is to solve problems and bring hope, not to find deep meaning systems.

Growth areas for the IAERP

Clearly this type needs to find them self on a spiritual plane. They need to find out at a deep level that this is not all there is. They need to pay attention to that self within calling them to an identity with God apart from the world. It is only through doing this that they will remain optimists and have the energy, insight, and courage to maintain the long road ahead. If they do not, the world will wear them down. They may become bitter and judgmental of others. The IAERP needs to let go of the mind a bit and trust their spirit and intuition. Solitude is perhaps the best thing for them although even this has its drawbacks. The challenge is to fight the need to be in the world. Sometimes people flip from one extreme to the other. They go off on retreat and are stunned by what they find, so they leave the world and live in the spirit. At other times their minds are so active and strong they can rationalize just about anything. Spending that much time outside a community of faith that is acting as a check and balance system leaves them to their own devices. It's very easy for them to think they are hearing the voice of God telling them one thing when God may be saying something else. This is why becoming part of a community on a spiritual level is critical for them.

Activities

1. Learn to meditate and still your mind. Find inner silence. Practice the classic disciplines of solitude and silence.
2. Push yourself to find other forms of meaning in a situation. What are the transcendent values you see?
3. Find an STMND and build a relationship. Listen to them and learn from each other. You bring balance to each other.
4. Take some risks. Trust your gut. Pray and move on your gut instinct rather than always on your mind.
5. Use your mind to find your spirit. Read the mystics and poets, see what they have found that you are missing.

Mark 2:1-12 (see page 102)

The IAERP is concerned in this story with what happens to the people, how the story helps life. They are thrilled the man can walk but are puzzled why Jesus needed to forgive his sins. They identify with those who lifted the man onto the roof. For them, that activity is a sign of faith. Who cares that they destroyed a roof? They see the big picture. They see that Jesus has a crowd and through his actions changed lives. They are angered at the scribes who have an outdated view of scripture and a poor theology. They want to believe the scribes changed, but have their doubts. For them, this is a story about Jesus changing lives in a very down to earth manner. Their "A" (Sacred) nature is touched that Jesus meets people where they are. Then ailing man is unique and special in the eyes of Jesus, they get that. But through their eyes, so is everyone else there, even the scribes.

Sometimes to grow we need to chastise or be chastised as the scribes were. Their minds wrap around the story with many pieces that Jesus is in complete control of. They marvel at his insight, intuition and ability to out think everyone. Looking at all the relationships in the story keeps them busy. While they are not the most imaginative of types, their mind can see all the different things going on in the story. They feel the tension, the excitement, and the joy. They are filled with questions and have answers to them that work for them, true or not. They are grounded in the worldly narrative and miss the spiritual depth that exists on a different level. This is true of all types. We view scripture through our personal lens. It can't be any other way unless someone guides us and we are open to receiving.

IAMND

Immanent, Sacred, Mystical, Inspirational, Idealist

This type is focused on the spiritual end of the spectrum except when it comes to making sense of it all. They are connected in all ways to the transcendent save when they try to understand things. At that point their humanity and their groundedness on this planet kicks in. The world is where they get their meaning. Internally, their soul has all the tools needed to process their lives in light of spiritual language, but the immanent part of their soul struggles to let go of the world. This is not a clinging to worldliness and materialism, but to what God has created and how we are all an integral part of that creation. Because this is only one of the five traits that is connected to the world to such a degree, it is usually dominated by the others. This type may not seek spiritual meaning, other things may be more important. They are happy to accept mystery as an answer to humanity's lingering issues.

The IAMND is by and large part of Niebuhr's Christ Above culture. Their connection to God and to the transcendent is deep and tends to make them feel that the spiritual is above what the world offers—and to a large degree they are right. This becomes an issue when that view of them self and the world gives them a "holier than thou" attitude. Knowing you are created as unique in God's eyes, that you are holy, that you have a mystical connection to the transcendent, have deep intuition, and lofty ideals are all good things. Having perspective as to our place in the universe is also important.

Their idea of being holy as a core of their self-identity is fed by the relationship they have with God and the Collaborative Unconscious. They may not see clearly why they are here, but they know they are here for a reason and believe they are seeking God's will as much as they can. Their purpose in existing has more to do with serving God than with serving them self or others. They serve others because that is what they are called to do and because of their deep understanding that they have been served by God. They savor times when they can be alone with

116

God, even in the world. Humans can be frustrating to them at times because they don't "see" things as they do. The IAMND enjoys the symbolic language of life. Dreams are attuned to and more quickly understood than for many other types.

Their intuitive nature and their connection to the transcendent realm and all it offers often help them move through life with a sense of "peace that passes all understanding." Many people gather energy from what others have done in the past. We may have a memory of a friend or family member that motivates us. We may have read a book or heard a story about someone that went through something that gives us insight and courage to do the same. The Collaborative Unconscious gives us the potential to access all experiences that have existed and how they can support and help us on a deeply spiritual and intuitive level. Often this access comes through dreams or meditation, but people can learn how to do it on a more conscious basis, in part due to the intuitive nature of their soul.

The sense of Call comes from their identity as found in and through God. Because they are holy, their desire is to bring the world into that understanding. At its root, the world is holy, we lost that sense of our being along the way. When this type moves in the world they are seeing things differently. They are not overly practical by nature and see things most of us don't see. Their call may seem awkward to many because it doesn't fit the mold. When we attune to the call of the transcendent amazing things happen in spite of ourselves. Look at the leaders of the bible. Who would ever have picked Moses, David, or Peter to be leaders? Their resumes would not have gotten to square one. Their listening to God's call and depending on God is what raised them above them self. We all have the potential to do remarkable things,(perhaps not to be Moses or Paul) but to do things in life we can't imagine. The AMND (Sacred, Mystical, Inspiration, Idealist) natures allow that to happen more easily. Of course, there is at times conflict between the soul and the psyche. Our spirits may be very willing but our flesh weak. This is perhaps one of the largest frustrations for the IAMND.

This type is generally attracted to more mystical forms of worship. Often they see no need for corporate worship. When they do, they lean towards the more liturgical or symbolic styles. They enjoy solitude and silence and the transcendent can penetrate their being more fully and they aren't distracted by songs or preaching—preaching which to them is often quite shallow. Communion tends to be of more importance to them because it is the supreme ritual where the transcendent and the immanent merge.

What the IAMND is attracted to

      The natural attraction for this type is others who are deeply committed to the spiritual journey. Because this journey is to a large degree internal, they are often quiet about it. They get nervous expressing them self fully because they know many won't understand them. They relish opportunities to be with those that do. They are attracted to monasticism or at least getting away in solitude or retreat. They also like being with those who talk about walking with God and fulfilling God's will for their lives. The IAMND is good at spiritual discussions and like bible studies that look at what is going on beneath the surface. They don't get hung up on literal words but on symbolic gestures.

Growth areas for the IAMND

      The IAMND sees no need to bond more deeply with the world and yet that is exactly what they need. Finding how God lives in the midst of the world, how God is trying to connect them to his creation in very practical ways and learning the importance of reason are important. The challenge for them is that in their mind, moving toward the world is the negation of what they are called to. They need to discover there is a difference between being in the world and of the world, that you can be holy in the midst of a world that doesn't manifest that nature. Making relationships in the world that help move the call forward is a key area for this type. As with all types, the M/E (Mystical, Temporal) facet and the relationships we develop impact all things.

Activities

    1. Look at your relationships. How can you change them to deepen them, to understand and empathize with the struggles and sufferings you see?

    2. Find an STERP, listen to them and learn from one another.

3. Along with your silent prayer, try some yoga, something a bit more physical.
4. Do some community service that helps you work with others to help others in a very pragmatic and down to earth way---- soup kitchen, hospice, beach clean-up.
5. Listen to your friends. Ask them to tell you about yourself and see how it differs from what you think.

Mark 2:1-12 (see page 102)

The IAMND finds their meaning in and through the world but self-identifies with the transcendent. This means that as they look at this story they are apt to feel kinship with people on a spiritual level, but the story will make more sense to them on the more worldly end of things. The paralyzed man can be self-identified as themselves for we are all paralyzed to some degree. They can see they have internal blocks that are keeping them from moving on in their lives and that Christ can heal those. Transferring this understanding to those around them is more complicated. They latch onto their uniqueness in God and yet because of where they find meaning, they struggle to sense that relationship in and for others.

They will wonder why the scribes don't get it, marvel at the faith of those who lift the man onto the roof, and join with the crowd that stands in awe. They may raise a few questions that are more practical in nature, but over all that is of no concern to them. Jesus came primarily to help people with their spiritual journeys and that is what the story is about. They see how everyone was helped in some way. This type more easily puts them self into the roles of those in the narrative rather than looking in from the outside. They note how remarkable it is that all of these types of people were at the same place at the same time. Different places in their faith journey, different spiritual needs, a variety of social statuses, and an array of understandings of their faith were all present as Jesus spoke to each.

IAMNP

Immanent, Sacred, Mystical, Inspiration, Pragmatic

The IAMNP gets their meaning system and call from the world while their self-identity, connections, and creativity are from the spiritual. Creativity plays into their meaning system as they seek to make sense of the world around them. They are firmly in the world and yet are very aware of their spiritual identity. Because they relate to the world for their overall meaning system, they see symbolic meaning in and through things of the world. Rituals and different types of art (like crosses and jewelry) are often important in that they are filled with meaning and also help fill the need of the other traits. They like iconography for the same reason. It reaches out to both their sense of immanence and transcendence. They are more prone to enjoy liturgical worship but can enjoy a more contemporary form with lots of singing and listening to others speak.

Because their connections are made more on the transcendent level, this tugs at their immanence. While these various traits may be out of balance, interestingly enough, they play off one another and things tend to work out. The only significant challenge is when each of these traits are at the extremes, the conflict can be intense. There is always a tension when a person finds their meaning through the world but their self-identity through the spiritual. Their Call too is impacted by this Immanent strain. At times they struggle to make sense of how they can be what they feel called by God to be in the world. They do not see the path clearly, yet the gravity of God is strong. Their Pragmatic nature collides with how they see them self and their mystical connections to the transcendent.

The IAMNP has a strong connection to the Collaborative Unconscious. As they build their spiritual identity this serves them well. They may struggle at times in relating to the world on the world's terms. The pull of the spiritual domain in their lives is strong. Again, there is a tension because they can't help but view the world through the eyes of their self-identity, yet their souls find meaning in and through the world. How can this be? Some people have jobs they don't like. They do the work well, but it does not define who they are. They can see how their work is helpful to others and useful to the world, but again, it doesn't define who they are. Our souls can be engaged with the world, understand it, learn from it, and still not have it be our personal core of who we are as a soul.

Their Pragmatic nature wants their creativity, which is spiritually oriented, to have an impact. They tend to be more doers than thinkers and their doing fits in with their vision of the world and the purpose for which they feel they were created, the Inspirational side of them. This type can be part of the world while living an internal life of solitude. They engage the world in order to do things, things that often are given to them from the spiritual dimension of life. In Niebuhr's world they live in the Paradox of a Christ in the world and in heaven at the same time. It is being in the world but not of the world. However, often while they are acting this out, it doesn't make sense to them because of the imbalance. They gather meaning from what they do in the world and for the world. But their primary connections, identity, and creativity come from God. They live in constant paradox, one side both feeding and frustrating the other.

They feel, and are often right; that they tread the line of works and faith well. Their works are found in how they respond to the transcendent and call traits while their faith is manifested in and through the traits of Holiness, Connectedness, and Imagination.

Biblically they flow back and forth. At times they are pulled by the sense of story, of seeing God in the world. At other times the spiritual beckons them. It depends on where they are and what those around them are doing. If they are reading the bible in the midst of being in the world, then the story will pull them. If they are in a bible study or gathered with a group of people focusing on the bible, the spiritual will probably come a calling.

What the IAMNP is attracted to
The IAMNP is both happy and torn in life. They are very adaptable as at least a couple of their traits are being fed and used no matter what they are doing. On the other hand, other traits are not being nourished, thus the frustration. They love solitude when focused on their self-identity and yet enjoy a sense of community when doing service and doing creative things.

If you ask where they are rooted, they will say both, but because a sense of rootedness comes more from self-identity they will tend toward the spiritual side of things. Words are important for this type. How you phrase something will have a large impact on how they respond. If you ask a question about meaning in their lives, they will focus more on worldly things, if you ask about their Call, it will also be more world oriented. Questions about how they see them self as people will focus more on the spiritual. This however is also dependent on who is asking the question. They are chameleon like in that they will speak to and in the language of the one asking the questions. It is natural for them, not a fight and not a lie. They enjoy biographies of people and like reading mystical authors at times. In literature they are more prone to literature than to murder thrillers.

IAMNP's like being with those who see deeper connections in reality than just what is on the surface. They are attracted to others who have a strong sense of self and an understanding that their lives to a large degree are a response to God's call to them.

Growth Areas for the IAMNP

The task for this type is to not only find balance within each trait but to merge the traits, to have them form a symbiotic relationship where they feed off of and into one another. The spiritual side of the soul's identity needs to find meaning in the spiritual and can do this to some degree by looking for how the spiritual connects to the physical. These two worlds are intimately connected, it just takes a different way of viewing reality to see it.

As our self-identity finds itself more in the world, everything shifts. Each part impacts all other parts. The nature of our call is enhanced by the depth of Holiness and Connection we have with the transcendent. Our identity as it comes from the spiritual realm lifts up those others that lean that direction while trying to raise questions with the more worldly. The other end of the spectrum is calling out to this spiritual side and telling it to listen to reality, to pay attention to all that is around it, all that God has created and given it to work with. This tension asks many questions and is constantly prodding this type to move forward.

Activities

1. Ask yourself what makes you you? Make a list of your personality characteristics as well as things that bring meaning to your life and what that meaning is. Where does this sense of meaning come from—what are their sources?

2. Develop relationships with others outside your normal group of friends. Expand your horizons, perhaps finding a way of serving others that will bring you into contact and relationship with others you don't know.
3. Look for an STERD and build a friendship. They are your opposite and you will be good for one another.
4. Find creativity in the world. See especially what humanity has done.
5. How can the gifts and talents you have be used to help God's work on earth?

Mark 2:1-12 (see page 102)

The IAMNP is able to see the story from many vantage points but because of the P (Pragmatist) they will usually end up with a bottom line. Because they find meaning in the world this type will look to how Jesus impacts people and things. The challenge to the scribes and the physical healing become the most important. The loyalty and faith of the friends are also of great importance. They do understand the idea of forgiving sins, but for them that is important because it leads to the physical healing. Internally the AMN (Sacred, Mystical, Inspiration) natures fight this because for them it is all reverse. You might think it's three against two in the nature columns. When interpreting a story, how we get meaning out of the story and what we do with the story, especially a biblical one, are at the top of the list. Because these two strains are more attached to the world, this is the primary way they will look at it.

For them, God is acting in the world through Jesus to heal, glorify, teach, exhort, challenge, and support those around him, great qualities for all of us to model. The beauty of the story for them is that Christ is like they are, going back and forth between the world and the transcendent. He speaks to the soul of the paralyzed man first, then to his body. He challenges the scribes and yet shows some compassion. Jesus is there for the people to meet them where they are. The IAMNP likes to think they do this, but in reality they jump back and forth rather than having a foot in each domain as Christ did all the time.

They are able to see the creativity of Jesus and how he brings people together, a merging of the mystical and temporal aspects of his soul in balance.

IAMRD

Immanent, Sacred, Mystical, Reason, Idealist

The IAMRD is one of the most conflicted of the types. The IR connection is very strong, especially where the person is intellectually oriented in life. This pull of the Immanent and the Reasoned way of perceiving the spiritual world is a very strong force for the AMD to reckon with. Finding their meaning through their external senses and what they receive from the world as well as having a need for it to be all rational makes it difficult at times to let go. On the other hand, this dyad grounds them in the world God created and helps them understand the purpose of the world and how things fit together. These are not people that will take the flying leaps of faith, but they are risk takers. Their Sacred and Mystical natures along with the pull of God's call deep in their souls help them to move out in a rational faith that makes sense to them. C.S. Lewis is perhaps one of the most famous people who had a very deep faith but was also quite rational about it---to a point.

While they see them self in the world, internally they know they are God's creation and God's child. They comprehend their unique nature and attach that to God's call. The challenge for them is to understand how it makes sense when often it might not. Fortunately the mind is very good at mental gymnastics and they can make things seem rational to them self when to others it isn't. To some degree we all conform to the world to benefit our way of thinking, this type is very good at that.

While their worldly relationships tend to be more on a surface level, they do connect to the spiritual world when they give them self to it through prayer, dreams, or meditation. This mystical side tends to the Sacred in self-identity and tries to lure and persuade the Immanent. The Collaborative Unconscious is hard at work in this type, working on both the spiritual and mental planes. Through dreams and helping them perceive things in a different light, the CU can use the mind as a vehicle for discovery.

Their Idealism comes through in many ways. They tend to be attracted to places of worship that breed hope, to serving the world in ways that bring hope to people's hearts and to places that raise up the strengths of individuals. For the IAMRD hope is a key word, it links all things and is what keeps them moving forward. Their hope is not in the world, but in God acting in the world. They have a very high degree of self-responsibility and loyalty. Their Idealism is based on their sense of call from God. Their idea of call in the big picture is very similar to that of Teilhard de Chardin who believed God wants to pull all of creation back to himself. Our goal as humans is to help the planet return to God and all that God purposed in the created order. This makes sense to them, what else could God want? The destruction of the earth is not God's desire.

Their creativity comes from how they see the world and how they go about building relationships that will help the world move to God. They are more linear in their thinking, but are great planners, internally and externally. They acknowledge the spiritual world and do not deny its importance, but they feel that time will come (after death). For now we are on this plane and need to pay attention to the more sense oriented domain of existence.

The IAMRD is in a bit of all the Niebuhrian categories. They are Christ Against culture when they see the suffering and injustice the world exhibits. They can be Above culture when their feel their views are right and they go out of their way to prove them right. In the midst of social action they can fit right into the political arena and join hands with the world as long as they feel the world is mirroring their values. They are in Paradox because they go back and forth so much and feel they are often stuck. In the end they want to be Transformers of Culture but are not truly convinced God wants culture transformed. Perhaps there should be another category; Christ in Conflict with Culture. They would surely fit there.

What the IAMRD is attracted to

As mentioned before this type likes to think about things, plan, strategize and then do them, not so much because they are pragmatists but because it's the right thing to do. There is a sense of duty that is wrapped up in how they perceive faith. They love being around visionaries who have a spiritual component to the vision. They also are pulled by deeply spiritual people even though they can't explain why. This connection feeds the AMD (Sacred, Mystical, Idealist) part of their soul. Even though various parts of their soul may be out of balance, on the whole they are well balanced because of how the five traits play off each other in the different domains.

Growth areas for the IAMRD

This is where the paradoxical nature of this type is seen the most clearly. The conflicting strengths both serve them well and keep them from becoming balanced. They need to trust their intuition more and let go of the need to have everything make sense. This goes along with learning to find meaning on a deeper and more internal and spiritual level rather than just through their sense. They also need to build deeper relationships with people that go beyond basic friendships but involved the struggle to be a better and more spiritual person. Their identities need to be found in those relationships and in what the world is telling them about them self. As they do this and while they are bringing hope to the world, some of their goals need to be more practical in nature. It's a matter of engaging the spiritual dimension with the very human one, of empathizing more deeply with the sufferings of the world.

Activities
1. Before you do something ask yourself this: Was your decision based on your mind or your heart? Do some things from your heart and give the mind a break. If you find that you do things primarily through the heart, then use the mind and see what is most useful for those you are serving.
2. Ask others to describe you, see what you learn about yourself from others.
3. Look at what you do in the world for God and see how practical it is. Use your mind and your heart to find a path that is both meaningful and practical.
4. Find an STENP and build a relationship, you will learn much from each other.

5. Look at your relationships with people. Pick a couple and see if you can't talk about moving it to a deeper level, more meaningful and spiritual.

Mark 2:1-12 (see page 102)

The questions the IAMRD will ask have to do with making sense of the story. How did everyone find out Jesus was there or even know about him? Where are the disciples? How did these people know the paralyzed man? Why didn't the man say anything? How does Jesus know people's hearts? Why don't the scribes get it?

For them, Jesus created the scene, he brought the pieces together for a reason, it is up to us to figure out what that reason is. Their idealism sees the hope in the faces of everyone there, the hope Christ brings to the world. They can identify with the man because they know they have faults and that Christ is the one who can free them from the obstacles in life.

This type feels and understands the tension of the scribes but want them to use their minds to see a different interpretation of scripture---just as they have. They acknowledge the faithfulness of many there but are more focused on the rational. They would be standing in the background watching most of the drama unfold, giving play by play commentary rather than engaging fully into the drama.

IAMRP

Immanent, Sacred, Mystical, Reason, Pragmatist

The IAMRP find themselves in a quandary. Their self-identity is found on the transcendent plane and is wrapped up with their connections to the Collaborative Unconscious and all things spiritual. When they try to make sense out of their lives and the world, they are pulled more towards the world. When they remember their dreams they are often filled with amazing images, but they struggle to make sense out of them because their meaning system and creative mind are attached to the world which doesn't really comprehend the meaning systems and creativity of the spiritual realm. Half of them doesn't get the other half. They are torn between two worlds not understanding that each is needed to fully understand and work with the other. When the traits are at or near the extremes there is little dialogue and much confusion. Their Immanent side sees some logic in how the world is working, what its needs are and how they might fit in. Their spiritual self can't really get it and struggles to become active because it wants to rest and connect with the spiritual, at times avoiding the more material. There is a going back and forth between the two realms, living out fully Niebuhr's Christ in Paradox.

Their sense of being sacred hits head on with the world telling them they aren't all that special. They are conflicted and struggle with having a foot in both worlds. When they give in to one, they often revolt and it makes them feel guilty or shamed. They question their motives and at times even their faith.

The Collaborative Unconscious is fully present to both worlds and yet can only work effectively to the degree the soul allows it to. Dreams are offered and yet often misunderstood. "Coincidences" are precipitated and the point missed due in part to the Reason and Immanent parts of their soul. The soul yearns to be in balance, has a strange attractor at its core (see Chaos Theory chapter) that pulls us to the center. That part of us that holds fast to reason keeps the soul from seeing fully the irrational side of life. Much of who God is and what God does is not rational in worldly terms. Our Immanent and Reasoning side keep us from seeing that just as being overly A (Sacred) and M (Mystical) keep us from understanding and learning from the world.

Like other IRP's (Immanent, Reason, Pragmatist) they are an active type, engaged in activities that move the world forward to become more fully the kingdom God wants it to be. Justice is very important to this type and in the works vs. faith debate they tend to side more with the works side even though they may not admit it. Their calling is to follow Christ's commandments in deeds. To love your neighbor means to do something, not just to pray about your neighbor. At times they lose sight that what your neighbor might need is more spiritual. Jesus did not always heal the physical body at first, sometimes he forgave sins. There is a distinction between what the world wants and needs and calls us to and what God wants, needs, and calls us to. God's call is never against the world's call if understood correctly, but pulls us to a deeper level of that call. The IAMRP sometimes is of the world rather than just being in the world.

The beauty of the IAMRP is that they have a grounding in both realms. They have the capacity to be fully present to each when they are able to give way, which to be honest, is rare.

This type likes all forms of worship---depending on where they are at any given moment. This type is more frustrated with worship than most types. They will probably find it uncomfortable to have the same style of worship consistently because one side of their soul isn't being fed in the way they would like. On the other hand they thrive in community so having a firm base in a consistent community of faith and worship is important—yet another paradox. Sometimes they will choose churches that offer a variety of styles and will jump around within a church.

What the IAMRP is attracted to

This type is attracted by just about everything. They tend to be very curious and willing to try new ways of praying, acting, worshipping, and being. They are not as bound by protocol or absolutes as some other types. They understand that with risk comes failure. They are spiritually adventuresome and enjoy the glimpses of heaven they get from those risks. On the other hand they are very practical people and want what they do to make a difference in their lives and in the lives of others. They are not spiritually patient and may try meditating for a few days and seeing it isn't "working," move on. A trial period of months is more called for but they lack the discipline to do that. Delayed gratification is not in their vocabulary. They like practical people who have a spiritual edge to them. They get along well with those who can live in paradox and chaos.

Growth areas for the IAMRP

Trusting intuition is perhaps at the core of the transformation of the IAMRP. The center of the soul is found through letting go of reason as the sole method of discovery. This type would do well sitting for a few months as part of a Zen meditation group. This is not to give up their Christian faith, but to expose them self to the nature of silence, internal listening, and being present to what lies within and beyond. Using their minds to pull them from a more mystical way of seeing things to find the earthly connections that deepen relationships with other people is important. As with all traits, one needs to teach and learn from the others. The Immanent side of the soul needs to foster and pull at the Sacred and Mystical, giving them a grounding on earth, even as those traits pull the Immanent to gain meaning that is deeper than what the world offers. They can also use their mind to help them see that God's call is to something more profound than the world's call, even though that is important.

Reality is different than what it seems. Paradox is what they live and reverse paradox is the key to finding balance.

Activities

1. Meditate in a way that helps you still the mind and listen. The best of all worlds is to join a group, Christian or other that fosters that style of meditation.
2. Find an STEND and build a relationship. Learn from each other.
3. Look for ways to discover a deeper sense of the spiritual in the things you do. Nothing wrong with doing, just wear a different set of lenses when you look at it.
4. Expose yourself to types of creativity that call for something outside the rational to understand; like poetry, abstract art and music.
5. Push yourself to deepen a couple of relationships you have with others. Join them and support them in what they like doing. Fight the tendency to push your agenda, fulfill theirs.

Mark 2 :1-12 (see page 102)

The IAMRP views this story like most people do. They ask lots of questions and yet at the same time are filled with awe, not unlike the crowd. In light of the notion of the call, they wonder if the friends were called to take the paralyzed man to Jesus? Were the scribes called to ask these questions? What was the call of the crowd? Perhaps solely to observe, bear witness, and give glory to God. Isn't that enough?

Their Mystical nature if allowed to show itself, will help connect the dots with other stories and ways God speaks to the world. They will find not only ways that Jesus relates to people but learn strategies from him about how they can relate to others. When not to be goaded, when to go deeper into someone's life and not settle for the surface issues, when to not worry about what is going on around you like a roof being ripped off, are all things we can learn from this simple story.

The mind of this type is working overtime. This narrative is so rich and deep with possibilities, they enjoy mulling them over in their minds. The key is to have their ideas merge with everything else they believe about life. If our lives are a puzzle, then all the pieces need to fit. The image of Jesus we have must meld with the one in this story. They will push hard to have everything make sense, to answer all the questions even if they admit to them self, there may not be an answer they comprehend. They love this story because of its depth and breadth in such a short space.

ITEND

Immanent, Terrene, Temporal, Inspiration, Idealist

The totality of the core parts of the ITEND comes from their relationship to the world. They find their identity, meaning system and relationships embedded in the language and ways of the world and how they find God there. This is not to say they aren't spiritual or are ungodly, but they find God and the transcendent in and through the world rather than internally. They are dependent on the world for who they are. They see them self as part of God's great creation, put on this planet for a reason, a deeper purpose than just existing. Their Immanent nature helps them see the world in ways others don't. They see God's activity in the world, feel his presence in others and in nature and relate to others as God's creations. We are not merely entities bouncing around, created by chance, but were created with a purpose.

Humans have a need for meaning in their lives. There are a limited number of ways to find meaning in life. Victor Frankl discusses at length this search for meaning in his book ***Man's Search for Meaning*** (Beacon Press, 1959). We can allow others to give us meaning, we can create it ourselves, or we can find it through the transcendent. Most people use a combination of at least two if not all three of these processes. Because the transcendent interacts intimately with the immanent we may never know how much of how we gather meaning is or is not from the transcendent realm of existence. The difference is, are we gleaning meaning through the lens of the transcendent or through the filter of the world gazing upon the transcendent. It would be like hearing second, third or fourth hand about a complicated concept. Would you prefer learning directly from the source or via how others have interpreted the source? The Immanent type learns primarily from secondary sources in relation to meaning.

Because their self-identity comes from the world as well, they are more motivated by what the world says and tend to become more of the world than in the world. It is their calling from God that keeps them from completely capitulating. This calling finds it hard to manifest itself because at times what is called for goes against everything the person believes about them self. Their self-identity comes from what their senses tell them and the lens their brain has adapted throughout life. They know they are in the world for a reason and there is tension between what they feel the world needs and what God calls them too. Because of the power of meaning and of self-identity, they tend to err on the side of the immanent.

Their creative side is linked to the transcendent. This allows for a unique way of being in the world because they have intuitive access to the infinite creativity of God and the Collaborative Unconscious. The soul's goal is unity with God and service to God. Through this creative avenue, the soul finds ways of bringing the spiritual into the immanent even though the person is dominantly driven by their more worldly natures. Keen insights, Zen thinking, and an appreciation for the spiritual are part of their life. These characteristics may not surface much and others may be surprised to hear them when they surface, but they are rarely very deep inside.

From the Niebuhrian perspective, the ITEND is primarily the Christ Of culture. Because their meaning and identity come from the world and their primary relationships are viewed through how the world sees them, they are in and of the world. Their intuitive side and the spiritual call from God may beckon them to look at things differently but these are often over-shadowed by the ITE parts of their nature. This type wants to find God in the midst of culture and to call out the best humanity has to offer. They may have hope that he world can solve its problems in and of itself.

They tend towards the less formal and more contemporary forms of worship. Ritual and worship for them are tied into the culture out of which they live. Doing a ritual that is thousands of years old and has no real ties to their culture other than historical ones are not meaningful to them.

What the ITEND is attracted to

ITEND's are in their hearts idealists but have a very practical nature. They are doers more than be-ers. They like being around others that understand God's actions in the world; the fight for justice and the responsibility of bringing hope to the world. They see the connections in the world and tend to enjoy nature. Over all they are thinking people who often do things more out of a sense of duty than of love. This goes against their intuitive nature and sometimes that part of their soul breaks forth. They prefer being around those who are active and like group activities. Worship that is active makes sense to them and fills them with God's presence. They are uncomfortable being alone with God and the larger the group, most often, the better.

Their sense of call is conflicted because internally they know and feel God calling them but externally if that call is not literally connected to what they want to do they might miss it. Their call in their mind and spirit is always connected to God.

Growth areas for the ITEND

This type needs to expose them self deeply to the spiritual realm of life, to see that it is not something to be feared, but is indeed part of who they are. This should be their focus of growth because if they focus on the ITE (Immanent, Terrene, Temporal) they will slide completely into the world. The ITEND should keep the ND (Inspiration, Idealist) part of their nature strong until the ITE aspects move toward the center. ITE's struggle with this transition. Often, the best way is to take a solo retreat for 3-5 days with nothing but paper and pen. The spiritual side of life is at times counter-intuitive to what ITE's think. In order to find the Spirit we sometimes have to let go of the rational –at least to some degree. Making relationships on a spiritual level is key for this type.

Activities

1. Go on a retreat, just you and God, just pen and paper.
2. Find a SAMRP. Build a relationship with them. Learn from one another.
3. Read poetry and the mystics, they will open your heart and eyes.
4. Learn to meditate and find meaning on a different level.
5. Pay attention to your intuition, trust your gut a bit more.
6. Write down how you think God sees you.

Mark 2: 1-12 (see page 102)

The ITEND is all about watching the story unfold. They love seeing how the people relate to each other and wondering what people are feeling and thinking. They easily identify with most of the characters on a worldly plane. The only ones that may be difficult are those that are undoubtedly present but not mentioned like the disciples and the owner of the house.

They like the tenacity of those that raise the man on the roof and feel they were called by God to do so. Jesus speaks to their faith and they self-identify with that faith. The forgiveness of sins is a bit of a blip on their screen, but not the focus of their attention. Their intuitive nature pulls at them to look at the relationships, to understand how Christ is relating to each and every one there and how they can get meaning from that. Jesus not only hears what people say, but reads their hearts. He simply knows the man needs his sins forgiven and that the scribes are questioning him in their hearts. He knows the faith of those that lower the man through the roof and implicitly knows the owner of the home is ok with it. The story does say "when Jesus came home"—perhaps a home away from home?

This type will wonder what the next step is. What did all the people there learn from this? What does it tell them about them self? How were their lives changed? How do they now see the world and others in a different way? What did they miss?

ITENP

Immanent, Terrene, Temporal, Inspirational, Pragmatic

The ITENP has only their intuition to connect them directly via their soul to the transcendent realm of existence. It's rather remarkable that this intuitive side gets through at all in light of the dominance in every other area of their soul. While their intuition may be at play in their lives, they more often than not do not trust it because of the other traits. The soul, inspired by God, seeps into the other areas and tries to lure them to the center, even as they lure their imaginative side to the world. The soul seeks balance and is constantly pulling all of us to the center, no matter where we are on the continua.

With these types that are so worldly in their traits we must be careful not to judge. There is a tendency to think we must be all spiritual, that that is the goal. In reality, to be purely spiritual is the goal for eternity, not for this life. We are in the world precisely because we are meant to bring the two facets of our lives together through the soul. It is not a matter of being in the world, but how we perceive the world through the lens of our soul which is distinct from the lens of our egos and psyches. This gets to the armor of God discussed in Ephesians 6. We start to see the world through God's eyes, gaining a perspective that is not possible with merely human eyes. The expansiveness of the transcendent sense of the cosmos is enormous. The world puts things in boxes, the transcendent dissolves them. The world categorizes and stratifies things, God shows no partiality. Those whose soul is truly of God but in the world see God at work in the world, they are rooted in the created order. This is the ultimate balance we should seek. We are not talking about mentally having this sense or catching glimpses now and then, but a sense of reality that is fundamentally different from the norm. This gets to the point of how honest we are with ourselves. We can all answer questions that make us look spiritual, even atheists can do that. But is that truly who you are and by not being up front and honest, who are you fooling? Yourself? Others? God?

This type can easily rationalize their way out of simply being in but not of the world and can become Niebuhr's notion of Christ Of culture. We see how quickly they adapt and lose sight of God's vision for them and others. Their hope starts to rest in how the world can fix things rather than on the hope of an eternal future through the grace of God.

Their identity and meaning come from how they see them self in relationship to others in the world. They are who others tell them they are and they have an internal drive to have that sense of self be good. So they go out of their way to be good in the world. They have a high sense of loyalty and morality at their best, but can slide into less ethical practices the more they give in to the world. Relationships are on worldly terms. They are not seeking a spiritual relationship or one of great depth. Relationships are a means to an end and the end is God's will on earth—which at times they believe they are a better judge of than God. This may not be what they say, but it is how they act. This is the path of some evangelicals who seek to simply bring people to the altar and not worry about what happens after they find God for the first time.

In relationship, God cares about depth. God knows us better than we know ourselves, but we still act as if God doesn't. We harbor thoughts fearful of what God might think. We tend to not take spiritual risks that call us to a deeper level of commitment and understanding of the world. It's much easier to just read the paper or look at the news to see what is going on in the world. What do you think a newscast put on by God would look like? What would the focus be? Evil?

The ITENP is very action focused and shows signs of creativity within that focus. They care deeply about injustice and believe we are stewards of the planet and are all meant to share in the bounty of God. Their spiritual roots keep them hopeful in the midst of despair. They struggle with suffering in the world but know God is in the midst of it.

In worship they are most at home with more contemporary forms of worship and prefer having things done for them. They like having the insights of preachers rather than spending a lot of time wrestling with scriptures and issues them self. They are trusting people and when they find a pastor they trust, they tend to accept what they say without asking questions. By showing up and being part of a community of faith, they are doing what God calls them to relative to worship.

What the ITENP is attracted to

Like all ITE's (Immanent, Terrene, Temporal), they love the world. They are refreshed when seeing amazing things. They love nature and those who are trying to be good stewards of it. They are drawn to those who want to make a difference and are thinking creatively about it.

Relationships are important to them, although as mentioned earlier, they may not be that deep. They enjoy seeing how they can best fit into the puzzle of life and now and then like a good theological discussion as long as it is grounded in reality and not some mystical notion. Their metaphors are very concrete and they struggle at times with very abstract ideas of the spiritual world. Their concepts of heaven tend to be more physically oriented. They enjoy biographies and books that are not overly spiritual in nature. Bible study for them is good when it focuses on the story and on how things change when touched by God.

Growth areas for the ITENP

This type needs to see God at work in a different way. God is in the world, but constantly drawing us to a different kingdom and a different set of values than what the world tends to offer. The ITENP needs to find meaning outside of what the world offers. They tend categorize with boxes and should work on ways of expanding them. While they see they have talents, they need to see that God loves them for who they are, that they are created unique. It is through this self-discovery of God's vision for them that they will gain new meaning and be able to serve God more fully in the world. The ITENP also needs to build spiritual relationships, asking spiritual questions of those they care deeply about. Learning to sit in silence and hear the still small voice of God will serve them well. This type also needs to understand that God gave them a brain for a reason and solely trusting what they view as the Holy Spirit or others is not necessarily a good thing.

Activities

1. Learn to meditate in silence. Listen, be still.
2. Find an SAMRD. Build a friendship with them. Listen to them and learn from each other.
3. Try putting on the lenses of God. How does God see the world? For what spiritual purpose is God calling you to?
4. Start focusing on your dreams, ask God to help you remember them and see what they are saying.
5. Go on a 3-5 day retreat with nothing but a pen and paper. Listen to and be guided by God.

Mark 2:1-12 (see page 102)

The opening to deeper and broader understanding for the ITENP is their creative side, the N (Inspiration). They are pulled by the narrative to see what Christ is offering the world. They are looking at the relationships being forged and being strained. They love the commitment of the men raising the paralyzed man. They have many practical questions being the pragmatists they are. This type can identify with each person or group in the story on a worldly level, but struggle to find the depth of faith that many see. It is their creative nature that allows them to glimpse the spiritual side.

The immensity of what Jesus is doing here is almost a burden to them. How can one person meet the needs of so many? How can Jesus forgive sins, heal paralysis, engage the crowd, keep the owner of the house from getting angry, deal with the stupidity of the scribes, and listen to the questions of the onlookers? To do all that with grace is astounding. Rationality does not do the situation justice, only intuition and the spiritually driven Jesus makes any sense.

In and through all this, the ITENP sees God at work. They find God filling everyone's minds with meaning, steeped in the traditions of their faith while changing the bar. Much of what happens in the story is implicit rather than explicit, is said between the lines rather than through them.

This type will not spend a lot of time on this story unless pushed—which they should be. Their grounding in the world helps them focus attention at what is actually being said and done rather than just assumed.

ITERD

Immanent, Terrene, Temporal, Reason, Idealist

The ITERD is well grounded in the world. Their sole trait that comes from the spiritual side is their calling. This characteristic tugs at them because we are created to be in the world for God's purpose, to bring all things back to the Creator. God's call comes through humans to engage the world. As Niebuhr talks about, they are Christ OF the world. They are not unlike the rich man who has done everything right in the world and is troubled when Jesus asks him to give everything away he has worked hard for. It makes no sense to him, it doesn't go by the Law of Moses. He was expecting a pat on the back and instead was given a challenge that was beyond his capabilities at that time. Spiritual ideas do not make a great deal of sense to this type unless they are firmly grounded in the world or in metaphors that make concrete the abstract. A deep understanding of grace and faith are difficult for the ITERD outside of seeing them in action.

Relationships, connections and hard work are core values and ideas for the ITERD. Their personal identity comes from those relationships. They are networkers, wanting to bring people together to achieve things for the benefit of all. They are idealists in the same sense the early church was as long as everyone is on board with them. In the Book of Acts we see everyone held everything in common. What a wonderful ideal to have. Their souls feel the world and are in pain with and for the world. Their souls seek to use the world to bring hope, to fix the problems and right the wrongs. What they have a hard time grasping is that this is just one world. There is another and you can't earn your way there and ultimately, this one can't be completely fixed.

The rational side of their being brings lists into their prayer life. They know who should be healed and why, what parts of the world can be changed and how to change them. Who and what they are as an individual is found through the senses. They are what they see and feel. They become what the world needs them to become. They want justice and peace and can become frustrated when things go in the opposite direction. There are times when the world doesn't make sense even though it should. They tend to avoid the spiritual because by definition it isn't supposed to make rational sense at all times. Their overall belief is that God works through the brain and the world, that the spiritual is for after they have proven them self here and are in heaven. That's when the soul takes over. Their being OF the world is not a bad thing, it simply means they are missing out on half the picture and half the fun.

Biblically, they are very narrative and tend to be somewhat legalistic in their thinking because they are so rooted in the world. Christ's commandment of loving one another as he loved us as one of two commandments instantly brings the ITERD into thinking practically; what would it look like? If we look at how Jesus treated people and use that as a template, most people can't conceive of that type of love, it isn't purely about logical actions, or even worldly actions. The narrative side helps them relish the stories of the bible, seeing how God is acting in the world and through people. They enjoy biographies because they describe action.

Obviously they lean more towards the contemporary styles of worship. They like worship that is grounded in a culture they understand and are part of. Mystery is not something they enjoy nor is more symbolic worship. For them, the deeper mysteries of communion being the body and blood of Jesus is a concept with which they don't wrestle. It's a memory, something we are called to do to remember, a story and to remember what Jesus taught. They enjoy sermons that make sense and make them feel good about them self.

Their creativity comes with and through others. They are very good at using what is available and being creative, but thinking outside the box, especially on a spiritual level is very difficult.

What the ITERD is attracted to

This type is attracted to the world and everything in it. This does not mean they are materialistic, but they enjoy the miracle that is the world. They appreciate the things humanity has done as well as being upset when humanity goes astray. At their best they are conscientious and move through the world with right motives and actions. At their worst they become materialistic and self-centered. They are attracted to others who enjoy what the world can give. Their souls are fed, literally, by good food. They understand the body is the temple of God and healthy ones enjoy taking care of that temple. They are good networkers, moving in the world to make connections that will push their vision of what God wants in the world. They enjoy sermons that are filled with stories, humor, and practical ways of living.

They read more biographies and science than most and are at times active in the political arena since that is where many important world oriented decisions are made. They tend to struggle with church politics because on the one hand they see that process as a vehicle for change and on the other as missing the point of what the church is called to.

Growth areas for the ITERD

Because four out of five traits show that the soul gains its energy from the world, any work that will shift those towards the center will help. This lack of balance in their lives may make them feel comfortable, but it also keeps them from experiencing the richness God has to offer. This type is pretty aware of their lack of spiritual focus in a transcendent way. Their perception is that they are spiritual. Their theology is created to back up their view of God in and of the world. They are acting as God's ambassadors in the world which means they must be of it. The core challenge for this type is to understand there is another world, another realm that offers them new insights and ways of seeing the world. Letting go of the world and attuning to the transcendent does not come easily. Many times this type needs to be "shocked" into a deeper understanding, not unlike the Zen notion of being shocked into enlightenment. They are led by their brains and need to come to understand the brain is not the only guiding principle that can run their lives.

The one area, the Call, where they do learn from the transcendent is so overwhelmed by the others it is barely noticeable. For a while it is helpful for the ITERD to let that go and use it to help balance the other traits. Once that happens then they can balance the call side of their being. They may find this a bit puzzling because the Call is what gives purpose to their lives. They want their actions to be purposeful in the midst of how they understand God and the transcendent.

Here we see a Christ Of culture. There may be times when they are so fixated on their view of what is right they stand in judgment of the world and in so doing become Christ Against culture, but this is rare. They want to see God in the midst of culture, to know that God is working in and through the activities of humanity. They see God in the foodbanks, hospitals, research facilities and even militaries of the world. They struggle to know when God is there and is not, but they don't fret. They are pulled by the ways of the world fairly easily and need to fight to maintain an understanding of the differences between God's domain and that of the human.

Activities

1. Probably the best thing for the ITERD is to go off on a retreat. The best would be a three day retreat by them self, next would be with others. Less than two days will not give the potential breakthrough they need.

2. Doing anything that is spiritually oriented will help. Books, prayer groups, bible studies, listening to sacred music.
3. Find someone who is a SAMNP and get to know them.
4. Try reading and writing some poetry. It may seem awkward but it will be good for you.

Mark 2: 1-12 (see page 102)

The ITERD attunes to the needs of the people in relation to the world in which they live. They can feel the plight of the scribes while not agreeing with it. Being idealists they want everything to be well. While they are ok with the man's sins being forgiven, they want him healed, especially after the efforts of those around him. They wonder why Jesus comments on their faith rather than on their works. Jesus does not seem to care what people do, it's their hearts he is more concerned about and this does not sit right with this type.

They want to feel what each person is doing there, how Jesus is going to touch each of them. They believe at some level everything is about being called by Jesus to be and do something. The homeowner is called to open his house and make it available to all who come to seek Jesus, even those who tear off the roof. Apparently the homeowner does what he is called to do. The scribes are called to raise questions but also to listen—which they don't do so well. The paralyzed man it would seem is simply called to be. For most in the story, the assumption is that their ideals are reached if not perceived, save the scribes.

This type would love to talk about this story, see what it tells them about their lives and the lives of others, and wrestle with the questions that remain unanswered by all the story doesn't say.

The ITERD wants to be able to move through the world like Jesus does. That often asked question, "What would Jesus say or do?" is on their hearts and they try to learn from this story about how to deal with the world. Much of the story does not fit into a logical world and that is a problem for this type. They tend to avoid the thorny ideas that are very faith dependent.

ITERP

Immanent, Terrene, Temporal, Reasonable, Pragmatic

ITERP is at the other extreme from those most transcendently oriented. This group is firmly rooted on the earth and has little contact with the transcendent realm of existence. Their souls, while they believe in them, are a distant reality and to a large degree taken for granted. Spiritually, they are more based on the idea that if they are good people and do the right things in life, the rest will take care of itself.

Their day to day relationship with God on a personal level is not that important. They trust their minds more than they trust their intuition. They are task oriented, even in relation to their spiritual lives. They read the bible daily more out of duty than for what it does for them. If they belong to a church they are focused on building a depth of financial security and numbers than on building spiritual community. They readily acknowledge that both are important, but leave the spiritual things to others.

Their lives have more to do with doing than with being. They are active people. One of the keys to understanding the difference between the I (Immanent) and the S (Supernal) is what lies behind the actions. The I's go to a bible study to see how they need to lead a good life, how the stories help them become a better person. The S does so to learn and see how God moves in people's lives and thus in theirs, how certain actions bring people closer to Christ or take people further away. Immanent people, especially those who are also P's (Pragmatists) like to act, they are engaged with and in the world. There is a greater tendency for the I's to become enmeshed with the world which is a danger. The I's use their five senses to orient them self in life and with God. They struggle with any senses other than the basic five.

T's (Terrene) may feel special, but it is because the world has told them so or they have created them self as special, not necessarily in an egotistical way, but in an honest and humble way. The root of their specialness comes from the world. Often they will have a skill or personal attribute that enamors them to the world. Because all is well with the world, most feel all must be well with God. They move towards that which brings them positive feelings and encouragement.

Because all of the attributes of their soul are founded on terra firma, the ground of their being is the world they walk in. Terrene is a very positive term for the earth. It comes with a sense of being rooted and grounded. The problem is that there is more to life than just this world. The ITERP's ignore the spiritual dimension of life to their detriment. The spiritual realm is connected intimately to the more physical one. There is a lack of wholeness at this extreme. They purport to be happy because they are so out of touch with the other world. They actually use energy to keep it at bay because to let the spiritual in would rain havoc on what they have already created around them.

This group connects well in the world. They tend to be more social and often have large networks. They can get things done because of those connections. They are more about using the connections to get things done than in building relationships with those connections. They enjoy viewing networks of people or things and seeing how all the dots connect in the world. If you ask an E (Temporal) how we got into financial woes in the U.S. in the early 21st century they will track various people, industries, and political decisions. If you ask an M (Mystical) the same question, they will probably say something like, "Greed." There will be few if any specifics, just the spiritual state of a culture. Global warming becomes a scientific issue rather than a spiritual one. It becomes more about percentages and amounts of certain chemicals than about humanity's stewardship of the planet. We need both views in life. There is danger in residing in only one.

ITERP's are more existential, they live in the moment and find their meaning in the world around them. They may be thinking of the future, but they are planners. They start with what is happening now. It's part of their pragmatism. They love to think things through. They write their sermons or speeches, use logic in most things they do and try to stay one step ahead of the game. While they may enjoy worship, it is not their favorite activity, they are too restless. They prefer music that is more in tune with the rhythms of the day or of their day. If they are in their 70's they may prefer the music they were rooted in. Their spirituality comes from the world in which they became grounded. Prayer for them tends to be more rote than open ended.

The ITERP fits into Niebuhr's category of Christ OF culture. At times they may come across as Christ Against culture because they are so outraged at what is happening in the world. It may simply be that they are angry at them self for not being able to change things in their lives or in the lives of others so they blame the world, they rationalize. Relationships tend to be more shallow and concerned with practical matters.

In worship this type is the most contemporary. Most will find liturgical worship very slow and boring. They enjoy worship that speaks to the issues of the day in a practical way, that uses words and music they are familiar with. The ITERP likes being part of a community of faith that is very active with their outreach ministries. They are prone to bring politics into the community of faith since they believe it is a major vehicle of change in the world.

What the ITERP is attracted to

The world excites this group. They see the world as filled with opportunity to serve God and fulfill their purpose which comes from their rational minds. They enjoy connecting dots and helping put the puzzle together in their mind's eye and through their actions. These people enjoy big projects that help lots of people. They tend not to think small because their value comes from what the world gives them.

ITERP's are drawn to actions that put them in contact with others. They don't like being alone unless they are busy doing something. Sitting in a coffee shop talking about life is not their thing. Talking about what they are doing or want to do is fine. Group work is enjoyable because of the energy, synergy, and camaraderie they feel.

Because they are so rooted in the world, their spirituality is more focused on doing things. They feel closer to God when things are going well, they are busy, and making others happy. They enjoy more practical sermons than lofty spiritual or theological ones. They are more intellectual than some, but mental games are not all that interesting to most ITERP's; it's what is done with ideas that matters most to them.

Growth areas for the ITERP

The ITERP is at the extreme and most of the time extremes are not healthy. While we are to have roots in the world, we need to have roots in the spiritual plane as well. To avoid our spiritual selves is to avoid a part of our reality that helps us more deeply understand, relate to and be in the world as it is meant to be. There is a difference between being in and of the world in our eyes or in God's eyes. This group needs to find ways to open their hearts and souls to the transcendent.

Their connections with the world are seen through the lens of doing and they need to move more towards being. They live on the surface and need to move towards looking under that to see what is happening on different levels. As they connect with people, these relationships should be more about connecting at the level of the heart. Seeking understanding is as important as simply doing things or looking at practical matters.

Intuition is not trusted much by this type. The hope is that they will find ways of listening to their intuition more. It's not a matter of not having it, just not listening to it. Perhaps one of the best things an ITERP can do is to meditate. So slow down, quiet the mind and listen to the other dimension. Their rational minds fight this, but if they spend time thinking it through, even their brains will let them know they need to move to the center more.

There is absolutely nothing wrong with attuning to the world, it's where we live. But if one believes in the soul and God, there is another world, another dimension we also need to attune to. For this type, finding that spiritual dimension in the midst of the world is a good way to go. They need to ask why something is the way it is through spiritual lenses.

Activities

1. Read more spiritually oriented books.
2. Meditate—doesn't matter what method you choose.
3. Do Yoga, a great physical way to create the internal space needed to listen.
4. Read poetry, pushes the mind to let it go and see things differently.
5. Write a description of God and what your core beliefs about God are.
6. Find an SAMND. Build a relationship, it will be fascinating. Learn from one another and be patient.
7. Finally, this type would be served well by going on a vision quest retreat that puts them in touch with their spiritual natures.

Mark 2:1-12 (see page 102)

The ITERP is fully world based. Questions of faith, sin, and the authority of Jesus seem odd and perhaps even a waste of time to this person. They are intrigued by the loyalty of the men hoisting the paralyzed man onto the roof. They want to know how they know him. They see this event as a golden opportunity; a large crowd, Jewish leaders and Jesus pulling out all the stops. This type wants to capitalize this event and yet no one else seems to, why?

Their practical nature wants to cease the moment and build upon it, something which Jesus appears to not be concerned about. This type is not afraid to challenge the strategies of Jesus. The import of Christ's forgiving the man's sins, the challenge of the scribes and the faithfulness of the men is all but lost on this type. They are focused on the action of the moment and how people are changing for the long run.

Within the story, they are able to sense what is going on with their eyes, ears, mouths, hands, and noses. This is an experience to be felt. They are conflicted with their emotions about the reactions of the various players in the drama. Their minds tell them different things than their heart, but they are so out of balance toward the world that is what they see and feel, that is how they perceive God in that moment,.

ITMND

Immanent, Terrene, Mystical, Inspiration, Idealist

This type finds its identity and meaning in the world but everything else in the transcendent. This may seem strange because outside of our identity and how we make meaning out of the world what is there? How can we feel a call from God without an identity or meaning? How can we relate to the transcendent in a way that is wholly immanent? Having the world try to make sense of the spiritual is a struggle. First of all, there are language problems. Human words do not capture at times what is happening on spiritual levels. The two realms are not the same. There are cultural differences on every level. The kingdom of the spirit does not play by the same rules as the kingdom of the flesh. Their language is different which is why in part, one of the gifts of the Spirit is tongues. We know on earth there are words that can't be captured in moving from one language to another. So much more so as we move to talking spiritually and transcendentally.

Their notion of uniqueness comes from what they hear from others and from whom they perceive them self to be in the world, not because of what they know to be true as a creation of God. They do not have an internal sense of being sacred in and of them self. Their identity is wrapped up in meaning. Spirituality is more something you do than who you are. We "go" to church, we "pray" or "study God's word." These are all fine but at some level, the soul simply "is." The ITMND has a hard time accepting its divine sacredness. They are well connected to the transcendent but have difficulty accepting or seeing that connection. On the positive side, they find God in their lives all the time. Being very grounded in the world while having the MND (Mystical, Inspiration, Idealist) adds a mysterious dimension to their lives they don't understand but accept. It is these connections to a different plane of being that at times conflicts internally with what they know and believe as well as not trusting a deep intuitive sense they do not trust, that keeps them from fully living out their soulful natures.

Relationships are important to the ITMND. Their earthly relationships are shaped through how they find meaning in the world and on their own perceptions of who they are; both of which are rooted in more worldly terms. Relationally however, when talking about the soul, they are mystically connected to the transcendent. The IT (Immanent, Terrene) part of their nature struggles with making sense of these relationships and the M (Mystical) struggles because it is already in relationship with the spiritual domain but can't make sense of it because the IT (Immanent, Terrene) is grounded in the Immanent. As these two learn to respect and feed off one another, there is a rich loam in which to grow. If they do not, their spiritual lives become frustrating and fraught with tension.

They struggle with their call at times because deep inside they know what they are called to do and be from the transcendent, but the IT part of their nature keeps them from fulfilling that because the IT is more practically oriented. This push and pull is found in all aspects of their being and one trait moving one direction or the other can have a significant impact.

This type can be a variety of Niebuhrian styles. They are Of the world because of their grounding in the world via their IT. They are in Paradox because of the tension between the IT and the MND. At times this tension may cause them to swing one way or the other making them

Against culture when the IT is feeling self-righteous and Above culture when the MND is dominant and keeping the IT at bay.

While they are comfortable with many forms of worship, they tend to prefer more modern forms of worship in many ways. They appreciate good long sermons and music that has meaningful words that draw them in.

What the ITMND is attracted to

This type enjoys both the world and the spirit. They are attracted to stories and use those narratives to make sense of them self and the world. They put them self into the context of those stories and how they perceive the world.

The ITMND enjoys the abstract as well. They are drawn to symbolic works of art, poetry, and music. They feel a pull to their dreams, but don't quite get them. They tend to be eclectic people who are open to many things and drawn on different levels to them. Depending on the day, they could love or hate a meditation session, a poetry reading, or a walk in the park. At any time they may find them self fully engaged with the world or fully engaged with the transcendent. It is at these times they most need to stop and listen to the other traits that are being ignored, to catch them self. Another tendency is to be spiritual followers; they listen and accept what others are saying more than they trust their own hearts, minds, and souls.

Growth areas for the ITMND

Learning to respect the inherent traits as they are is the biggest step. The IT (Immanent, Terrene) needs to pay attention to and respect the MND (Mystical, Inspirational, Ideal) and visa versa. As they learn to do this, each trait will be pulled more to the center. Finding spiritual and more metaphysical meaning in the world and listening to others describe them are both growth edges. Their personal psychologies can impact the perception of how they perceive them self spiritually. Finding ways to push that notion to a more spiritual plane will go a long way to helping them find their uniqueness in God. The ITMND would also be helped by trusting them self more fully on a spiritual level, by listening to what they feel and going with it rather than simply accepting what others say is right.

Activities

1. Find ways of identifying the IT (Immanent, Terrene) parts of your nature as well as the MND (Mystical, Inspirational, Ideal) parts. Write these down. This will take some concentrated effort and time.
2. Serve the world in silence. This type is prone towards more social ways of serving. Find some behind the scenes work where you will have to be with God in your service.
3. Keep a dream journal and ask yourself what patterns you see, what God is trying to tell you about your spiritual lives within them. Ask God in prayer to give you discernment.
4. Find and SAERP. Build a relationship and learn and support each other.
5. Look at your relationships, see if you can't get them to a deeper level. The tendency is to not have many deep friendships, one where you enter into another's world or pain. Find out why and see if you can't break through that.

Mark 2:1-12 (see page 102)

The ITMND views this passage in an interesting way. Because their meaning system and self-identity in regard to the spiritual domain come from the world they struggle finding spiritual language to describe what is going on even though the Mystical, Inspiration, and Idealist parts of their soul are from the transcendent. They enjoy parables where Christ uses worldly metaphors because those they get. They will struggle having direct expressions of the soul other than through the world.

This type identifies more with the paralyzed man standing and walking than with having his sins forgiven. They join with the crowd being in awe of what Christ did TO the man more than what Christ did FOR the man. They focus more on the commitment of those bringing the man to Jesus than Jesus remarking on the depth of their faith. This is not to imply that faith is not important, but its value comes in and through how it is lived out in actions.

The ITMND feels an internal sense of call, is inspired from the transcendent, and relates to the Collaborative Unconscious and to God, but all of those are through the lens of the their perception of seeing God in the world. They tend to be big picture people who look more at the totality of the story than one piece. They see this story as a snapshot of culture itself; culture, with all its biases, struggles, conflicts, loyalties, power struggles, and yearnings.

Few stories in the New Testament have the depth and breadth of this one. It's Jesus at perhaps his most masterful of bringing factions together, showing the priorities of life, the variety of his power, the depth of his love, and how he meets the needs of all. The ITMND gets this but gravitates more towards fulfilling the more worldly needs than the spiritual ones.

They do understand that they are called to do similar things, that in and through Christ they have the potential to change the world, or at least those around them. They tend to feel convicted by this story to act more out of faith than they currently are.

ITMNP

Immanent, Terrene, Mystical, Inspirational, Pragmatic

The ITMNP find them self in an odd place. Their identity and their source of meaning comes through the world as does their practical nature and yet their relationships and imagination are transcendent in nature. It is as if they are pulled by what we perceive as internal things but cling to the world for who they are and how they perceive meaning in their lives. Let's remember, this is not ignoring God but rather seeing God through the world rather than independent of it. But this same God is trying to shout out his purpose to them, gives them full access to the Collaborative Unconscious which they receive, and lures them through a creative vein others can't see. They have a deep sense of intuition but often don't trust it because of the IT (Immanent, Terrene) aspects of their nature. It's important to see that our imagination and relationships are filtered through our self-identity and meaning systems we have created. One of the reasons we don't hear the clear call of God is precisely because our identity is not found as much in God as in other places. The ITP finds it in the world and thus misses the deeper sense of Call at times. They are so grounded on the planet, the more mystical nature of their soul finds it difficult to break through.

This type will have large and significant breakthroughs. A mystical experience may come upon them at the oddest moments. They may feel a deep call by God to do something or they may have an insight that puzzles them as to where it came from. The degree to which they can honor these breakthroughs and follow them through is the degree to which balance will be found. These experiences can to some degree be planned, or at least one can make the possibility greater by doing certain things. On the other hand as in the Zen tradition, insight comes out of nowhere, when we least expect it. The woman at the well, Peter at the Transfiguration, and all resurrection experiences are examples of this. The empty tomb was not expected and at first everyone missed it, they were all too rooted in the world. God's power breaks through our barriers when we make ourselves present which all of those people did.

The ITMNP struggles with spiritual language although their soul relates to the transcendent through its mystical nature consistently. The transference from the soul to the psyche and to language is a challenge. When they are able to let go of their connection to the world, the words flow. Their spiritual nature is deeply internalized and becomes manifest in odd and different ways. As we said before, it may show up through their creativity, insight, or actions, but will more often than not be a surprise to them.

Their Call comes from God in the world so they fail to see the larger picture. Just because someone is a P (Pragmatic) doesn't mean they follow through with it, simply that the soul understands and tries to move forward, gaining their Call from the world. They may fail to see how to connect the spiritual laws of love with the realities of the world.

Their Terrene nature gives them confidence in the world, that they are here for God. They may be very curious and inquisitive people, challenging much of what they see, both in the world and spiritually. They don't just accept pat answers to questions, but push for deeper meanings although being an N (inspiration) fights against rationality. Here again we see Niebuhr's Christ of Paradox in culture. Their souls are torn but for the most part on the outside they are not. This presents a double paradox. Not only is the soul in paradox because part is of the world and part of the spirit, but how they manifest their spirituality is in paradox because of their relationship to the world. One minute they can appear very worldly and the next quite spiritual. They are fluid and go back and forth with ease and often don't see or feel the tension of doing that.

The ITMND is at home with most types of worship, but gravitates more towards the contemporary and less ritualistic and symbolic. They can value and enjoy any type of worship in the moment, although worship is not their favorite way to be with God, action is.

What ITMND's are attracted to

For the most part they enjoy the world. Because of the paradox they are comfortable in spiritual settings as well, for short periods of time. They enjoy people who are engaged in the world for spiritual reasons. They see a deeper side of life than just getting through the day and like people with vision. The ITMNP is also attracted to those who pull at their MN (Mystical, Inspiration) side. Internally, the soul knows this exists and needs to be fed. They move toward deeply spiritual people even though they aren't sure why. They are puzzle solvers and enjoy thinking about a great many things and challenging the status quo even though they are part of it. They do their puzzle solving more via their senses and intuition than with their minds.

Growth areas for the ITMNP

The ITP needs to listen to the MN (Mystical, Inspiration) and visa versa. The IT (Immanent, Terrene) parts need to begin to find their identity more in the transcendent, to find meaning through the eyes of God and the Collaborative Unconscious than through the eyes of the world. They perceive them self only as unique as the world helps them see. The truth is that God created them unique in and of them self no matter what the world says. Their M (Mystical) nature can help guide them to this realization. This type will be well served by slowing down and listening to the inner voice of their intuition and of God.

Activities

1. Spend time in prayer and meditation. Learn to still the mind.
2. Look for God in unexpected ways and trust your intuition more.
3. Find an SAERD. Get to know them and learn from one another.

4. Find very practical ways of serving God and then look for the spiritual meaning and happenings in those activities.
5. Pay attention to your dreams and what you are hearing in your meditative silences.

Mark 2:1-12 (see page 102)

The ITMNP is another of the types that goes back and forth in the story. Over all they are practical people who find meaning, purpose, and identity in the more worldly end of things. It's the relationship with God, the Collaborative Unconscious, and their intuitive nature that pull them to dig deeper. Because of their pragmatism, they like seeing results and believe they can identify how every person there had the opportunity to be touched and used by Jesus. They understand at a deep level that that is part of the call of Christ, to be used to change the lives of others.

The Mystical and Inspirational natures help them understand that people need help on many levels, not just the existential and world based ones. Internally, they are identifying with the history of the world, the vast array of human experience as found in the CU. This touches their hearts and soul and helps them perceive the spiritual dimension of the story even though the other parts of their nature may not.

They do struggle a bit with Jesus forgiving the man's sins first, because for them, the man's paralysis was the most obvious need and we are called to take care of people's needs. Their Immanent and Terrene natures tie them to this reality and trying to change things on earth for the better of all. Looking deeper into someone's life for other things that may need change is not high on their list.

They do see how Jesus meets people where they are, that he is part worldly and part spiritual, that his intuition is critical and that he uses what he has around him in the moment to change things. This is a key for them, to use what is available as the starting point for change. One need not wait for something to happen, just use what is there and move forward with the help of the Spirit and intuition knowing that God is fully present.

ITMRD

Immanent, Terrene, Mystical, Reason, Idealist

The ITMRD has several conflicts occurring within their souls. They gain meaning and identity from more worldly parts of their nature and relationships. Their connections are with the spiritual and Collaborative Unconscious while their creative edge comes from the world. Finally, their Call is premised upon what they feel God is calling them too on a spiritual dimension. Like other IT's, because their purpose and meaning systems are so tied to the Terrene realm of life, other aspects have to fight for their territory. Because they are all working towards the same end, just with different tactics and visions, things most often work out. The key challenge for all types, especially for the more potentially conflicted ones is to listen to all the traits. There is a tendency for IT's to be absorbed into the world because it not only makes sense to them, but is where the vast majority of information comes from, the senses.

This type finds dreams a problem because they want to find a more rational explanation for their dreams, they want to make concrete sense of the images they see, and they want to believe things as they appear in the dream. This is not often true, especially in dreams that are created from the transcendent realm. The Collaborative Unconscious doesn't work that way. Metaphor and symbol are their language and they are using all previous knowledge from all people that have ever existed along with what God brings into the dream. The CU is a profound believer in novelty, in seeking where things are not found, in hiding treasure where ultimately you are the only one with the map.

This Mystical aspect of their being goes along with the sense of Call that doesn't always fit how they perceive them self and the world about them. They try to fit God's vision into their vision or perhaps a more broadly based world vision of who and what we should be as citizens. God doesn't work that way all the time. God's lenses are different than ours. She sees the entire puzzle when we see but a few pieces at best. Abstraction does not work well with this type. They are concrete thinkers and feelers. Love is an action to them more than a feeling. Some people love and then act because they love. Others act and out of their actions they fall in love. Sometimes we simply act because we are supposed to and love has nothing to do with it. Their minds are sharp but lack a deep ability to trust their intuitive nature. They tend to distrust miracles and most theology doesn't matter to them, it's all speculation and doesn't do much for anyone. This may seem odd coming from a person who loves to work with their mind. The deepest theologians are those who love the mind but have meaning or identity in the more Transcendent realm. This type is firmly grounded in the world and theology is over all a mental construct that is not grounded in the world. Even Liberation Theology which claims to be grounded in the humanness of Jesus and in oppression is actually a mental construct.

They are pulled time and again by their sense of Call. They lack the tools to explain it, but it is there nonetheless. Their soul finds itself in the relationships of this plane of existence, of the depth of relationship they can have with others. They have this notion of what an ideal Christian looks like and how that takes form in the world. For them, it is a life of love being shown through action. It is this aspect of Call which they follow. Their Call gains strength and energy from the Collaborative Unconscious. They feel a connection to the spiritual even though they are very grounded in the material, in the best sense of that word.

In relation to Niebuhr, they have an affinity with both the Christ OF culture and Christ the Transformer of culture. They are intimately tied to culture and the world around them, yet this connectedness to the transcendent and their call coming from God help give some perspective to this idea of transformation that the ITR (Immanent, Terrene, Reason) parts of their soul don't get.

Biblically, they are more prone to view scripture from a pragmatic and narrative perspective, enjoying the stories and morality while at times finding the deeper and more subtle meanings when the M or the D can break through. They are happy to worship in a variety of settings but are probably more comfortable with contemporary styles. The communal orientation of contemporary worship along with its pace feed the IT parts of their being.

They do struggle at times listening to sermons that don't fit with their view of the world. They are pulled by more ritualistic forms of worship and to their own individual time with God because of the Mystical and Reason sides. Their minds need to be fed and work, not just to have information pushed onto them. They enjoy wrestling with ideas in them self or with others.

What the ITMRD is attracted to

They are attracted to those who find energy in the world, with those who thrive on being part of it but see that it needs changing. They love talking about change but are not usually the best at figuring out how to get there, especially using spiritual tools. They enjoy talking about what God wants of them and of others and how God wants them to be in the world to change things. They see them self and the church as the light of the world, the only hope the world has. Their minds help them be a good part of group work that is focused on these tasks. They do not normally do well on their own, either spiritually or in more worldly things, they like being with others. They enjoy the experience of abstract things like art or symbolic movies, or poetry, but they don't claim to get them. They have an odd attraction to people that do.

Growth areas for the ITMRD

As with all IT's they need to discover that part of their identity and where they find meaning in life that comes from the Supernal. It is not enough to just pay attention to your dreams on a concrete level, this type needs to find ways of opening them self up more directly to the spiritual kingdom of God. On the other hand, they need to see more clearly how God is connected to and through the world and to use their sense of identity and meaning as it is, to make their calling more pragmatic and to connect it to the world. The ITMRD should learn to have the one part draw out the other. The ITR needs to pull the MD towards the center and the MD needs to have that same impact on the ITR. This does not happen just on its own, but takes conscious effort.

Activities

1. A retreat is probably the best thing for this type. Getting away and just spending time with God is the best change the MD (Mystical, Idealist) has to impact the other elements of their soul.

2. As odd as it may sound, the reasoning ability can help. Use the mind to push questions onto all segments, including the mind. Provoking them self into asking challenging and thoughtful questions is important. Journal writing can be very helpful to this type.

3. Find an SAENP. Get to know them and learn from one another. They are your opposite.

4. Look for evidence of God in the world.

5. Do a spiritual timeline/lifeline, find your identity and purpose and see if you can't find ways of shifting it a bit. Read biographies of saints.

Mark 2:1-12 (see page 102)

The ITMRD is very cerebral. They like looking at this story with their mind. This is true not only because of the Reason, but also because their meaning systems and self-identity are found in the world. They rely on their senses to show them who they are rather than a direct experience of the transcendent. Their minds explain away purely spiritual ideas and use metaphors to discuss issues of faith and spiritual relationships. This makes a lot of sense because talking about the spiritual on spiritual terms is difficult at best. Even the mystics used metaphorical language. In truth, to talk in a spiritual language is an oxymoron. The transcendent is beyond language. The mystics, probably the best examples of people on the other side of the spectra, use symbolic language. It makes no sense to most unless you are able to find meaning, identity, and creativity from the spiritual domain. They are so abstract it's like a foreign language.

This type is filled with questions and enjoys working with a wide variety of answers. They tend to be very open minded and rarely cling to absolutes in relation to biblical story interpretation. They enjoy pushing people's biblical buttons, at times actually liking making people squirm a bit. Discomfort in relation to God is not a bad thing to them. Jesus does it all the time, in this story with the scribes.

They can identify with the scribes in that they too have many questions. They believe however, that unlike the scribes, they listen to what Jesus has to say---most of the time. They are not so arrogant as to make the claim they always are obedient or listen. They are well aware of the strength of their egos and the weakness of their will.

This type is concerned with follow-up. What happened to all these people? What were they doing a week, month or year later? Were they like some who go to evangelical rallies, get converted and then quickly fall away? What did the paralyzed man do with his life? They want to see how spiritual change is manifest in worldly actions. Because their relationships tend to be more surface oriented, they struggle to see the depth of change Jesus is after. They don't grasp that change at a deep level because they don't understand it. They see people in the story acting out their call in their doing rather than their being.

ITMRP

Immanent, Terrene, Mystical, Reason, Pragmatic

The ITMRP is deeply rooted in the world. The one area where they have a transcendent grounding is in the area of relationships where their connection to the Collaborative Unconscious (CU) is strong. The problem with this connection is that what it gleans from that relationship is often over-shadowed by the other traits. Remember that it is this trait that can most easily lead the way to internal transformation if they give it room. The pull of the CU is very strong to begin with and when it is a strong trait of the soul, it becomes all the stronger. They find the mystical angle poking into their lives in strange ways. Dreams are clearly one avenue, but quick and deep insights that come from nowhere, or seeing underlying connections where others don't are two ways the M (Mystical) may also manifest itself.

Finding meaning in the world through God is a good thing. God created the world and endows it with meaning. The ITMRP tends to miss this meaning in the world and finds their meaning from the world. In the lives of those who seek God, there is always a tension between the spiritual and the mundane, the Supernal and the Immanent. This type can fool them self into believing they truly and deeply understand the world and yet those perceptions are coming from the world. It's like scientists who believe they have made an earth shattering discovery only to find they were blinded by their own egos and missed a few critical pieces. Our world is not the Kantian version of the clockwork universe where God winds it up and lets it go. Kant claims God creates and disappears. We make the claim God creates, endows, and pursues the created world. To not see or seek God's vision for the world is to miss out on its very created purpose. There is a detachment from the spiritual life on an ongoing basis for this type. Their world makes sense to them and those parts that don't are either ignored or chalked up to mystery--- comfortably. For the ITMRP the spiritual is found in and through the world.

Their self-identities are wrapped up in how the world sees them. In Niebuhr's terms they are clearly in the Christ OF culture camp. They engage culture where culture is because they believe the world will only change through worldly processes. They are often politically oriented and very focused on social justice and the practical ways of pursuing it. They need to seek more balance in that the end goal is not to change the world, but to change people's hearts for an eternal vision of their lives, not simply a temporal one. Yes, we need to be caring for those around us, but God pulls us to something deeper. Scripture clearly tells us that when we seek God's kingdom first, all else will follow. If all hearts and minds in the world were truly focused on God, things would change rapidly. The world will never heal itself or live in peace as long as it uses the ways of the world to do so. It has been a bankrupt system from the beginning. This is not a call for everyone to drop everything and solely focus on the transcendent, but the world has swung the pendulum so far towards the world that we rarely hear truly spiritual truths from leaders, even well-known spiritual ones.

The ITMRP loves the mind. They gather information like a sponge. They are not prone to read spiritual books or more spiritually oriented biographies. Worship for them is more about networking for God than worshipping God, although they admit gathering as community to be present to God is important. Feeding the five thousand, healing the sick and distressed, forgiving sins that get in the way of leading a full life, and proclaiming the call to feed the hungry and clothe the naked are their biblical loves.

In the end the ITMRP are down-to-earth people with little interest in the spiritual or mystical. They believe their lives are spiritual as they act in the world. They don't have to retreat to connect with their spirituality or speak to the spiritual that may turn people off. There is no need to speak spiritual lingo, their actions speak for them. They are doers in the best sense of the word.

What the ITMRP is attracted to

"Be doers of the word and not hearers only," is what the Letter of James tells us. This is the focus of the ITMRP. They thrive around doers. They identify with those who change the world on God's behalf to bring God's kingdom to the earth. Being around people that think and plan also excites them. They are goal setters and find meaning in accomplishment. While faith is important, they are people of deeds and are attracted to others in the same vein.

The Mystical aspect of their soul connects them to the spiritual domain and helps them feel that their work has an eternal and transcendent quality. By having this connection to the Collaborative Unconscious they catch glimpses of a bigger picture and are exposed to a much larger source of ideas.

Growth areas for the ITMRP

The roots of the ITMRP need to shift. It's like a plant that is very sensitive to the light of the sun. They quickly turn and bend to find the light. Turn them around from the sun and again their stalk shifts. This type needs to shift focus to the spiritual light. Part of the way to do this is to build deeper relationships with others on a spiritual level or to just be with more spiritually oriented people. We do not worry about transitioning the M (mystical) because that pole is helping pull the other traits to the center. If that trait were to move toward the world more quickly it could stall the changes needed to find balance.

Activities

1. Build spiritual relationships with others. Ask them how God fits into their lives. Read more spiritual books.
2. Find an SAEND and build a relationship. Learn from one another.
3. Learn to meditate and listen to the transcendent.
4. Pay attention to your dreams and ask yourself what God is trying to tell you on a spiritual level.
5. Go on a retreat, preferably for at least 3 days.

Mark 2: 1-12 (see page 102)

The ITMRP would see this in a very practical way. They will identify with the friends who go out of their way not only to take the paralyzed man to Jesus but to get him on the roof, dig a hole through the roof and lower him down. They are willing to take risks based on their faith. They believe that Jesus can do something for this man in a very practical way. They are puzzled by Jesus's forgiving the man's sins because they don't see that as his deepest need. Because they lack the spiritual side of most of the traits, the idea that redemption is an important part of healing may be missed by them. The Mystical attachment to the transcendent does enable them to see the power of what Jesus can do. While they may not understand the deeper meaning behind Jesus's words and actions, they know that he comes from a different kingdom and brings that with him. They see them self as helpers, as people opening their homes, helping those in need and supporting the needs of their Lord. They gather meaning from the healing and its manifestation of the power of God.

They could also be like those that challenge Jesus. They question everything and are steeped in the ways of tradition and the world so this person who claims to have the power to forgive sins is out of the box. They tend to like boxes.

SAEND

Supernal, Sacred, Temporal, Inspiration, Idealist

The sole way this type connects with the world is through their relationships. But these relationships are at times strained because the SAEND relates on primarily a spiritual level and often misses many of the more human dynamics that go into a relationship. They are always trying to get the other person to meet them where they are. They are unable to come to their level because they have no real grounding in the world. This is not to say they are psychologically deficient. Remember, we are talking about the soul. The author's belief is that this is another rare type because most people are more grounded in the world than in the spirit. Usually this type person has had a profound experience in their lives that so impacted and shifted their understanding of them self they have let go of the world as a primary source of meaning, identity, creativity, and call. Their attention is always toward the transcendent. They may seem aloof or a bit off to most people.

The SAEND clings to relationships because they know they need them. They just aren't quite sure how to make them work. These relationships on the temporal plane are the only lens through which this type takes God's call into the world. One of the struggles for them is that they are very at home in solitude and yet know they need relationships to ground them in the world. All people need relationships, but many take them for granted, knowing they are just a natural part of life. This is not so for the SAEND. Relationships are a struggle. The lens through which they view the world, people, and relationships comes from the transcendent. At this level, worldly filters are limited. They see people differently than others see them or than people see them self. Their perspective is unique and at odds with the worlds at times. They are remarkable in that they have a way of intuitively seeing what someone can become and what binds them to the world. The Bible for them is simply a history of God acting in the world, seeing the relationships born and developing through time. They see how those relationships change from the early chapters of Genesis through the covenants with Israel, the shift to relationships of the heart in Jeremiah 32 and the one on one relationship with each person through Christ. Niebuhr would see them in the Christ Above culture group, not because they are necessarily better (they wouldn't know) but because their spirit resides in a different place; beyond more than above culture. They do not see them self as better than culture, just as different. Contrary to Niebuhr, they do not find solace in the institutional church but may feel the institution has missed the boat and is overly immersed in the world. The church needs to take a step away from the world and focus its energies on more spiritual matters. This is not a call to isolate the church, but to reorient its priorities. For them the primary goal is to heal the world, not to fix it. We start that process internally, with ourselves.

That is often the essence of their calling; to be a spiritual force in the world, so extreme that people notice. Their idealism calls people to become what God created them to be. The bar is very high for this type. They are much more likely to be people of faith than of works, people of grace than of guilt. The Call is to be an ambassador of redemption for God, creating new and deeper relationships. They find their identity in the context of these same relationships, in seeing how what God has created on earth is part of Rudolph Otto's "Holy other." It is the mystical understanding that in our true nature we are part of the divine. It is their worldly relationships that keep them humble.

They are creatively mystical people. Symbolism and metaphor are seen everywhere. It is how they relate best to the world.

They are deeply intuitive people and just sense the spiritual dynamics around them. For the SAEND, meaning is spiritual, everything has a transcendent tone to it. Their identity revolves around their perception of how God perceives them, created them as unique and holy.

This type leans towards the more symbolic and ritualistic in worship. They can attend a more contemporary form of worship but the sermons are usually too long and not nearly spiritually deep enough. It is the singing that attracts them in these services. The sacraments have a deep hold on them.

What the SAEND is attracted to

Clearly they are attracted to deeply spiritual people. They love all things spiritual; rich ritual, sacred music, symbolic art, silence, mystical writing, poetry. If it's not spiritually oriented, they probably won't be interested for long.

They feel at peace with God and their strongest desire is to serve God. They just wish they could do that in heaven rather with humans. They are pulled to groups that feel the same way. They struggle a bit with overly pragmatic people and love to be around dreamers—literally and figuratively. They do enjoy getting to know new people, but relationships may not last long if there is not a spiritual component to the relationship. They do suffer, but they focus more on their spiritual suffering, on their dark night of the soul.

Growth areas for the SAEND

While a life in the spirit is great, we are to have some grounding on earth as well. There is little to bring this type down to earth at the level of the soul. God is certainly trying to get them to do so and their dreams and symbolic ideas will point them in that direction if they can listen and watch. They fear losing what they have—the closeness to the transcendent. They fear being pulled away from God and becoming worldly and of course that is a potential danger albeit highly unlikely. However, this is what they need to do. It is through their relationships that they will find the way of attaching to the world in a way that works for them. They need to become more concrete in their thinking and in their being. Even when works and faith are in balance the SAEND needs to do a bit more work in the world to identify with human suffering and growth. Biblically, they would do well to read the stories of the bible and identify with each character. They need to learn to live the stories out in their minds; to ask what any given person in a story would feel, think, see, smell, taste, or hear. The SAEND needs to start to walk the world in other people's shoes while not letting go of God's vision.

The SAEND loves ritualistic worship. Symbolism is critical for them. Potentially transformative services touch them at a very deep level. Communion, baptism, marriage, and others are important parts of their worship experience. If they are part of a contemporary service they will often lose themself in the music, almost feeling they are alone. Sermons rarely hit them deep, in fact most will seem trite and boring, old news. They yearn for meat and are being fed cereal.

Activities

1. Find a ITMRP and see how they live. Learn from each other, you need one another in a big way.
2. Community service of a very practical nature is important. Find a way to engage in the day to day sufferings of others and be with them where they are.
3. Look at your relationships. Think about how to deepen them on non-spiritual levels. This is not a call to forsake the spiritual, but to understand there are many levels to relationships.
4. Listen to what the world tells you about yourself.

Mark 2: 1-12 (see page 102)

The SAEND relishes the power of Jesus in this story. They see how he is in complete control and knows everything that is going on. Most people would be overwhelmed with any single element of the story. Jesus attunes to the needs of each in that moment. Naturally, some have greater needs than others. He focuses on the men, the paralyzed man, and the scribes. He knows that the needs of others will be met in and through his working with those people. They marvel at Jesus's intuitive nature and are transfixed by his power.

This type does not question much. They are not hung up on whether this is historically true or not. They see Jesus in relationship with each of the characters and that speaks to their hearts. When they see the men lowering the paralyzed man through the roof they don't think about the practical aspects of this, but about the faith and commitment of the men and how it must have touched the hearts and minds of all those there, including the scribes.

Deep inside, this type knows they are called to this kind of power and intuition in their lives. They know that they too have a block and need healing. At that point, many will identify with the crowd who stand by and watch, standing in awe. They are reticent to take risks of faith, but love seeing people who do. Nonetheless, they are pulled by the story. Because they are more intuitive, their minds do not push them to become more faithful, but their spirits do. They are called to build deeper relationships whose core is the relationship with the Creator. They are comfortable with the knowledge they are unique and holy in God's eyes, but often are not so comfortable sharing that with others, especially those who do not have that understanding.

This type likes talking about what happens to the characters after this experience with Jesus. How have people changed? Did the scribes go away and convert? What did the paralyzed man do? How many of the crowd stayed with the faith and how many drifted away? What did Jesus think and feel about everyone around the campfire that evening? What does he expect of us when we have been touched by his power?

SAENP

Supernal, Sacred, Temporal, Inspiration, Pragmatist

The SAENP finds their identity and meaning wrapped up in the transcendent while their activity is wrapped in the ways of the world. They find them self in conflict because of the difference between how they think and feel and how they act. This is not to say they are bad, their actions are simply more reflective of acting for God through the world than acting through God in the world. At times it feels like they are in neutral in relation to the world and relationships. Their Call is premised on their inner drives to work with and for the world.

Their connections are primarily worldly which may seem odd since their identity and meaning systems come from the spiritual. They find their way in the world intuitively, trying to find meaning in the world when in reality it often makes little sense to them. Being practical people on the spiritual side of their lives they seek routines that work for them and become comfortable with set ways of doing things. They struggle at times to be fed by and in the world. The world is filled with ways of nurturing their spiritual sides but they don't often find them. On the other hand they can be very creative. This is the central place they find a connection to the Collaborative Unconscious. The CU is the amalgamation of all that has been along with the creative nature of God. To use these brings novelty to the world.

The SAENP is somewhere between the Paradoxical and Transformative view of Niebuhr. They are pulled in both directions and yet are always looking for ways to change the world. The question is why? When we seek to change the world solely because the world needs changing, people are in need of things, or it helps us, our motives are not where they should be on the spiritual side of life. If we seek to change the world solely to convert it and bring eternal hope then we have not been good stewards of what God has given us and the responsibilities of having that abundance. A balance between these two perspectives is what should be sought.

This network they create in the midst of fulfilling their call is one of the signs as to where they are in the spectrum. The broader and deeper, the more important the network is, the more they are living in the paradox and feeling the pull of the world. If they simply have the necessary connections to get done what they need then they are more pulled and swayed by their self-identity as spiritual beings and are doing what they need in the world more out of duty than anything else.

What does it mean to have our identity founded in the transcendent, to have the lens of meaning come from the spiritual dimension of life? Their uniqueness, the quality of their being comes not from what the world tells them, but from God. They believe it when God tells them they are his child, that he believes in them, that he writes their names on the palm of his hand. SAENP's see the world through more spiritual eyes, at times ignoring the pains of the world. They remember Jesus talked about the two kingdoms and they feel more based in the spiritual one even though they are currently bound to this one.

This type can find the bible hard to work with. The SAI (Supernal, Sacred, Inspiration) part of their soul pulls them to find the spiritual realities in scripture while the EP (Temporal, Pragmatist) looks to the story line and the more practical applications. This sounds great and when things are working well it can be. But frustration can also come into play because these two are battling at times for the lead role in the thought process. The Collaborative Unconscious is intimately tied in with the transcendent, so it's not possible to have their identity and meaning system be transcendent without the connection to it. However, because of their attachment to the world they miss the big picture of the transcendent and focus on a few narrow pieces. They are inspired by the feeling of God's presence in their hearts and minds and use that energy in prayer and in relationships.

What the SAENP is attracted to

Because of the pull to the spiritual realm for identity and meaning, this type enjoys some solitude and contemplation. They like good art and seeing how God's creative nature finds itself in the world. They are often prone to have a creative outlet. They like being around people who make goals and stick to tasks, especially when they feel those tasks move their idea of what God wants in the world forward. At times they are very social and at times feel and act almost anti-social depending on which trait is in charge, if any, at that time. They tend to enjoy worship, especially that form which helps them let go of the world and enter God's world, if only for a brief moment. This can come in the form of more traditional and ritualistic worship or in a service where the fervor of the community has its own mystical energy.

Poetry, music, icons, and anything else that gives insight and an avenue to the transcendent attracts them. They have a tendency to like new age things and to be open to what other religious traditions can teach them in light of their solid core beliefs.

Growth areas for the SAENP

Having a grounding in creation is important in life. It is the context in which we live, and move, and have our being. While it may seem appropriate to be rooted in heaven, the reality is that we are put here for a reason and as we seek balance we need to deepen the relationship with the world. It's that fine line of being in the world but not of it. The SAENP should find ways of transforming the world into what it was intended to be through God's eyes.

By opening them self to the Collaborative Unconscious through attending to their dreams and in the stillness of their heart listening to the voice of God, they will move and gain more of their identity through the world. This does not mean to become worldly, but to find God in all things in the world. Becoming more empathetic of people's suffering in the world rather than just saying there must be a reason for it is another goal to be sought. Part of this attuning to God is to hear what God's plan is for their life. Relationships are important and need to be sought out and deepened. This type has the innate ability to build connections but at times shies away---don't. Find the connections that are below the surface. This will not only shift the E (Temporal) towards the M (Mystical), but will also impact your Sacred and Supernal natures.

Activities
1. Work on stilling your mind and heart, silent meditation is good. But also find more active forms of prayer such as yoga or visual prayer.
2. Listen to what others tell you about yourself, trust them. Build relationships and don't fear going deeper.
3. Keep a dream journal, the Collaborative Unconscious wants to help you.
4. Find an ITMRD. Build that relationship and learn from each other. The two of you complement one another in the life of the soul.
5. Write a one page biography of yourself. One page only, not a memoir. Note where any shifts take place in your life.
6. Do a spiritual time line as outlined in the appendix.

Mark 2: 1-12 (see page 102)
The SAENP loves this story, it may be or become one of their favorites. The depth and richness of all the characters, the worldly and

spiritual needs of the people and how Jesus meets those needs all come to play in how their soul works in the world.

Their practical side sees the interweaving of relationships and how they feed into and off of one another. They love how the friends of the paralyzed man rise to the challenge, how the scribes are there to ask questions that point to the essence of what Christ is about, to his calling and purpose. The men clearly show the depth of commitment once a call has been issued. Note that no one rises to challenge what they did, only that Jesus has the audacity to forgive sins. The story is rich with a spiritual understanding of what it means to be a human. God knows our inner most thoughts and our hearts and that is the most important part of our humanity. Houses being torn apart, questions of theology, healing the physical side of a person are all behind working with the soul. Christ calls out the faith in the people present and most respond.

The paralyzed man needs to internally accept the fact that he is God's child, unique and holy in God's sight even though culture has been telling him different his entire life. Jesus releases him from that bondage and ultimately, in so doing, commands followers to do the same in his name. Christ's intuition and creativity are displayed on all levels in this story. Read this story along with 1 Corinthians 13 and see if Christ does not display unconditional love.

Because the SAENP is more drawn to the spiritual dimension, they are not as full of questions as many of the other types. They look at relationships for what they say about how God is working in them and in the world. The process of becoming is more important to them than the end game.

SAERD

Supernal, Sacred, Temporal, Reason, Ideal

The SAERD finds their identity and their meaning system in the spiritual side of life. They watch the world as it passes by on those two levels. The world may give them ideas about who they are, but they are often ignored. They have a spiritual self confidence that is reassuring. Understanding that they are unique in God's eyes comes naturally and they see the Spirit active in the world about them. These two attributes, the S and the A are the foundation of the soul because they create the lens through which we see and deal with the world.

By finding their meaning through the spiritual lens of life, our souls work with us on a different plane. The perspective is from a place where time and space are not as relevant. They tend to be "big picture" people because of this. Their calling ties into this as well. Because they are more idealists and see their calling from a spiritual perspective, they are not as hung up on results as many are. The goal is to entice the world to see life as they see it—for them, as God sees it. While they are concerned about injustice and suffering, those do not loom as large for them as for many other types. Bringing hope to the world, helping the world to see the temporality of it all in light of eternity is what makes sense to them.

They are caught by the TR (Temporal, Reason) in their lives. The Temporal brings them into relationships in the world. Their Reason helps them to use their minds to make sense of things and to find creative ways of fulfilling their calling in the world. The problem lies in the fact that how they perceive them self and where they find meaning are not in the world so the ER attributes struggle to be heard. The SAERD is not an idealist in day to day terms because activity in and of itself is not what connects one to the transcendent. In this sense, this type is very Buddhist in nature and that can be a good thing. There is an odd detachment from the world, not isolationist, their E (Temporal) wouldn't allow that, but a deep sense that this world is not as important as we all seem to think. Their human relationships are very important to this type. Part of their calling is to build relationships that enable them to forge tight bonds. They can get frustrated when people are not into spirituality as much as they are. But they are more playing at spirituality, they too get a bit uptight when an M (Mystical) pushes them to deeper levels of what a spiritual relationship looks like. They are also frustrated by people who put God in a box and fail to see the vastness of God's presence in the world.

This type bounces around the various ways Niebuhr discusses Christ and culture. They can be at one time the Christ Above culture and at other times Christ in Paradox with culture. Their identity puts them above and their relationships and mind put them in paradox. Life is a riddle for the SAERD and they are trying to figure it out. They are comfortable with many forms of worship and biblical study although a more narrative approach appeals to them more.

Their spiritual nature, along with their calling to present the kingdom of God to the world and their desire to be rational often puts them at odds with authority and the institutional church. They have little time for petty arguments, bureaucracy, and theological infighting. They are not impressed with those who proclaim that social justice ranks supreme. As they meet the world their tendency is to pull the world to them rather than meeting the world where it is. The depth of their ties to God will determine how much angst they feel in the world. They can become judgmental and prophetic or they turn and become more aloof.

The imagination of the SAERD is bound by the ideas the world offers. They do not have flights of fancy but are grounded in what they know. Even this can be a struggle because they internally get the spiritual realm and yet often have a hard time expressing it because the R (reason) is looking for human rational for it which does not exist. They lack a deep connection to the Collaborative Unconscious, even with the SA(Supernal, Sacred). The SA will pull them to the M (Mystical) because of their need to be in relationship on their level.

What SAERD's are attracted to

Depending on the day, the SAERD can be attracted to very spiritually oriented people or more rational types. They are pulled to the spiritual side of life, although not the mystical. Being with people who enjoy thinking and talking gives them pleasure. They are more into discussing what can be than what is although their strategies for getting there are not that important. The SAERD is most comfortable around those who are spiritual in nature, whether it's in their own religious tradition or another. Being eclectic by nature opens many doors for them as they seek God in all they do.

Growth areas for the SAERD

The beauty of this type is that each trait is inherently seeking to balance the others. The SA tugs at the ER and visa versa. There is a natural tendency to move to the middle. Learning to let go and pay attention to each of the traits goes a long way for this type. By identifying how each trait plays out in their lives and learning to respect them and learn from them, balance is found. They do need to push them self to become more practical and to learn from the world what gifts they have to be used to make the world a better place because we are told to feed the hungry, clothe the naked, and visit the lonely.

Activities

1. Get involved with a service project that actually helps change people's day to day lives. A soup kitchen, hospice, tutoring, or shelter are good examples.
2. Find an ITMNP. Build a relationship and learn from one another.
3. Listen to your dreams and trust your intuition. Use your prayer time to ask some questions, listen for answers and trust them. Not all things are rational.
4. Ask yourself how to more practically do what you are called to do by God? How can you more fully engage the world?
5. Ask others to tell you about you. What do they see, feel, and hear about you?

Mark 2:1-12 (see page 102)

The SAERD sees this passage from a couple of different angles. While they are primarily driven by the more spiritual ends of the spectrum, their relationships being based more in the world and their need for a rational spirituality pull them in a different direction. On any given day, one side may pull them more than the other. They live in this paradox, able to see both sides and yet they find it difficult to fully identify with either. They understand the men carrying the paralyzed man to Jesus, but struggle to grasp the depth of faith and conviction needed to lower him through the roof. They are puzzled by the man's lack of response or engagement with the entire process other than being a willing person in the drama. Knowing that the man may have internal issues that need to be resolved, they accept the fact easily that Jesus forgives his sins first and heals his body second. Their minds are wondering what they need to let go of, and what steps of faith, what risks, they should be taking to deepen their faith?

That aspect of their soul that works with the notion of a calling joins with the supernal and holy side. It recognizes that many people in the story are indeed called to do what they are doing. They may ask why the scribes are there but rationalize that as someone who is not in the call of God, who does not seeking meaning and purpose through God, but through the world.

Their temporal side empathizes with everyone, even those who are not present. They can become part of the crowd, the disciples, the owner of the house and the rest. They understand the surface and deeper issues although rarely at the same time. For this type, each time they read the story, something new turns up and they are attracted and identify with a different person—which in and of itself is a puzzle to them.

SAERP

Supernal, Sacred, Temporal, Reason, Pragmatic

The SAERP finds their identity and meaning in the spiritual realm while their relationships, call and creativity are in the world. This can prove to be difficult because they are deeply spiritual people who at times struggle with the world. Christ as the Paradox of culture is their norm. They really want Christ to come and be in the world, transforming it as the disciples wished he would. Their expectations rest in their view of the world in spiritual terms. But the world can't comprehend the spiritual on solely rational terms. Their more rational approach to creativity and the relationships with the world make it difficult to break free of reason. Their spirit wants them to just be while their other soulful attributes want to do things that make sense and have a goal.

Because they see them self as unique in God, they have little need for the world to validate who and what they are. In fact, at times the world may see them very differently than they see them self. This type loves the mystics, but because their creativity and relationships are rooted in the world, the mystics are still a puzzle to them.

The Collaborative Unconscious is a key part of our lives. How we relate to it provides a critical link between the soul and the psyche. It is what weds our humanity to our spirituality, it is the stuff that creates the links that help us make sense of our spiritual lives. When our connections are primarily through the world, the SA (Supernal, Sacred) lacks the linguistic system to break through to the psyche. This type is rare because most of the time when our identity and meaning systems are based in the spiritual, the Collaborative Unconscious is not far behind. This type tends to have a greater distinction between the psyche and the soul than many other types. Most people blend the soul and the psyche and struggle to differentiate them. For this type, the distinction is more clear. For them, the two worlds are distinct; the realm of the spirit and the realm of the world. They do their worldly work and they do their spiritual work. On a rational level, they understand the concept of how they blend, but in day to day life, the two do not mix well. Our souls are in a struggle to unite our entire being with the transcendent. It is what they exist for. The soul have a desire to listen to, learn from, and act upon what comes from the spiritual realm of life, even as that Spirit infuses the world. That is why those who are on the more worldly side of the spectra still find God, because God is in the world.

The SAERP enjoys networking and connecting the dots on earth. They want these relationships to go deeper. That is the SA pulling them, but they find them self holding back unless those with whom they are talking lead the way. This shift back and forth between the traits is constant. Like a chameleon they blend in and are comfortable in a wide variety of settings and circumstances. This is not a bad thing, they are not avoiding or changing to please, but adapting to understand. They tend to be active people that use their connections and mind to solve problems. Their creativity comes more from what already exists and how to do things better or a bit differently than from an out of the box idea. Their rationality hits a road block when confronted with spiritual realities, especially those that go against logic.

Being pragmatic, they love serving God and feel fulfilled as they do. By bringing God's hope and love to the world, they see their spiritual purpose being fulfilled in a way that serves others. They view the bible as stories of God acting directly in the world and in and through others. For them, it all makes sense, there is little mystery when you accept who Christ is and who we are called to be and the tools we are given to carry out that call.

They struggle with worship. Because they both love mystical liturgy as well as more pragmatic and engaging liturgy, they are frustrated people. There is always something missing for them. They enjoy worship, but the needs of the traits of their soul tend to go unfulfilled. Sermons are not deep enough or pragmatic enough. The singing is either too modern or too traditional. This is all the traits trying to get what they need out of worship and being frustrated. At times this type will just give in and let go and enjoy wherever they are, allowing some traits to dominate for that time. A good strategy to keep peace in the soul.

What the SAERP is attracted to

This type enjoys just about everything. They are pulled to what is happening around them. If they are engaged in active ministry, the ERP takes over and they feed that side of their soul and thrive in working with others. If they find them self alone, the SA may pull at them, allowing them to find that inner voice and the sensation of God in their lives. In this sense they are very lucky. They tend to be optimists and God's hope is strong throughout their being. They deal with suffering in the world through offering hope. They may get frustrated at times with the pace of how others deal with what needs to be done, but they put one step in front of the other and join with others in seeking to change people's lives.

Growth areas for the SAERP

The SAERP needs to listen to the world to see how they see them. God speaking through others is an ingredient to our identity. While understanding that they are unique and holy in God's eyes is of great value, God also gave us gifts to use on earth. We need not deny our worldly nature as we deepen our spiritual one. Their connection to the transcendent needs to deepen. Finding the Collaborative Unconscious is very helpful for bringing balance to the other traits. Trusting their intuition and finding the spiritual dimension to their Call is also important.

Activities

1. Ask friends to tell you how they see you. Look for common threads and broaden your self-perception.
2. Find an ITMND. Work with each other to see how you can learn from your opposite.
3. Trust your intuition. Take some risks.
4. Still your mind and see what God is calling you to do in the world, but on a spiritual level.

5. Keep a dream journal and ask God to help you understand them.

Mark 2:1-12 (see page 102)

The SAERP struggles with this story if they read it on their own and then are guided by the group when reading it with others. The internal turmoil that goes on between reading it for meaning and through the lens of how they perceive them self versus seeing the more worldly relationships and practical aspects along with trying to make sense of it all with their minds causes them to have brain freeze. In the best of all worlds they will see it all and at the least they will just move on.

They identify with the scribes because they too have this struggle. They are trying to have their view of scripture make sense in light of what Jesus is doing. They know of their uniqueness in God's eyes and their system of meaning comes through how they have seen God act in Jewish history for millennia. The scribes are the intellectuals of the age and their relationships are based on the idea of family and of law. Faith and grace are secondary, not primary. There are rules and protocols, especially for the Messiah, and Jesus is not following them.

But the SAERP can also understand the friends of the paralyzed man. They have faith in what Jesus can do and just need to get the man in front of him. Either their relationship with the man, their faith, or their ability to see the man for who he is in the eyes of God, persuade them to do whatever it takes. This type is driven by a sense of purpose and it is through fulfilling that purpose they find their deepest meaning and sense of self. Certainly many were horrified as they watched these people drag the man onto the roof, rip the roof off and then lower him in. They feel vindicated at the end when he walks away and Christ affirms their faith.

This type is very self-confident in what they believe and can struggle at times to be open-minded. Because their self-identity is not founded primarily on the world, they have an internal sense of them self that is not easily swayed on spiritual matters. This can bode well for them most of the time, but can lead to missing things and to be delusional at other times. The hope is that their connection to others will prevent this from happening very often.

SAMND

Supernal, Sacred, Mystical, Intuitive, Idealist

The SAMND is as soul oriented as you can get. They seem to live on a different planet, almost floating around the world. Some may consider them delusional and they can stray that way if they disconnect from the world. They feel awkward in this world and yearn to be in the next. They believe they talk to God and hear God's voice more often than do most. Their orientation in life is to the spiritual. More worldly things are of little import to them. They normally have few material belongings. They tend to be more idealistic and see things as God would want them to be. The Collaborative Unconscious is an active part of their lives as they feel mystically connected to all things. The SAMND's want others to see the world as they do. Their obsession with the transcendent realm drives their lives.

This person knows how special they are, not in an egotistical way, but in a way that accepts them self for how they were created, as a sacred being. They are very accepting of others because they see the sacredness in them as well. This causes tension because they connect easily with the spiritual in others but often struggle to make more concrete and pragmatic attachments. They feel they are in the world but not of the world. Often they are loners because of this lack of ability to connect with this world and a desire to be with the world they know.

Their language is often very metaphorical or symbolic because there is no language to express what they experience. They will have mystical experiences, visions, remember many of their dreams, and enjoy just sitting in the presence of God. SAMND's enjoy conversation, but they always move them to more transcendent dimensions feeling lost in the world of politics, science, and other more immanent arenas.

At times this type will struggle with problems because inside they feel they should be easily dealt with. Because we are body, mind, heart, and soul, we can't live fully in only one of those, we need them all. To live in just the transcendent part of our being and ignore the mind or live in the heart and ignore the soul leaves large gaps. This type tends to ignore or not give credit to those other areas of their lives.

SAMND's are prone in life to be more imaginative artistic types, broadly speaking. They have a bent for sensuality because that part of life is beyond words. They are guided by the inner voice rather than external realities in their lives. This may sound odd because aren't we supposed to listen to the inner voice? In a perfect world yes, but all of us can be delusional, we can think we hear God's voice when in reality it isn't. God gives us the other parts of our lives as a check and balance. We say that and then we need to point out that at times we are called to do things everything else says we shouldn't do. There are moments we must simply take a leap of faith based on our internal experience. These are very limited. The person who is this type needs to be very careful solely listening to the internal voice.

The SAMND is remarkably inspirational. They are often what many of us aspire to. They ooze spirituality and are very comfortable with that. We see they have a deep relationship with the Creator and may even be envious of them at times. Many of us think about God, they experience God.

Niebuhr would see this type as Christ Above Culture. While they do not judge the world they understand how far short it falls from the desire of God. They believe that being deeply spiritually oriented as they are is the answer. They look down on culture with a desire and hope to have culture see what they are missing. The problem with this is that culture does not change like that, it takes engagement, something the SAMND struggles with.

The core of their calling is to bring God to the world, directly and through prayer. They believe in the power of prayer and of the activity of the Holy Spirit in the world. They often disconnect that they are what the Holy Spirit wants to use in the world. God and the Collaborative Unconscious are trying to push them into the world but they resist. They are not unlike Peter, James, and John at the Transfiguration. They want to stay there, to build tents. Why would you want to go back into the valley and into the woes of the world when you are sitting with Jesus, Moses, and Elijah? Because it is what God calls us to do.

What SAMND's are attracted to

SAMND's are attracted by spiritual things. They tend to be very open-minded spiritually and are not put off by investigating and learning from other religious traditions. They have clear boundaries and God is a significant attachment figure in their lives. This means they feel safe leaving the confines of a tradition and exploring others because they know they can return home to the secure haven of God. They are aware of the boundaries within which they need to stay. They love music and art that helps deepen that connection to the transcendent.

These people are intrigued by the world but do not see it as others do. They see the transcendent in all things and have a winsome way about them in general. They believe there is this world and that of the transcendent and they choose to relate more to the transcendent. SAMND's enjoy solitude and the interior plane. The world is attractive to them in so much as the transcendent can be found there.

They are also attracted to poetry since symbolic language talks more to a way that makes sense to them. Abstract art and mystical literature are of great interest to them as well.

Ritualistically they tend towards the more sublime and liturgical modes of worship and ritual. Things that call forth mystery and are different than the norm pull at their spiritual strings. They are more apt to listen to music than to join in, to think about what is said or read on their own than to pay close attention to a sermon or homily, and to be drawn into the mystery of the sacraments.

Growth areas for the SAMND

The SAMND's are at extreme end of the spectrum. Every aspect of their lives is transcendently oriented. The danger is that they lose perspective in the world and miss what the world offers them. They lose sight of the fact there is a reason they are here. They need to find ways of connecting or reconnecting with the world. Very few SAMND's start life as such, they grow into it normally either through mountain top experiences or trauma. The key is for them to look at the five aspects of the soul and see which one(s) they would be most comfortable moving more towards the center. The SAMND would be helped by using their minds at times rather than just their intuition, gut, or spiritual self. The hardest part of this shift is understanding that we are not called to be completely transcendent while living in the world. One might think that is the goal, but we have been given bodies, minds, emotions, and a soul for a reason, they all need to be functioning. If the Creator had not wanted us to use our brain, we wouldn't have them. If relationships and emotions were not important, we would not have them. But each of those things brings something to making us whole.

Activities

1. Find a hobby that joins you with other people doing something that is not purely spiritual.
2. Do some community service that will help you build relationships with those struggling and meet them where they are.
3. Discover what gifts and talents God has given you to share with the world. If your gift is sharing what you know about God, that is fine, just make sure you do so in contexts that will help you be with others. This is not preaching to the choir. Getting together with other SAMND's doesn't work to pull you to the middle.
4. Read some different kinds of books, even a junk novel. Science books are great.
5. Look at your life and see if you can find a place where you could be more organized, practical, or realistic. This isn't a call to go buy things and become materialistic, but to understand there are wonderful things in the world.
6. Try a different form of worship for a few months. One shot deals rarely work, give it some time. This is not to get you to change churches, just to expose you to other ways of worshiping that are equally of value and may broaden and deepen your own perspective.

Mark 2:1-12 (see page 102)

The SAMND is on the extreme end of being transcendent. The soul's attachment to the world is only through necessity and through the lens of "what may be." They wouldn't ask practical questions in this story other than to figure out why people don't get the deep spiritual significance of what Jesus is doing. They are drawn to faith. Everything for them comes from within. Scripture for them comes from within. They get frustrated with those who analyze spiritual truths from God. This type wraps their arms around the Jesus who meets the spiritual needs of those who come to him, even those who may reject him.

Being on the extreme end in all five traits, there is no grounding to the realities of the world for this type. This is not to say they don't

181

have a grounding, just that their spiritual parts don't. The SAMND yearns to be close to God, to physically feel that bond. They are less than thrilled to have to do anything other than be with God, even as God is calling them into the world.

This type identifies with each person in the story, but to what they feel is the person's heart, not necessarily what is presented. They will bring up things no one else sees and sometimes things that no one has a clue what they are talking about and yet it seems obvious to them.

They exist on a different plane than most. Their identity and relationship with the transcendent is so out of balance they miss the point of being in the world for the world. For them, the world has had its chances. They do see how Jesus speaks to the faith of those that brought the paralyzed man forward. But they would note that he speaks to their faith, not their tenacity, friendship, or insanity. They focus on what is not seen more than what is, such is the life of transcendence.

SAMNP

Supernal, Sacred, Mystical, Inspirational, Pragmatic
This type is deeply grounded in the transcendent. Virtually everything in their lives comes through the filter of the spiritual if not the mystical. Their identities are so focused on the spiritual and the inner workings of their being they can seem aloof in the world. The SAMNP becomes a stranger in a strange world because what they sense is not what they see with their mind. The relationship they have with the Collaborative Unconscious runs very deep and connects them to the world in what may seem like psychic ways. This type has more direct access to the CU during their waking hours than most types. We all have some access in our dreams and through our intuition but the level of the M (mystical) trait is only part of the puzzle. It is when our meaning, self-identity, and imagination also come from that vein that the CU can truly reveal the power of its presence. Imagine that everything that ever was existed in a computer and you had the password. Because the soul as an entity is not bound by space and time (other than it lives in a body that is) it can access any part of the computer instantly. That is the potential

of the CU. Because the SAMNP is concerned with the spiritual, it is that part of the CU they seek.

We all know there is great power in numbers. This is true whether you are trying to change a culture or pray. The SAMNP has access to amazing amounts of internal power and strength because they have let go of them self and live in another realm---at least their souls do. This may sound good, but we still have bodies and live on the earth. If there are no connections made to the worldly, the spiritual is lost. Because they struggle to make sense of the world on the world's terms, people often ignore them and their worldly "backbone" is not very strong. This leads them to avoid the world, to look down on it rather than to live in it. Niebuhr would see this as a case of Christ Above culture. It's not so much they are better than culture, they just don't get it, they are polarized from the world. They are much more concerned with what can be than with what is. If this type becomes judgmental of culture they become Christ Against Culture, but normally they are not concerned with the way so of the world because their soul is focused on the larger more eternal picture where worldly concerns do not exist.

The P (pragmatic) is in a tough spot for this type. It wants to be practical and do things in the world, to find the call of God and act upon it for and in the world. The other traits are so dominant that the action rarely happens. They see their prayer and spiritual life as actions for the world and indeed they can be. What if everyone felt called by God to pray all day? Most of us are so far removed from this lifestyle the world need not worry. This style comes with such a great cost and amount of discipline that the odds are that if a person feels this is their calling we should be grateful. The P/D continuum has to do with being in the world for the world in the name of God. As with all traits there are tradeoffs. It is difficult to be acting on behalf of the world through God if we don't understand the suffering of the world. Scripture tells us Christ knew all things, endured all things, and was tempted in every way as we are. This is hard to do if we are enmeshed with the spiritual and keep the world at bay. We might feel a pull to go out into the world to share and serve and yet do not have the capacity to do so internally because our traits are so out of balance.

The SAMNP thrives on an abstract sense of imagination. They love mystery, symbolism, and the quest for depth rather than breadth.

They are at home trusting their intuition and relying on God for all things. They understand they are here for a reason and that they have been given gifts to use on God's behalf, but lack the connections to the world to see how best to do that. Because they tend to be more alone in their spirituality, they lack the sense of community that can help them in a reflective way. They are often misunderstood because the language they use is not the vernacular.

Their purpose tries to get them to engage the world, but the rest of their soul wants to find purpose elsewhere, in the spiritual. This does not mean they have no purpose, just that internally they are confused by it. They say one thing but feel another. For the most part, if they are frustrated it is with the world. But internally and spiritually they are frustrated with them self because the piece of the puzzle that deals with purpose just doesn't fit with everything else that seems to neatly fit together.

What the SAMNP is attracted to

The SAMNP loves all things spiritual. They are very eclectic as a whole and open to other means of finding God outside the tried and true. They are by nature mystical and therefore tend to not be as community oriented as other types. Nature is a strong pull to them as are more abstract forms of art and music. Discussing the spiritual, the quirky, and the interconnectivity of life brings them great joy. They are pulled to the more liturgical forms of worship and enjoy hearing a good chant that draws them into a different realm.

Growth areas for the SAMNP

Having a depth of spiritual connection is fine, but while we live on this planet, connections through the spiritual to the earth are critical for a balanced life. The SAMNP needs to make those connections. That is at the root of their imbalance, discovering God in the midst of the world and its struggles. Instead of running from the world, they need to run to the world. This is not a call to become worldly or materialistic. God wants us all to be spiritual beings, but to serve the world and empathize with it where it is. There is no judgment in love or understanding and the SAMNP needs to let go of judgment and allow their spiritual base be tugged on by the needs of the world and how God is working there. The P (Pragmatist) will especially benefit from this.

Activities

1. Push yourself to get involved with the community without the need to be overtly spiritual. Interestingly enough, most of the world fears being spiritual in the open, the SAMNP fears that by not being spiritual they will give in to the world. This is highly unlikely with the imbalance they have.
2. Find an ITERD. Build a relationship. Learn from each other.
3. Read more practical books on culture, science, and around issues that concern you.
4. Read the bible and put yourself into the shoes of those you are reading about. What were they thinking and feeling. Get out of yourself and into others that are different from you.
5. Listen to what others say about you. Ask your friends to describe you. What is it you give to the world? Your friends? Your family? Yourself?

Mark 2: 1-12 (see page 102)

The SAMNP sees all things spiritually—with a practical end. This type loves to see the future through the lens of the transcendent. They would probably guess that the man's sins need to be forgiven as well as what was going on in the scribe's hearts. Their intuitive nature that comes from the inspirational side of their soul helps them get under the surface of the story. Just as they enjoy the symbolic nature of poetry, music, and art, so too they enjoy stories with as much left unsaid as said. They are good at filling in the gaps. This is made all the easier because of the mystical relationship they have with God and the Collaborative Unconscious.

They identify most with the faith of the men who bring the paralyzed man to Christ. Faith in action is paramount to this type. They can empathize with the scribes even though they are saddened they can't let go of past ideas that no longer hold true in the presence of the Messiah. They are deeply touched by the humility of the paralyzed man who asks for nothing and receives everything. He waits upon the Lord and is rewarded.

Their intuition helps them engage the story at a deep level and their relationships in the transcendent realm help them to identify the spiritual dynamics within and between the players. Once there, the story and its meaning unfold effortlessly. While their opposite, the ITERD, struggles to find this depth and settles for what makes sense, the SAMNP wants to tug at the heart and soul strings of all the participants. They want people in a bible study to become part of the story, to learn from it and to see it unfolding in their lives, even today.

For this type, spiritual truths never die or change, just the world in which they are revealed changes. They love seeing the crowd glorifying God at the end of the story. People have changed their lives because of how Christ responded to the world around him. They don't really care that the disciples are not mentioned and that there are so many unanswered questions. For them, Christ met the needs of those who were there who wanted their needs met.

If this type has a question it is why did Christ heal the man physically? He'd already taken care of his soul and for the SAMNP that is the critical part. They miss that Jesus isn't against the world, he simply wants people to put it in perspective of eternal life.

SAMRD

Supernal, Sacred, Mystical, Reason, Idealist

The SAMRD is transcendentally oriented in all things but their creativity. They have a mind that loves to figure things out which is in conflict with the rest of their soul that is more comfortable with mystery, intuition and the spiritual. They see and feel things around them constantly that do not make rational sense and most of the time, they let it go.

Being very transcendentally oriented in their souls has a tendency to pull their psyches that direction. Remember, the soul and the psyche are linked, they impact each other—consciously and unconsciously. This type speaks spiritual language more easily than many types. Because they have relationships that are founded more on the internals and spiritual than on the externals and temporal, that is what they speak too and seek in others. They may appear to be displaced around IT (Immanent, Terrene) types because their worlds use different foci in dealing with the spiritual world and at times with the physical world. IT's are more apt to be science oriented while SA's are apt to be more mystically and symbolically oriented. They are able to speak well of their spiritual journey because of the R (Reason). Their minds kick in to help linguistically.

The SAMRD is drawn to the symbolic nature of the Gospel of John. They are more interested in spiritual truths and eternal realities than with how that all looks on a day to day level. They tend to lean more toward the liturgical forms of worship that emphasize mystery and deemphasize long explanations from one person's perspective of what God is trying to say. Part of this comes from what they glean from the Collaborative Unconscious. They have a grasp on the depth and breadth of God and know that humans try to put God in boxes that don't work. They spend more time tearing down their own boxes than in building new ones.

Because their self-identity comes from the transcendent, they understand how special and unique they are in God's eyes. They know at any given time they have a unique purpose and they use the other traits to help find and live out that calling. They find great meaning in and through not only the calling, but the process through which they go to comprehend it and fulfill it. Who and what they are is found in the special gifts God has given them. This type also understands at a deep level that identity is found in and through community. God created them as social animals, to be on this journey with others. Again, this speaks to their enjoyment of process more than content. They love having a deeper and heady or emotional conversation, but the joy comes in how that discussion brings them and others closer to God, not in the specific information traded or learned. At times this is in conflict because the M (Mystical) does not form relationships easily in the world. They are so into the spiritual side of things that those who aren't tend to shy away.

They are connected to the great repository of life in the Collaborative Unconscious. Because they seek meaning and identity on that level as well, this proves to be a vast resource that feeds them through their dreams, art, music, and other venues. Because they do not tend to trust their intuition as much as their mind, they may struggle with getting what they learn from the CU out into the open, but it does happen because of the force of the other traits. They can be spiritually very wise and at times on a worldly level, very naïve.

The SAMRD also has a deep pool of faith and hope. They know the world will never solve its problems so their hope is not in the more world oriented systems like politics, but in what they know to be at the core of all people; love. One of their purposes is to witness to that and to call it out in others. They see parts of people many of us miss. They see the good behind the sin. They are prone to be very peaceful people with gentle minds and hearts. Appearing to be out of touch with reality is not quite accurate. This type may not hold claim to buying into the world—this world—but they understand reality, the deeper reality lying within all things.

Having said this, there are times when the SAMRD does not identify with the pains and struggles of the world because their vision sees past this. It isn't that they don't care, they just view suffering in a different light. This type is Niebuhr's Christ Above culture. It is not a holier than thou attitude, just one that stands outside and above culture looking in and offering a new way of seeing things and being. There is certainly the possibility of judgment since they do feel their view is closer to that of God, but their meaning system tells them not to judge so usually they don't.

What the SAMRD is attracted to

This type loves all things spiritual and symbolic. They love good music that is uplifting and glorifies God and creation. They like poetry and art that is filled with the potential for meaning. Their minds like to think about these things even as their other aspects just enjoy it. They thrive in environments with others who are more spiritually oriented and get frustrated around those that are task oriented and goal driven. While they do enjoy their solitude, they are drawn to groups because they feel called to be social creatures, to be in community. Things that help them draw closer to them self and to the transcendent appeal to them. Dream work, journals, retreats, workshops, and meditation are all on that list.

Growth areas for the SAMRD

The SAMRD needs to build bridges to the world, God's world. They become so attached to the spirituality of God they forget the worldliness of God, that God created and is fully present in the world.

This planet was created for us. There is a need for this type to build relationships that go to the heart of people's struggles and pain. A need to listen to what others say about them, to learn from those in the world about how they are in the world. Their calling needs to become more specific and practical than they perceive it. Finally they need to trust their intuition more and their minds a bit less.

Activities

1. Look at your relationships with people and start to ask questions that allow them to be vulnerable with you and you with them. Reach out in your struggle and listen to theirs.
2. Find an ITENP. Build a friendship. Learn from each other.
3. Take one of your ideas about what God has called you to do and find a very practical way of doing it. Enlist others in your work.
4. Read some books that are more science oriented, learn about the world in which you live. Find God in the material, not just the spiritual.
5. Trust your gut and take some risks—in relationships, groups, work, and service.

MARK 2: 1-12 (see page 102)

The SAMRD views this story through the spiritual lens. They are drawn to the depth of faith of the men and the amazement and change in the crowd. They are awed by the lack of understanding and perception of the scribes. They almost take Christ for granted since he after all, is God. They would have been stunned if Jesus had not taken care of the man's sins first. For them, the healing is an after-thought and not truly necessary except to prove Jesus's power and authority.

This type enjoys thinking about what happens to everyone after the story. How has their faith truly changed? How have their lives been touched by being part of this remarkable event? What did the paralyzed man do with the rest of his life? Did any of the scribes get the message? How many of the crowd followed through with what they saw and learned? This plays both to their spiritual curiosity and to their need to find answers.

Their more mystical nature is always looking under the surface for deeper implications and meaning. Who were these men that took the paralyzed man? Where did their faith that Jesus speaks to come from and what was it in? How was it they even knew this man, cripples were not the center of many friendships in that culture? Why put their necks on the line? What drives them to destroy a man's roof?

They want to know how this story speaks to the people reading it. They want to know which people they identify with in the story and what God is saying to them. This type sees this story re-enacted every day in the world and wants people to open their eyes and see what they see, experience what they experience.

SAMRP

Supernal, Sacred, Mystical, Reason, Pragmatist

The SAMRP lives primarily in the spiritual domain but rationalizes it all and acts out that rationalization in the world. This is perhaps one of the extremes of Niebuhr's work. They are living out the Christ in Paradox with culture. Their souls find meaning and identity through the transcendent, being connected to the Collaborative Unconscious and yet living in the world using their minds to exist and make sense of it all. Understand that we all use our minds all the time to explain things. What is meant here is that they use the transcendent to explain things rather than the world, but reason is in the background. Reason and rationality are the way to get answers and to find creativity, not intuition and more Zen like thinking.

Because God created the world, God can be in both worlds at the same time and we have the potential to do that as well, as Christ showed. Most of the time we fail at this venture, we tend to separate the two. We often hear that people go to church on Sundays and then forget about God and being a Christian; it's no longer at the forefront of their minds. This isn't to say they are bad, it's just very difficult to keep two kingdoms ever present and balanced within.

The spiritual world is not always rational or pragmatic. Perhaps the largest irrationality of the bible is the New Testament and what God chose to do in and through Jesus the Christ. Rationally, the Old Testament and the Law made sense. The do's and don'ts of being with God. There was some social and cultural logic to the Law and you knew where you stood. There were concrete ways to overcome what sins you had committed. The New Testament radically shifts that paradigm. Faith is the bedrock of relationship, not the Law. In the scope of life, it does make some sense. How many of us have deep relationships that are solely based on what someone does or doesn't do? There is a large degree of trust and faith in those relationships. How rational is it that God chose to die, innocent, for us? For you? Not very. Unconditional grace and love shift everything. They are glasses we find it virtually impossible to see through and yet that is what we are called to do. The SAMRP feels it in their bones yet can't bring their minds to let go enough to get it. Their practical nature clings to the idea that they can "earn" a relationship with God even though spiritually they know they can't and don't need to.

The SAM (Supernal, Sacred, Mystical) part of their nature gives them access to an amazing depth in the transcendent world. When they allow them self to be found by God, there is a depth that is extraordinary. They understand their holy nature, that God believes in them and accepts them for who they are and for what they can become. They are able to move into different layers of consciousness and experience the transcendent, not just talk about it. This in turn helps them to feel the presence of the Collaborative Unconscious, not just have dreams, but experience the web of life as a whole. Their rationality when working well helps them connect the dots and the pragmatic nature of their Call enables them to put all of that into a balanced way of being in the world.

What the SAMRP is attracted to

The SAMRP loves the spiritual. Rituals soothe their souls and draws them deeper into the world where they feel more comfortable. They are comfortable with solitude even as they enjoy serving others. Their service is more enjoyable for them if they can do it alone or quietly within a group of people. Networking and socializing on a spiritual level does not often come easy for this type. They do enjoy thinking and planning when it comes to the world, but they need to separate them self from that which they enjoy most. This is more out of duty than desire. They are open and attracted to experimenting with their spirituality; trying different styles of worship, prayer, creativity, and social action.

Growth areas for the SAMRP

While they feel pulled by the kingdom of God, they are still in the world and God has something for them to do while here. They need to find out what that is and find some grounding in the world. As they move more towards the earth, they need to be careful not to overdo it. People can be like a pendulum and swing from one extreme to the other even though we are called to find balance. Building relationships and deepening the ones they have is the most important aspect of their growth. It's great for them to deepen spiritual relationships with others, but they should learn to accept and appreciate their humanity as well. This type often avoids suffering, they feel they are just giving it to God, but in reality, they are probably burying it because they lack the tools needed to deal with it on the human level. God did not give us hearts and emotions to ignore but to help us process internally and to use as tools to relate to others and to the transcendent. This type also needs to find a deeper sense of call with God. Use the place from where meaning and identity come from to give new depth and perspective to the sense of call and creativity.

Activities

1. Build relationships, become more active in a group and follow their lead, engage them.
2. Find an ITEND and work with one another to move to the center. Affirm and strengthen what you see in that person.
3. Trust the Holy Spirit and bring different people together. You intuitive side will do that and those you bring will help you move more towards understanding the world.
4. Read biographies of people that struggled in life yet thrived.
5. Write a biography of yourself, very short, that shows the fruits you have born in the world and the influences you have had in your life other than spiritual ones.
6. What does the world tell you about who you are?

MARK 2: 1-12 (see page 102)

The SAMRP sees most things spiritually with a reasoned mind. They enjoy looking behind the words to see the larger picture of events. Context is important to them, but the spiritual context is the most critical. Why did Jesus do this now? What was the transcendent purpose for this gathering? In this story, they focus on the collection of individuals assembled, what they witnessed and what they left with.

The central character, who never talks, arrives on the shoulders of friends and leaves on his own two feet, walking and forgiven of his sins. The men who put him in front of Jesus arrived with faith and leave with that faith being justified and validated. The scribes arrive with questions and leave with more questions and with answers they don't like. The crowd arrives wanting to see Jesus do something and are not let down, leaving amazed and glorifying God. Jesus arrives to meet the needs of people and does so on many levels.

The SAMRP wants to talk about this on levels that most don't. They want to get at the story behind the story. They want to sit down with all the players and have a cup of coffee to discuss what happened to them, how they were touched by Christ. They have a desire to impart this wisdom to others, to share how they see them self in the lives of those in the story. They can identify with everyone who is mentioned and some of those (like the home owner) who aren't. This type is able to enter fully into the lives of the characters because they have attached to the Collaborative Unconscious while at the same time use their minds. They can separate the wheat from the chaff most of the time. Being practical, they do want to see results, but are fine if those results are internal. There is as much unsaid as said in this story and they like thinking about what wasn't said (or at least written down) and why.

STEND

Supernal, Terrene, Temporal, Inspirational, Idealist

The STEND's Call comes from a sense of the transcendent as viewed through the creative lens of the soul's relationship to that same transcendence. There is a passion about their imagination and the ways they find to serve God in the world. Their submitting to God's call becomes a meaning system in and of itself. The supernal side of their soul helps them to feel attached to the spiritual and find meaning within, even while what they think and do may not make sense to many in the world. Many missionaries at least start at this place in their souls. Their connections are in the world which is why they are willing to go to the ends of the earth to serve God. Their identities are wrapped up in who they are in the midst of a culture that is far from theirs and very world oriented even as they seek to bring the spiritual into their midst. Their faith and imagination allow them to see things others don't see, to be hopeful in the midst of despair, to allow God to bring about transformations when many of us could not.

Because of the depth and connection between the SND (Supernal, Inspiration, Idealist), their self-identity takes a back seat. They find them self in God and in their work. Who and what they are does not matter as much. The notion that God must increase and I must decrease, that we die to ourselves in order to find ourselves have great meaning for this type. They have a much easier time seeing others as sacred than how they view them self. One of the spiritual questions we must all ask, and especially this type, is, are we running to something or from something? At times, the lack of self-identity within the soul, is avoiding harsh truths. We placate the soul by doing good things, by heeding God's call. What they fail to comprehend is that God calls us to do things in part to make us whole, to show us why we were created, to have us be in full relationship with ourselves, not to run.

The STEND at times wants to flee the call. Look at Elijah on the mountain, despondent that he was misunderstood by the world and ignored by God. He keeps looking for God to speak to him in and through the world. But God is not in the fire, the wind, the earthquake, or other things, God is in the still small voice. When he finally listens and submits, he finds himself and moves forward with God. Elijah is also a great example of how at one time we can be very close to God and shortly thereafter be distant. Relationships ebb and flow, are organic and are constantly shifting.

The tendency of this type is to see them self as Christ Above culture but desiring to transform it. Their identity being grounded in the senses means they are relying on the senses to make the transformation. The connections they have are primarily in and of the world. They network well, but because they can't understand the self-identity of the soul on a transcendent level, there is no vision that drives the transformation. Their imaginations lead them to feel they have the answers but reality paints a different picture. Their idealism paints a wonderful picture of streets paved with gold. They foresee a future that is heavenly, their optimism is at times grandiose. They long for the second coming because their identity is grounded on and in the earth yet they yearn for a deeper spiritual existence on this plane. Christ coming would fulfill that vision.

This type is torn in relation to worship. On most occasions they will go with the flow and enjoy whatever is presented. At other times they will feel frustrated because whichever traits are dominant at the time will not be getting fed. Their creative and meaning sides enjoy the symbolic nature of ritual. Their Terrene and Temporal sides prefer something more hands on and pragmatic. They enjoy hearing about "being for others," more than about how to change them self.

What the STEND is attracted to

Being driven by the pull of idealism, they are attracted to other idealists who have a wonderful vision for the future, even if it entails pain for many. They are big picture people and understand they have a role to play in bringing that future to fruition. They enjoy groups because of their social nature and because it gives them a place to hide their lack of spiritual identity. They are chameleon like in that they can conform to just about any system. This type is very tolerant and enjoy variety and diversity on all levels. They are attracted by people of passion. The STEND likes being around those who feel the pull of God and yearn to hear God's voice calling them to a particular thing or type of ministry. They may not enjoy talking about it, but they love being around people with deep feelings.

Growth areas for the STEND

The center of growth for this type lies in finding the meaning of God more deeply in the world. As they begin to see God at work in the world and in them, they will identify them self more and more with that new lens of reality. This in turn helps them to create a sense of identity that is more in line with the transcendent view of the soul's identity. This connection to God also merges with a more mystical connection to the transcendent web that includes the Collaborative Unconscious. As the STEND works in the world for God, they need to attune to the needs and sufferings of the world, to push to make a practical difference in the world and in the lives they touch. The STEND should be trying to look at their relationships and finding spiritual connections with those people.

Retreats and meditation go a long way in exposing this type to the transcendent.

Activities

1. Find an IAMRP. Build a relationship and learn from one another.
2. Listen to your dreams, keep a journal of them.
3. In your prayer time, spend more time being quiet and listening.
4. Look for connections in the world but on a different level. What is the spiritual significance of what is going on around you?
5. Read more poetry and mystical literature, especially biographies of deeply spiritual people.

MARK 2: 1-12 (see page 102)

The STEND finds deep spiritual meaning in this story. The piece that is missing for them is to find them self in the story because their self-identity is wrapped up in the world. They will identify with the characters but more on a practical level than on a spiritual one. For example, they might see that the paralyzed man's sins are an obstacle to a full and abundant life for him, but won't transfer that understanding to their own lives.

They would certainly identify with those lifting the man on the roof. They see and feel the depth of faith and commitment, are touched by Jesus's acknowledgement of them and are humbled by the man's humility in the midst of the healing. They can envisage the men sitting around talking about what to do, seeing an opportunity with Jesus to help their friend and encouraging one another to take the risk. One for all and all for one.

Their grounding and relationships in the world help them understand that what people go through while their search for meaning and intuition ground their more spiritual side. They enjoy flipping back and forth as they read the bible.

The STEND finds a call in their idealistic views of the world, hoping for what God wants. They have a natural desire to be in God's will and enjoy seeing others heeding the call. Finding biblical stories of people responding to God is a faith builder for them. They see in this story that Jesus does not always get the response he wants, but the offer is always there. Christ always offers a way to find yourself in God by responding to his call. In this story some chose to follow, others didn't. He condemned no one for their choice.

STENP

Supernal, Terrene, Temporal, Inspirational, Pragmatist

Persons of the STENP type find their meaning and creativity in the spiritual world or more internally while their self-identity, relatedness, and sense of purpose come from the world. When we talk about meaning coming from the transcendent we mean that there is a depth to their understanding of what things mean. They don't settle for the world's answer to the big questions. They may believe in the Big Bang, but they don't stop there. They ask the question, "Who created the Big Bang?" "Why was there a Big Bang and what does that say about our place in the universe?" Their meaning in life comes from a place beyond concrete human concepts. They are more apt to see the big picture, to hear the still small voice of God that Elijah heard on the mountain, and to find God in the spaces between things.

The soul finds its identity in the relationships it builds in the world. Overall, these two aspects of the soul, Terrene and Temporal, are the dominant ones in this type. Because relationships are so important in life, where they are found and how they are used help form our identity. Because of the TE nature of this person, their self-identity is in the world as are their relationships. They connect to build a very strong bond that is hard to break. Purpose and meaning take a back seat to these and even creativity is seen more in light of relationships than in a more abstract notion of creativity and imagination. They think about the church as what the church could be in the world, how it is a place where relationships can be real and bound together for and through God. The struggle is that for them, there is a lot of talk about God in the midst of relationships, but they lack the ability to actually bring that to fruition because of their rootedness in the world.

The STENP is another practical networker. They are often seeking ways of bringing their ideas of what the world could and should be, into fruition based on their special talents and gifts. They are often extraverts and use that social ability for what they believe are God's purposes. Biblically, they are drawn to both the story and the meaning. They see the relationships within the stories as central, especially how individuals relate to God. On the other hand they relish a good discussion about the meaning behind the story and can push these spiritual ideas to very deep levels if they can overcome the pull of the temporal in their lives.

This is another type that is on that fence between seeing Christ as Paradox and Christ as Transformer. They are pulled back and forth between the spiritual and the worldly. They are able to see Christ's worldliness as well as his transformative abilities. They see and feel how they are called to transform culture and yet they find it hard to let go of that which they know well. There is a comfort in the world as it is. Their relationships and networks for the most part work well, why change them?

Their imaginations are entranced by the spiritual. Poetry draws them in because of the meaning that lies within them. Transcendent systems of meaning are different from worldly ones. Our souls can see things transcendently, but our soul's meaning system is impacted by whether it connects itself more to the Supernal or Immanent end of that spectrum. Listen carefully to how people describe a story in the bible and you will see where they are in this spectrum in relation to their soul. Again, there is no good or bad, just a different way of perceiving. Or try this: Look at a flower or a tree or a person. Ask yourself how the world would describe what you are looking at. What characteristics would they note? Then ask yourself how God would describe the same thing. Do you think God would use the same language?

What the STENP is attracted to

Because of this strong TE (Terrene, Temporal) bond, they are most attracted to things of and in the world. Their networks and relationships are hugely important to them. They like building new connections and bringing others into the fold. They are good evangelists and church builders in the sense that they have a passion for God but are practical and relational. The best way to spread God's message is through relationship. They have a wonderful imagination and enjoy being around those who like creativity. On the other hand they are very grounded and don't enjoy pie in the sky ideas. They struggle with the idea that with God all things are possible. They can say it, but acting on it is different. Their search for transcendent meaning doesn't mean they see things in that vein, just that they interpret what they see that way. They are task oriented in their spirituality and mission and enjoy being with others of the same vein.

Growth areas for the STENP

While relationships are critical for all people, the STENP needs to spend more time focusing on their direct relationship with God. This is very hard for them because of their more worldly orchestrated relationships which they believe at some level are from God (but they can't replace God). At times, their pragmatic nature needs to let go so they can take some leaps of faith. They dislike failure of any kind and yet failure is a part of a life of faith. Find someone in the bible who didn't fail. That person doesn't exist. Let's remember that failure is not always our fault but at times is the fault of how others respond to our success. Elijah saw himself as a failure after proving to the group of Baal worshipping prophets that Yahweh was God. It was the prophets who failed God, not Elijah.

This type needs to learn from the world, not just from close relationships. Science has a great deal to teach us all about God's creation. We are in a physical world for a reason and the world is filled with meaning for those who have the eyes to see. The STENP needs to let others open some of those doors, to see that relationships can strengthen their connection and relationship to the transcendent.

Activities

1. Find an IAMRD, your opposite type. Build a relationship and listen. Learn from each other.
2. Read more mystical poetry and some more spiritually oriented books. Richard Foster's book, **Celebration of Discipline** (Harper Collins,1978) would be a great place to start. Combines a depth of spirituality with pragmatism.
3. Find out what makes you unique outside the things you have done, outside the skills and talents you have worked to create or strengthen. What internal strengths do you have that are either innate or you can't really explain?

4. Look for the remarkable amount of coincidences in the world, the connections that make the world tick, but weren't planned by the world. Write them down. Consider them.

5. Look at what you are working on. What are you part of changing? What are you transforming things into and why?

MARK 2: 1-12 (see page 102)

The STENP is an intuitive pragmatist. They look for meaning behind what the world sees but want to see results. They get bored with simple sermons, but love a good thought provoking message and this story certainly delivers all that and more. Jesus uses what is in the moment as his message. He feeds off what the paralyzed man and his friends deliver to him as well as the questions and hearts of the scribes. The depth of this passage is not lost on the STENP, He/she could work with this for hours.

The intuitive and creative nature of Jesus and of others abounds in this story. Think of the men trying to figure out how to get the man in front of Jesus. How many would have thought about and dared to haul the paralyzed man onto the roof, dig a hole in the roof and then lower the man? How many of us would have known the hearts of the scribes and the soul of the man and responded as Jesus did, surrounded by a crowd?

The STENP can see how everyone in the story was served in some way. From having their faith challenged and deepened to being healed on the inside and out, each player gained from this experience with Christ. STENP's enjoy the narrative flow because it engages so many players. It speaks to relationships, faith, loyalty, fear, and Jesus's primary focus of changing people's lives.

For this type, God is inspirational, reaching down from heaven to meet everyone with a need they have. All the players in the drama impact one another in untold ways that God brings together. They enjoy taking this story and finding ways of seeing it in their lives, to see God at work in the world.

STERD

Supernal, Terrene, Temporal, Reason, Idealist

The STERD finds meaning in transcendency. Their call can only make sense when seen this way. Because their call is also primarily from the spiritual domain, these two traits make sense together. Meaning comes from a more intuitive side of their being. Life however needs to make common sense to them. They have a need for order and that is called forth with the TER traits. Their groundedness in the Terrene plane along with their rational soul and the connections they have on earth move them through life with ease. The tension is finding out how to discover meaning on earth and to find their identity in the sacred.

Some may say that we should all be SD (Supernal, Idealist); finding meaning and our sense of call solely through God. We do not claim we should ever be apart from God, but God has always worked in and through nature and others as well as directly. To ignore the abundance of what God gives us on this earth as part of our call and as a source of meaning is to miss the point. There will always be this tension between the transcendent and the immanent, no one will ever find a perfect balance with all traits at all times. We bounce back and forth across all the continuums. We will catch glimpses of what balance is like and the more we learn to use the language we are talking about, the more able we are to find imbalances and to correct them, or perhaps to understand why (for a time) we are called to be out of balance.

We are grateful for mystics and prophets who are certainly well out of balance on many of the scales. They are pulled in those directions to give the world something we would not have were they balanced. This book is not about judgment and we understand that for some of the people some of the time, imbalance is what they are called to. The pull to those extremes is clear and not usually for lengthy periods of time. We need to rely on our own prayer, wisdom, discernment, and that of others to validate where we are.

The STERD finds their identity in and through their relationships in the world. They are called to build relationships, to connect people to each other and to use their confidence and their minds to bring forth God's kingdom. The connections they make are more in the world than in the spirit. Their spiritual identity is found more in who and what they are in the world for God than in an internal and spiritual sense. This makes sense to them, the creative side of their soul finding God's work in the world and gaining identity through that. Their creative side draws people into God's influence by helping others see how God is at work in the world. Social justice is important to the STERD and they feel that who they are as God's creation is attached to how the world is.

Stewardship is vital to them; they need to believe they are good stewards of the bounty God gives them and the world. Their minds play an important role in their lives. Our brains are part of our created nature and are to be used by us to bring forth God's vision for the world. Asking questions, pondering deep things, and taking risks of mind are all acceptable for this type. Their search for meaning is tricky because they find meaning in and through spiritual language even though their self-identity is found in more human terms. They will often use more human metaphors to speak of spiritual meaning.

Their tendency is to be more of a Christ of Culture since most of their view of the world comes from the world and they see God in the world. They move towards the positive elements that exist in the world and can identify with the world's suffering. In the midst of suffering, they see God working through humans as the hope of the world.

On the worship end of life they are pulled more toward forms with longer sermons and contemporary music. They like large churches because it speaks to community and they can visually see and feel the impact of God on people in that space. The S (Supernal) side of their nature does enjoy symbolism. They enjoy messages that use metaphor because it feeds that aspect of their being.

What the STERD is attracted to

This type is attracted to socially active people in the world. They enjoy the struggle for justice, networking, and worship or bible studies that focus on those types of issues. Pure spirituality is often difficult for them. Their call tends to attract them to other dreamers and idealists, people who have a grand vision of what the world can be, even if they lack some of the tools to get us there. On the other hand they enjoy a good spiritual conversation, one that is tied to the world but sees the activity of God in their midst. They enjoy using their minds, are curious and find the bible most helpful when used in a practical way. They are more likely to enjoy contemporary forms of worship and ones with less formal ritual and longer practical sermons.

Growth areas for the STERD

Because the STERD is pulled more by the more worldly side, their challenge is to move towards the spiritual. They need to find their identity in God and allow them self to be more fully found by God. They need to trust their intuition more and their minds less. They need to turn their idealism into realism and use the wonderful gifts they have to make real what they dream about. While they are finding a sense of self in the spiritual, this type needs to find meaning in the world, in the created order that was given to us. By listening to their dreams they will start to discover many new areas of their life that a connection with the Collaborative Unconscious can reveal.

Activities

1. Find an IAMNP. Make friends with them and learn from each other.
2. Keep a dream journal, watch for patterns and ask God to guide you.
3. Find a meditation group to join for at least 3 months.
4. Take risks that align with your intuition, trust it more.
5. Find something in the world you would like to change and move to do that in a practical way.

MARK 2: 1-12 (see page 102)

The STERD identifies with the people's pull to Jesus. His charisma, wisdom, and intuitive abilities are a marvel that this type catches glimpses of in their lives now and then. Being more driven by their minds they tend to want to explain everything rather than accepting the mystery. Because they get their ideas about who they are as a person primarily from the world, they may not grasp or be interested in some of Jesus's actions or statements. On the other hand they get their meaning from the transcendent realm so they do have a more spiritual source of insight as they move through stories.

What makes sense to them are the relationships between the various players in the story. They can see how Jesus is like a benevolent director moving the people around the stage in a giant drama, using one to help another. Of course the actors and actresses have free will so they must heed the advice of the director—which they often don't.

Their active minds want to ask questions and are more than able to give answers which may or may not be accurate, but work for them. How well did the men know the paralyzed man? Where are the disciples? What was Jesus' relationship to any of the people in the story? What did the crowd think of the men who brought the man forward?

While their perception of them self and their mind may keep them from seeing a deeper level of meaning in this story, their search for meaning and their call, pull them the other direction. They see God in the midst of all this and feel a sense of call that is affiliated with at least one of the characters. Do they feel called to help someone in desperate need like the men who took him to Jesus? Do they feel called to raise questions? Are they called to simply listen, honor, learn, and glorify God? Are they called to be healed of something blocking their path to God? Are they called to open their doors and give of their resources so that others may experience Christ? All of these are things people are called to in the story. The STERD wants to serve God and uses this story as a vehicle to see what that call is about.

STERP

Supernal, Terrene, Temporal, Reason, Pragmatist

The STERP discovers most things in their lives in and through the world. The transcendent becomes visible through its impact on the world, not as distinct from it. This type finds their identity through what the world reveals to them about their nature rather than an internal search. Relationships in the world are very important, but tend to be on the surface rather than plumbing the depths of the human persona and spiritual dimension. They are thinkers and need for things to make sense, including God and the transcendent world. Because that world is so foreign to them and can't be discovered purely on rational grounds, they simply let it go as a priority. This type does find meaning beyond what the world offers. They see God's action in and through the world but part of them get a glimpse into a more eternal sense of meaning. This type is a big picture person when discussing meaning and spirituality.

They see them self as fairly normal, their "specialness" coming more from what they have created than through a deep understanding of who God has created them to be. They are pragmatic people focusing more on those things giving them benefits they can see rather than feel. They serve God more by doing than by being. There is always a tension however because of the pull of the transcendent in their life. Even in the spiritual life they have they struggle to accept it and understand that part of their being. Their connections are with the world. They may find those who are heavily into meditation and more religious things as being naïve or out of touch. For this type, God put us in the world to use the gifts we have been given to make this a better place. They are powerfully impacted by the world around them; by the culture and environment in which they live. The goals they set for them self and for others come from a vision driven by the world and its needs, including their own. The STERP's are not speculators or deeply creative. They move through life engaging the world as it is, using what is presented to them to move their lives forward.

STERP's have moments in their lives of deep spiritual openness and clarity. This is when they let go and give in to the pull of the transcendent. Most of the time they are busy doing what they feel is right. They are rooted in an understanding of how the world works and they fit into that model. Their prayer life tends to be more read prayers or petitions, asking God for things, telling God of their needs and the needs of others. They may even have a bit of fear around the idea of sitting still and quieting their minds. Certainly that is a difficult task for them.

Worship for them is an end in itself, not the means through which to enter a different plane. At times worship can be frustrating because, "what does it do?" For them, action is a type of worship although they may not acknowledge it as such. They become annoyed with those who love worship but don't do anything outside of it.
They serve others because it is the right thing to do. They socialize with people very similar to them self, through which they normalize their identity. They do this because they are so action driven. They become frustrated by those that are more into being than doing. These people are very salt of the earth, they keep the world moving.

The STERP is part of the Christ OF Culture domain. They see Jesus as completely aware of the culture around him and responding to it, not reacting. They consistently see Christ as being part of the world in which he lives while calling out its deficiencies in light of the call to all people to love unconditionally. This type would make comments such as: " Jesus didn't speak specifically against slavery, racism, sexism, or ageism because at that time they were all very acceptable in his culture. What he did do was to treat all people with respect and dignity."

What STERP's are attracted to.

STERP's are prone to the pragmatic. They like to get things done and to see positive results. They like understanding and having a firm grasp of their world and they like to be in control of them self, internally and externally. Those heavy on the P (Pragmatist) end of the spectrum are driven. They may even have a sense of self-destiny. They are well connected people socially if they are heavy on the E (Temporal) end of things. They enjoy their social natures and are attracted by more social than spiritual conversations. For them, the relationship with God is defined more by what God does than by who God is. They admire creative people and may be a bit frustrated with their own lack of imagination, although they appreciate them when seen. This admiration comes because they are surrounded by God's creative order and as they try to be good stewards of it, the lure of that creativity tugs at them.

Growth areas for the STERP

The challenge for this type is to bring spiritual balance to their lives, to enhance those aspects which find more grounding in the world. Their transcendent nature is pulling them, but all other parts of their being are fighting that pull. They need to make a conscious decision to trust their transcendent side, to trust their intuition so that it may move their lives in the world. They need to find their connections to the world in new and deeper ways, to know that creativity comes in many ways and to discover what God is calling them to and how that might be different from what they are driven to do. Relationships should be more deeply founded in the spiritual rather than solely on worldly needs. It's important for this type to understand that all humans have spiritual needs that in the eternal sense are vastly more important than the temporal ones.

Activities

1. Focus on how you are unique What sets you apart? How does God see you?

2. Do you fear letting go and trusting your intuition? What could you do to build your intuition and trust it more?
3. Learn to meditate in a disciplined way.
4. Find an IAMND. Build a relationship and learn from each other.
5. Responding to God's call, to the voice of the soul, will be difficult. For so long you have been driven by other things. Ask God to help you with this. What is the motivation behind what you do? Do you think God may have some other motivations for you? Might it be that your drive and God's call are the same? How will you know?
6. Try doing something way out of your comfort zone, even in the privacy of your own room or mind. Try drawing, painting, writing a poem or a story, doing something for someone else that makes you a bit uncomfortable. Giving someone a phone call or a hug can be a very creative endeavor. The context of our actions speaks to its creativity in our lives.
7. Pay attention to your dreams. Look for patterns, see them as metaphors of how God is using your transcendent self to speak to the rest of you. Make a consistent and persistent commitment to remember them and write them down.

MARK 2: 1-12 (see page 102)

This type struggles with this story a bit. They are looking for meaning on a spiritual level (of which there is plenty) while most of their internal lives are focused on the world. They identify deeply with the crowd and with the friends of the paralyzed man who know the meaning of faith and loyalty. The relationships of the people in the story give a deeper sense of meaning to this type. They are pragmatists who love using their minds so they will be full of questions, many of which can't be answered.

The STERP enjoys being with others in bible study, feeding off what they learn from others, asking penetrating questions and not being afraid to challenge others—at least internally. Their supernal nature allows them glimpses into the mind of God, a view of how God perceives the world and all that goes on within it. They will find things others don't see in the dynamics of Jesus with others.

Their biggest challenge with the bible is letting go of their mind. Reason reigns supreme and having a more open approach where the laws of nature and the rules of the road in the world do not always work. Jesus doesn't usually play by the same rule book that the world uses.

STMND

Supernal, Terrene, Mystical, Inspiration, Idealist
The STMND is mostly driven by the spiritual side of their being. The sole place their soul attaches more to the world is in their self-identity. This is an interesting twist because how does someone get their identity from the world and everything else from the transcendent? It raises the question more than most types of the relationship between the soul and the psyche. We know they influence each other. We are all, by nature, more aware of our psyches than our souls. Just look at how many books talk as specifically about the soul as they do about our psychological makeup and issues. Look at how many people go to counseling and how many people go for spiritual direction. The psyche by and large is the dominant force in most of us. We forge an identity in and through the world. In order to allow the soul to make significant headway into who we are as people, a breakthrough needs to take place. If this doesn't take place, the rest of our soul, as in the case of the STMND, can be spiritually oriented while our identity is still based in the world. For most people, the world is what we know. It is what we sense and where we gather most of our information. These types are often not secure in their self-identity. They find it hard to let go and believe they are holy, sacred, and unique. They enjoy spiritual matters until it comes to talking about them self as spiritual beings. When they do, the words might sound right, but there is a lack of passion behind them. They know they should believe, but like Thomas, they have their doubts about them self.

This being said, their self-identity does not get in the way of their service or ministry because they believe they are created for others. Mother Teresa may have been a good example of this type. No one doubts she was a deeply spiritual person and served God in remarkable ways. Yet she doubted herself and her faith, her perception of herself in relation to God. They find meaning in and through doing what they are called to do in the most imaginative ways possible. They see others as God's children even if they do not perceive them self that way. The STMND strives to be unconditionally loving and can be frustrated when they aren't. This tugs at the Terrene part of who they are. God does not put this pressure on them, they do.

They tend to be more mystical than most. They are always looking for the spiritual dynamic in all things. Life is filled with both worldly and spiritual dynamics. Martin Buber's book, *I, Thou* (Touchstone, 1970) is perhaps the best at discussing this. There are "its" and there are "thous." We are called to serve and be in relationship with thous, not its. When we objectify others we negate the creation they are, the reason they have their being. At times the STMNP will fail to see their worldly needs because they are so focused on the spiritual.

The STMNP is an ambassador of hope. They deeply understand how God is the hope of the world and they feel compelled to share that with the world in what they say and do. At times their identity gets in the way because they are not so self-assured on the outside. They may be spiritually shy with others about their passion. They can be remarkably optimistic even in the midst of crisis and despair. This is in part because their hope is based on an eternal view of life, not on a temporal one. They feel the context of the transcendent. They are able to gather strength from the Collaborative Unconscious as a wonderful cloud of witnesses. Internally they feel that power.

This is Christ Above culture. Niebuhr might say the STMND are so transcendent in their lives they look over culture. This is not necessarily in a judgmental way although it can fall into that quickly. It's more like "Hey everyone, look what I have, it's a better way of doing things, better than what you have figured out." This may well be true, but the effect of how it is presented comes across as condescending. When a person is above culture, they put a gulf between them and the reality of what people face in their lives. We need to be the bridge between the worlds, to find the balance, not to stand apart or above.

The STMND is pulled to more formal and symbolic style of worship that pulls for the mystical and internally creative sides. This is not to say more contemporary forms can't do this, it's just not in their normal milieu. The STMND enjoys being pulled out of this reality and into another more mystical one. This is all done internally but external rituals, music, art, and nature can help the process along.

What the STMND is attracted to

Being optimists, they like being around other ambassadors of hope. While they have a deep reservoir of hope, it needs to be fed. They enjoy spiritual discussions, worship, prayer, retreats, reading spiritually oriented books, and discussing dreams. They tend to be more abstract thinkers so poetry and sacred music along with more abstract art are attractions. The STMND have little time for material things or pleasures. Over all they lead simple lives. Feeling and responding to God's call is very important to them and they like working with others around the issue of call. They are very creative, but their creativity may seem at times well outside the box because it isn't coming from the world. On the other hand they enjoy talking about them self with people who do not push the spiritual identity button but accept them as more worldly focused because their identity is wrapped up in the world, as are their relationships. They can at times seem a bit chameleon like in that they adapt to who they are talking with around the issue of self-identity.

Growth areas for the STMND

The two clear areas for growth are to understand the world better and to find them self in God and accept their sacred and holy natures. This can be a challenge. As they focus on looking for meaning in the world, seeing what the world needs and identifying with its pain and suffering, there is a tendency for their self-identity to become more firmly embedded in the world. The hope is that they will move to accept their sacred nature and that will give them strength and insight as they move more into the world. This type needs to build relationships based on the humanity of the people they are relating to, not just their spiritual parts. The STMND should find ways of putting their faith into practice in ways that help fill the more temporal needs of the world.

Activities

1. Write down how you think God sees you and others. Are they similar or different? What makes you special in God's eyes? If you do not see yourself as unique and special, dig and find out why.

2. Look for meaning in the world. How does what you do come across to others? Listen to them. Ask them how they perceive you. In powerful worldly events see how others see it.
3. Build relationships and within those, try to find the challenges others have in the world; their pain, suffering, and joys. Especially find an IAERP and deepen that relationship, learn from one another.
4. Try to use your mind to become more pragmatic, more practical. In your service to others be more focused on the here and now rather than the future.

MARK 2: 1-12 (see page 102)

The STMND sees this as a very powerful spiritual story. In it Jesus meets the spiritual needs of the paralyzed man and challenges the spiritual inadequacy of the scribes. Jesus sees that the man does not really need to walk, he needs the burden of his sins forgiven. Perhaps this is his past or his present, it doesn't matter. He clears the man's heart. As he does this, he feels the hearts of the scribes and calls them out. They are questioning his spiritual authority and Jesus rises to the challenge by healing the man's paralysis. The people who observed this are changed, spiritually. They glorified God and were amazed---who wouldn't be? All the activity going on around these two events are secondary to the STMND. They don't see the import of the four people carrying him and of their faithfulness. They would be standing in the crowd unaware of the crowd. They wouldn't care that a house had just been trashed. It wouldn't matter to them that the man said nothing. They get the spiritual message of Christ's power and sovereignty. They understand that the inner person must be healed, this does not come as a surprise to them. This for them is what life is about, sitting at the feet of Jesus, watching him, learning from him. Because of their Terrene identity, they do not really think much about them self as a person in this story. They are focused on others and the spirituality of the big picture.

STMNP

Supernal, Terrene, Mystical, Inspiration, Pragmatist

The STMNP is another example of Niebuhr's Christ in Paradox with culture. Because their self-identity comes more from the world and is less dependent on the spiritual kingdom and their relationships and meaning systems are more transcendent; they are torn between the two realms of worldly and transcendent. At their paradoxical best they are feeding and learning from one another. At their worst they are in conflict and slowing the process of maturation and individuation down to a crawl.

Being pragmatists they want to get things done on behalf of the soul. Their view of them self is also more action oriented. At the same time they are connected well to the Collaborative Unconscious and interpret dreams and ideas through the lens of the spiritual. Their actions become reflections of who they are as God's creation. Because of the SMN their actions are often more spiritually oriented. They go back and forth in what their actions look like. Their pragmatism wants to see results on a more earthly plane while the SMN doesn't really worry about those types of results. They are more interested in helping God's creation connect with the Creator.

We talk about being in balance. The best form of balance is when all the traits are balanced within them self, not that 3 traits on are on one end of the continuum and 2 are on the other. This type of balance can actually lead to more confusion and perhaps avoidance because of the turmoil between them.

Creativity for the STMNP can be quite amazing. Because they find meaning and connections on the spiritual level, their creativity comes from a deep source that touches the souls of all people. They are a bit quirky in that way. Their work leans towards the more symbolic and tugs at the roots of our souls. This imagination shows up in their minds, words, and actions. They see something new in a bible study, have a subtle twist on an idea, or creatively find new ways of helping others. They are on the lookout for how to pull people more deeply into the spiritual world.

They find them self in the world as ambassadors from another place. They realize they are here for a brief time and have no problem being part of the world while knowing this is not their final destination. The Collaborative Unconscious is working on their soul, pulling them to find their identity more in God as well as luring them to find the call of

God in the midst of their call from the world. This is done through dreams and pieces of wisdom that come from within, helping them see things and drawing them to creative avenues that reveal God's deeper nature and connection to the world.

The STMNP finds deep meaning in prayer, worship, and God's creation. This meaning reveals God's larger vision of what He is trying to do in the world and in and through that person. Their vision is comprehended based upon the depth of our relationship to God and the transcendent. The intuitive nature of this type helps them find their way in the world with who they are. At times they feel like an exile or a stranger in a strange land. They can struggle to make sense of the world on the world's terms which makes it difficult at times to act on that which they feel called to. On the other hand their MN (Mystical, Inspiration) helps them make sense of the world through God's eyes when given a chance. As is true with all traits and types, the goal is to not only move to the center but also to have the traits listening to and responding to each other. It's important to remember that all traits are working towards the same end, the soul's maturity in God.

This type is often uncomfortable in worship because they are pulled in so many directions and thrive on the intuitively creative which worship services rarely are. If they are spiritually content and aware they can respond to all types of worship and find God within any style.

What the STMNP is attracted to

This type is torn. They live in paradox and enjoy both the world and the spirit. They enjoy what the world gives them that teaches them about them self. They like relationships that feed their need to be known and understood. They also thrive in a creative environment surrounded by people who have a passion for creativity and a deep imagination. They move comfortably between these worlds and yet it is this very comfort that at times gets in their way from moving forward. They are goal oriented in their spiritual quest and often like to be part of a group that is seeking to deepen their faith. The STMNP is constantly on the prowl for outlets. How do I act upon my call? How do I show my creativity? What does all this mean in light of what I know about myself and God?

Growth areas for the STMNP

The biggest challenge for the STMNP is to not become complacent. They feel balanced because the various traits are fairly evenly distributed. The trick is discovering which traits are not in balance on their continuums. On a specific level, they need to find their self-identity more in God than in the world and to find meaning in the world. What does the world say about this and that? They need to see deeper issues and concepts like redemption, grace, and abundance in the midst of suffering. While they are connected to the transcendent and have a good relationship with it, they need to relate more to the earth and its inhabitants on a deeper level. They also need to find out what makes people tick, enter into their world and their pain, join with others in their joys and in their sorrows from the perspective of those they are attuning to.

Their Call should find a more rooted means of engaging the world. This ties in with strengthening the bonds with humans on the level of needs. Putting a bit of reasoning into their spiritual lives will not hurt the STMNP even though they may think it will. Remember that God gave us brains to think—wisely.

Activities

1. Use the relationships you have in the world to find out more about people. Have conversations about what is going on in their lives, don't be afraid to push. It's about them, not about you. Take a Myers-Briggs or Enneagram Inventory and see what they say about who you are.
2. Find an IAERD. Build a friendship. Learn from each other and push each other. You are opposite sides of the same coin. Journal about this relationship and what you see and learn from the other side of your continua.
3. Enjoy the creativity of the world. What have people done with their imaginations? Can you see a difference between the creativity of the world and that of God or are they mixed? Take an art class.
4. Use a journal to think about who you are. Write about how you believe God sees you?

MARK 2: 1-12 (see page 102)

The STMNP lives in the world of paradox, jumping back and forth between which pair of lenses to view the world through. On the one hand they want to use what they know about the spiritual realm from the SMN (Supernal, Mystical, Inspiration) aspects. They find spiritual meaning in how Jesus treats people, how his intuition is vast, his insights pure, and his creativity remarkable. Faith reaches out to them and they see how each person's faith in the story is stretched and how each person may respond differently to those challenges. Seeing how each player in the story deals with their own faith gives them hope. They see Jesus's response to the faith of the friends. They see how the scribes are so attached to their view they can't see anything else and their faith dwindles.

This type believes because of God's call to them and their intuitive nature, that we can all have a much deeper intuition than we give ourselves credit for. The Holy Spirit and the Collaborative Unconscious are constantly leading us into relationships to change people's lives. We are the obstacle to that change, not God.

The STMNP needs the world to work. Their identity comes in and through their works and the works of others. Friends helping friends, Jesus changing lives, and even the scribes asking their questions are part of the activity the world needs. They find them self in and through what they do and how the world responds. Certainly many of the people in the story are this type. Wanting to see results and yet knowing it's a journey of faith, that works alone do not bring a person to the transcendent, to God is the essence.

This type is very creative in how they see the story. Their intuitive and creative nature mixed with their connection to the transcendent allows them to dig beneath the surface and get insights into the story that are both spiritually deep as well as very practical. They will find ways to make the story meaningful and helpful to everyone they meet.

STMRD

Supernal, Terrene, Mystical, Reason, Idealist

The STMRD has a mix of soul traits that is probably rare in the general population. They are very connected to the spiritual dimension of life and their centers of meaning and purpose are to be found more internally and spiritually. They have a serious calling to be something other than what the world wants them to be. They are idealists in the purest sense of that word and are always on the lookout for new ways to move toward those ideals, many of which are for all practical purposes, unachievable. They bring the relationships forged with the transcendent through their mystical nature into their psyches which are creating a self-identity based on what the relationships in and with the world are telling them. The Terrene side of their soul is deeply engaged with the psyche. This relationship can at times cloud how the soul works and how it relates to the other traits. Persons of this type are not fully comfortable with their souls because the human side wants to be heard and at times might feel ignored.

The mystic nature of the STMRD lets this type feed off the Collaborative Unconscious. Because they are drawn to more transcendent ways of finding meaning in their lives, listening and being sensitive to the Collaborative Unconscious comes more easily. The struggle in their dream life tends not to be remembering them, but figuring out what they mean because their identity is wrapped up in the world while the symbolism of dreams often is not. The creative side of their soul is more based on reason than on inspiration and intuition. This conflict between the abstract and symbolic world and the more concrete one comes up often. When they read the bible they enjoy finding the spiritual meaning within stories more than identifying with the human struggles found there. Their view of life comes from a more spiritual perspective even though their identities are founded in the world. They look for deeper meanings in what is happening in the world. They are prone to think more about heaven and the second coming because those things are the ideals for what will be. Heaven is the ultimate transcendent experience for a human and the second coming is the full merging of heaven and earth. They will be able to let go of their earthly part because the transcendent will be taking over, at least that is their perception. The Idealist part of their nature dreams of what the world can be, but is stymied at times by the more rational side of their creative nature. They perceive spiritually the world they want, but aren't sure how to get there. We need to be reminded that we are talking about the soul here, not the psyche or other brain functions. A person can be very creative in their worldly nature while being more rational in their spiritual nature. What this does is to diminish the depth of their creativity. Imagination that comes both from the soul and the psyche tugs at the totality of humans. Mystics have a vivid sense of creativity, but it is lost on those who do not share their vision of the spiritual world.

Another tension for the STMRD is that their self-identity is rooted in the world while their connections and where they gather meaning in their lives is from the spiritual. As these forces collide within the soul there is tension until a balance and a sense of respect is acquired where they feed off one another. Each tones down the other.

There is an odd tendency with this type to listen to what the world says about them and accept it, but to look for more spiritual meanings about things taking place in the world.

The STMRD is comfortable with all types of worship depending on the day. They are usually not comfortable all the time in the same place. If they belong to a church they will say that one day was fantastic and another boring while others view the same services as very similar. It depends on whether the SMD is dominant at the time or the TR.

Because our identities are so important in our lives and because most of us most of the time have a difficulty distinguishing between our spiritual selves and our earthly selves, in Niebuhr's terms this is a difficult one. They are more prone towards the Christ in Paradox with culture and but can easily be swayed to the Christ OF culture because their self-identity is tied to the world and their thinking brain needs to make sense of it all.

What the STMRD is attracted to

The STMRD is pulled in many directions. They enjoy thinking as well as just being. They can be happy with an intellectual discussion or a quiet walk in the woods. When talking about spiritual matters, they will rely more on intuition. When discussing more worldly items, reason takes hold. They are pulled to one world or the other, but find it hard to be in both at the same time. They are able to see a connection between dots others don't see, to come up with new ideas where others may be at a loss. This type enjoys being around others who are very facile with their souls, can jump in and out of both worlds and not be bothered with that fact. As their sense of self comes from the world, they tend to be attracted to others who also find their identities in the world. Most of the time they are very comfortable with chaos and do well helping others in crisis, especially spiritual crisis. They are able to detach more than other types and are interested in what other religious traditions can teach them while maintaining their own faith.

Growth areas for the STMRD

Finding a way to balance these conflicting pulls is not easy. The more out of balance a person is in any trait, the harder it will be to align them with the other traits. Dominance tends to overcome balance.

One of the keys for the STMRD is to find a way of discovering who they are as spiritual beings, finding a strong sense of identity in the transcendent, not just the immanent. It is helpful for them to find their spiritual core, their uniqueness in the eyes of God rather than just in the eyes of the world. Trusting their intuition and fostering relationships in the world are very important. They should be looking for ways to bring their spiritual ideas and values into the world, not just into their lives, but into the lives of others.

In Niebuhr's world they lean towards Christ Above culture when the SMD are strong. Their souls are pulled by the spiritual and they feel they are a bit better than the culture around them and are above it. They can at times be judgmental. Because they are not as connected to the world this is easy for them. Their meaning system comes from inside and via the transcendent. They are not existential in the sense they are not creating their own meaning as much as accepting that which they feel and believe from within that comes from a different place.

For growth, the STMRD needs to look at what they do in life and why they do it. Their Call comes more from their internal life with God. They need to find ways of making that call active in a practical way. It is this tension of listening and being connected to the spiritual realm on some levels, but on others not paying attention that causes strife. By specifically asking, seeking, and expecting to find what their call is from God, and moving out with that understanding into the world of action, they will move towards the center.

Activities for the STMRD

1. Meditation—Learn to be silent.

2. Service—Seek to find a means of community service that allows you to build relationships with others, perhaps tutoring, mentoring, or discipling young people.
3. Find an IAENP, your opposite, have a nice chat, build a friendship. Learn from each other.
4. What gifts do you believe God has given you apart from what you have made in the world? How can you use those gifts to change people's lives and draw them closer to God and their souls?
5. Find ways to find and appreciate the imagination in the world.

MARK 2: 1-12 (see page 102)

The STMRD likes to think. Because their identity comes more from the world, they use their minds to relate to those in the story. They enjoy getting into the mindset of what others are thinking and feeling, the mystical end of things eliciting emotions on a spiritual level. They see the grounding of most of the people in the story. For them, the people who carry the paralyzed man forward want him healed, physically. The scribes want questions about their tradition and scriptures answered. The people come primarily to see Jesus perform miracles. This type can easily identify with them. Their faith is enhanced by seeing great acts of faith. They have questions for God but may be reticent to share them publicly. The identity of the STMRD is tied to their senses and perceptions of the world and what the world tells them about them self—even as spiritual beings.

The SM (Supernal, Mystical) and D (Idealist) help them understand the importance of faith in this process. They know you can't earn your way to relationship with the transcendent. They, like many in the story, don't quite get what you are supposed to do because most of them are so grounded in the world.

This type treads that fence between the spiritual and the immanent. As they read the story they may see both sides or just one if those traits are what they are surrounded by. They are very fluid in their adaptability to scripture. There are few absolutes and just as Jesus met people where they were, so too that is what they feel called to.

Because their minds are a driving force when working with scripture, they like to make sense of things. The SM connection helps them let go of that need from time to time, especially when an internal spiritual nerve is touched by someone. They accept the fact that their rational mind can only take them so far in the spiritual world and that at some point they will just have to let go and experience---just as the paralyzed man did. He did not say one thing during the entire story; he simply experienced and was blasted (in a wonderful way) by God.

STMRP

Supernal, Terrene, Mystical, Reason, Pragmatic

STMRP's find them self either doing battle internally or blissfully moving through the world. Our identities, even as spiritual beings, are wrapped up in our self-perception. These ideas come from the information we gather about ourselves both internally and externally. Because STMRP's are very rational and pragmatic people, and their identity comes from what they glean through the world more than through the spirit, they find them self stuck with an image they want to break. Their search for meaning and their mystical connection to the transcendent are pulling them to find a new sense of identity, even as that very identity tries to make more connections in the world and find meaning there.

As humans, we are very good at rationalizing just about anything we want. This modality seeps into the realm of the soul and clouds the reality of a God beyond space, time, and a rationality we can comprehend in this life. This is not to say God is truly irrational, just that our very finite minds are incapable of conceiving that level. It would be like asking people at the time of Jesus to comprehend quantum physics. Ideas in and of themselves take time to ferment. The wonderful PBS series and book by the same title by James Burke, **Connections** (Simon and Schuster, 1978), took a modern day invention and traced its history back to its infancy. For example the invention of plastics was followed from the development of the fluvt, a type of Dutch cargo ship. Many things needed to happen to prepare the way for the invention of plastics. This same process is true with ideas and with the maturing of our souls.

There are times when God is able to make leaps and create significant change in a very short period of time. What it takes to make it happen is unknown. This brings up an interesting query. Was Paul ready for the conversion experience he had? While his soul may have been in the right place, his psyche certainly was not. There was no glimmer of seeing Paul as ripe for conversion, yet he had perhaps the greatest conversion of all time with regard to his impact on the world for God. The transcendent meets us where we are and tries to lure us deeper into balance.

The STMRP is more firmly attached to the Collaborative Unconscious than most other types. Their search for meaning is endowed with understanding that comes from the CU and from how God uses it. While this may grate on the Terrene side, over all it is not that problematic. While their souls and minds try to find the reason behind things, they still relish mystery and accept it, knowing that someday all will be known. The use of dreams, poetry, art, and other symbolic ways of expressing and seeing the world are helpful to them even though at times they are kept at a distance. This type falls into Niebuhr's Christ in Paradox with culture because they find their identity in the world but their meaning in the spirit. They go back and forth between worlds and are on the mystical quest for how they come together. This is what the search for the Holy Grail is partly about. Symbolically the seekers were trying to find the spirit in the midst of the immanent; the physical grail holding the spiritual Christ. If you go to a church where they serve communion in a silver chalice, look and see what the inside is like. Many are gold. Silver is the human side, the external representation to the world. On the inside is the gold, the divine and eternal that feeds us. We are all chalices, human on the outside with a core that is transcendent. Our quest is to merge the two.

For the STMRP reading the bible is an adventure. They are able to grasp many levels. They see the storyline and love the narrative even as they enter into the lives of those in the story and understand their sufferings and dreams. They can move to a different level and see the moral and spiritual truths behind the narrative as well. Their attachment to the mystical relationships helps them see new ways of looking at scriptures they have read dozens of times. They are uncomfortable with strict interpretations of scripture even as their minds tell them there must be a pure interpretation.

The STMRP likes all types of worship—it just depends on the day. At times they enjoy the pageantry and mystical nature of a wonderful liturgy. They become lost in the presence of the transcendent, words of the prayers, liturgy and music are important to them as they draw them into the sacramental nature of what worship is supposed to do. On the other hand they also enjoy a more "pragmatic" service that has a focus on preaching—practical preaching. They enjoy the liveliness of the music and the sense of community. Their souls are fed by both of these. If the SM traits are at play the more contemporary style may seem shallow. If the TRP is at work then a rich liturgical form of worship will seem tedious and very boring.

What the STMRP is attracted to

Because they live in paradox, they are attracted to and shy away from everything and anything at any given time. One day they love the world and seek to serve it. The next day they may struggle with the world and want to flee to a monastery or convent. They enjoy thinking and talking about things, usually practical in nature, but not always. They are inspired by dreams and are seeking to find meaning in all things. The STMRP is committed to bringing hope to the world in a way that also brings change. They are as concerned about people's day to day lives as they are about their spiritual lives. This brings them into contact with others on the same journey. There is a sense of quest for this type and they savor being on the quest with others.

Growth areas for the STMRP

The problem with living in paradox is there is often no direction in the quest. They bounce back and forth so much, the left hand may not know what the right hand is doing. These two parts of them self both feed off one another as well as do battle. The challenge is to use each part to seek balance. That is the ultimate quest. It is not a quest for something "out there," but rather "in here." This type needs to move inward, to trust their intuition and to listen to the voice within. Sometimes God isn't just about being practical, God is about just Being. Paul Tillich talked about God as the Ground of Being (***The Courage to Be,*** Yale University Press, 1959). This type needs to find that grounding and settle into it.

Activities

1. Read the bible and put yourself in the place of the characters and see God through their eyes.
2. Find an IAEND and build a relationship. Learn from one another, see the world through their eyes.
3. Trust your intuition and learn from your dreams. Take some risks that may go against what you think but do not go against your core values and principles.
4. Deepen your relationships in the world. Move them to a more spiritual depth. Raise spiritual topics with your friends.
5. Learn to meditate and quiet your mind down.

MARK 2: 1-12 (see page 102)

The STMRP is by and large a pragmatist. While they find meaning in how God relates to and through the world and they are connected to the transcendent in relationship, their identity and mind have a significant impact on how they tend to read the bible. The mind can be an enormous asset and it can also get in the way because God does not always play by linear or logical rules. The SM (Supernal, Mystical) aspects do give them the edge of being able to see the characters on many levels. They want to look at the story through the lens of faith, but struggle in doing so. They have a need to understand what is going on and why it is going on. They want things to happen. They are people like Thomas who need to see to believe. Blind faith is very hard for them and they encourage others to not have it.

The STMRP identifies with the humanity of each player in the drama. They can feel for the paralyzed man and his struggle over time. They know about friendship and loyalty as well as an underlying faith that believes Jesus can do something about it if he chooses. Understanding the questions and tradition of the scribes is also in their minds. This type is all of these people at the same time, pushing that paradoxical nature that at times brings comfort and at other times, angst.

Their melding of the spiritual and the immanent leads them to have lots of questions and often confusion. They want the mind to be able to figure it out, even though they know spiritually it can't happen. What they desire most of all is to get things done. If it takes faith, then find faith, if it takes organizing, then organize. Over all they are very bottom line people. Their mystical nature pulls them to dig deeper into the passage and when they give into that side of their soul, they come up with some amazing insights. This can happen by them self or in the context of a group where others may well be amazed.

DREAMS

This is a chapter on the importance of dreams in our lives. It is our belief that dreams speak to our deeper and spiritual natures. The diagram on the next page gives a visual representation of where we think dreams come from and how we understand them. Our desire is that people pay attention to their dreams and learn from them, that we ask God help us understand them.

The ideas we present are obviously not our original ideas. They come from a variety of sources including Carl Jung, Sigmund Freud, Robert Johnson, and John Sanford.

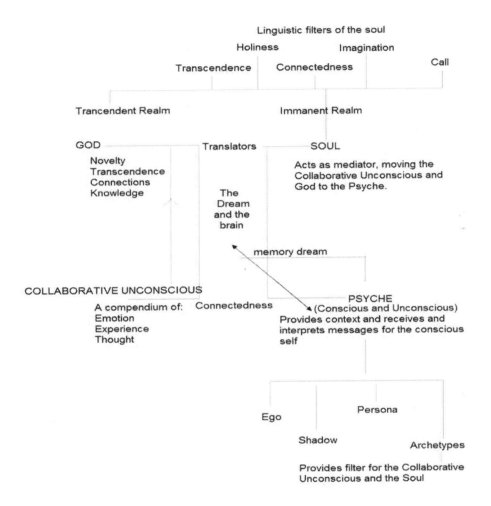

Linguistic filters of the soul

Holiness · Imagination

Transcendence · Connectedness · Call

Trancendent Realm · Immanent Realm

GOD · Translators · SOUL

Novelty
Transcendence
Connections
Knowledge

The
Dream
and the
brain

Acts as mediator, moving the
Collaborative Unconscious and
God to the Psyche.

memory dream

COLLABORATIVE UNCONSCIOUS

A compendium of: Connectedness
Emotion
Experience
Thought

PSYCHE
(Conscious and Unconscious)
Provides context and receives and
interprets messages for the conscious
self

Ego · Persona

Shadow · Archetypes

Provides filter for the Collaborative
Unconscious and the Soul

225

Dreams have been part of the human condition since we arrived on the planet. Every religion talks of them, every civilization writes about them and paints them. Freud's work along with many others, use dreams as one of the foundations of internal work. Reductionists will try to show they are simply chemical experiences within our brain, nothing more. We would like to offer another version of dreams. As with most ideas in this book, there is nothing radically new, just a different way of putting the pieces together. We offer no proof other than thousands of years of human experience and your own when you see if this perspective fits with your own personal experiences. We hope you follow some of suggestions and see if dreams speak to you.

Let's remember that from a reductionist's standpoint, love is nothing more than chemicals. All things are reduced to chemical reactions in our brain that are simply innate or learned responses to experiences we have in the world. Most of us think there is a bit more to life than this and to be fair, there are very few pure reductionists in the world. Proving something you can't measure is difficult.

We can't see the wind, we measure and see its impact. You can't pinpoint when a "wind" starts. We have no pictures of atoms, technically they are a theory, but there is so much evidence that backs up how we believe they will behave in certain situations we have come to think of them as facts. We believe the proof of dreams is no different.

Our view of dreams comes from the underlying theory of this entire book; we live in a universe with an infinitely powerful God as its creator. That being desires to know us and has created humanity in such a way that part of us is temporal and part of us is both eternal and transcendent; our souls.

God has also created a myriad of ways to communicate with us, dreams being one of those manifestations. One of God's purposes is to bring his creation into complete and full relationship with himself. Dreams are a way God can speak to us without our brains directly interfering. We can always (and often do) misinterpret dreams, but dreams are in and of them self, pure.

Dreams on one level are like the parables of Jesus. They are a mystery without understanding until you have the desire to understand and open yourselves to the truth of the message. Like parables, dreams can be misinterpreted.

Are all dreams from God? As you will see shortly, dreams are part of a process that includes God, our souls and psyches, and the totality of everything that has existed before us. All of these are part of our dream experience. Pinpointing who, what, and why a specific dream is created is not always easy. At times dreams are obvious and clear as to their origin and/or meaning. Other times they are wrapped in mystery. We do believe that in the end most dreams are created to move us towards a deeper self-awareness and to bring us closer to God, even if in a seemingly round-about way. Let's look at each of the types of dreams and then at the participants in the dream world in more detail, seeing what they bring to a dream.

Below is the essence of how we see dreams working and their relationship to the different entities that work to create and translate the dream.

DREAMS OF MEMORY

We have dreams that are based on recent or intense memories. Perhaps we had an amazing time with a friend or relative, tasted a remarkable flavor, saw something inspiring or scary, or had an experience that will remain etched in our brains for a long period of time. These memories trigger reactions in our brains and while sleeping, trigger dreams. We can relive the memory in our dream or perhaps shift the reality so that it becomes more epic or legendary. We go on a fishing trip and catch a nice 10 inch trout and in the dream it becomes a battle and we land a 20 incher. We either have a wonderful sensual experience or have a sense experience that triggers that in our mind and we have an erotic dream. These can be triggered by any number of memories. There is no distinct meaning behind them other than the memory that created them. Dreams that are purely of memory tend to be isolated incidents rather than repetitive and they tend to be close to the time when the memory was created. We dream about the beach shortly after having been to the beach.

The other types of dreams can use our memories as a vessel to get our attention but their purpose is different---there is a purpose. Dreams of memories really have no set purpose, they exist because our memory is intense and it just comes forth.

227

God and the unconscious are not beyond using powerful memories to create meaning. Nightmares are a good example. They are scary because they are based on a real memory. God wants us to work with the memory to get through it, to lessen the impact of it on our lives. People with PTSD often have these types of memories.

THE UNCONSCIOUS AND DREAMS

All of us have an unconscious. How much of our personality is unconscious is unknown. Some would say up to 80%. Some would say you can bring that number way down with effort. Things in our lives remain unconscious for two primary reasons. First, there is just too much information and experience to be consciously aware of at any given point in time. We can't handle being completely conscious, we pick and choose what we are consciously aware of. Secondly, we don't want to deal with something in our lives. Our psyches want us to be whole and yet we repress things that happen in our lives. We bury bad memories and even change good ones. We have an image of ourselves we want to protect and things that get in the way of that protection go into the unconscious. The unconscious prefers we deal with things when we are able and that we put forth effort to do so. It gets our attention by acting out, odd behaviors, and through our dreams. When we are awake, we can shut the unconscious out unless a trigger is pulled and we react act to an event we do not understand. Panic attacks are a form of this. People do not want panic attacks, they just happen because the unconscious is triggered and the person reacts rather than responds.

Dreams are a vehicle the unconscious uses to help us understand what is going on. It uses memories and things we have gleaned from our lives. They are by and large symbolic in nature and the things and people we remember from our dreams may not (from the perspective of the unconscious) actually be those things or people. For example, you may have a dream or series of dreams about your mother or father. Either or both of them may be deceased, but perhaps when you think about them they symbolize something like courage, faith, control, or cowardice. This is especially true of dreams where the person in the dream is someone whose imprint is on our lives from the first couple of years, someone with whom we are attached emotionally as we have spoken of before.

Our unconscious wants us to deal with things it holds that need to come to the surface and be dealt with. It wants us to mature.

Dreams have patterns to them, some are recurring. Some deal with issues in our day to day lives while others deal with issues from the past. A great many deal with relationships we have. If you feel an inner tension in your life, your dreams are probably speaking to that tension and giving you insight as to where it comes from and what to do about it. Ignoring our dreams is a way of telling the unconscious or God they are not important or that we don't want to deal with something. Our unconscious exists whether we acknowledge it or not. Wouldn't it be better to see it as an ally rather than an adversary?

Dreams of the unconscious tend to be more emotionally focused. Those who struggle with emotions often have a difficult time remembering dreams because they raise what they are trying to avoid.

The unconscious will give us the same issue in a dream until it is dealt with. You may have a variety of dreams, but the pattern will be the same, that is why we look for patterns and themes.

SHADOW DREAMS

We all have part of our human nature that lies in the shadows. It's the side of us that took the bite out of the apple in the Garden of Eden. It's the side that Judas listened to when he may have thought he was doing a good thing, only to learn he'd betrayed the Messiah. The shadow is not evil, but its perspective is more focused on a pure sense of self or selfishness than of balance. We have dreams where we do bad things even though we are good people. We may do something against our morals. We hesitate to share them with anyone for fear of how we will be perceived. If I dream that I killed someone, does that mean I am a murderer? No.

Our shadows exist to give balance, to bring perspective to our lives and to help forge us into a work of art. We have three choices with regard to the shadow and its dreams. The first is to ignore it which we do at our peril. The shadow is very crafty and manipulative. It knows our buttons and enjoys pushing them when ignored. The second is to give in to it. The shadow is tied to the ID, our more animalistic and instinctual nature. It wants to be at the top of the food chain and is not overly concerned about what or who goes under foot on the way there. Our news is filled with people and at times entire cultures that give in to the shadow side of our personalities. The third way of dealing with our shadow is to acknowledge and befriend it. Many of us have friends we vehemently disagree with, but we respect them anyway. They bring something to our lives we would miss without them. Our shadow is part of us, to claim differently is to deny part of who you are. We can accept who we are or deny it. We still are who we are. By accepting our shadow we take away its power to control. We acknowledge it for what it is and build a relationship from there.

Our dreams from the shadow side will change depending on which of these three we are using. The more we ignore our shadow the more intensely they push into our dreams. Shadows can be like volcanoes, you can only keep the lava down so long. If you keep it buried the explosion can be dramatic. Better to let it ooze out and enjoy the view.

Shadow dreams speak to the potential for darkness within us. They may come across as very unemotional, but dig a bit and they are perhaps the most intensely emotional of dreams. The Shadow understands the power of emotion in our lives. We need to understand that the Shadow is not out to destroy us, but to give us perspective. The Shadow has no problems with us making good decisions, it simply prefers we know why we are making them and gives all decisions a context.

GOD AND DREAMS

If God is the Creator, then God is also the penultimate source of novelty. Being pure transcendence, God is both above all and through all. By being in and through all creation, God is at a sub-atomic level connected to all things. God is more than just the space between things but is infused in matter. Computer folk talk about the day when a computer will be able to truly "think." Not just do trillions of calculations per second and have the appearance of thinking as in a computer playing chess, but actually think. Put every synapse that has ever fired in a human mind into one phenomenal brain. Imagine a mind that has thought every thought, seen every sight, felt every feeling, experienced every sensation and understood them all completely—not just on earth, but in the universe. If most of us fully comprehended and understood even five seconds of pure experience we'd probably collapse. Not only does God "get it", God uses all of that to lure us into her domain—the territory we have been discussing in this book. God is greater than the sum of the parts however.

In our dream world, God has a unique perspective. God alone knows the totality of who and what we are and what we can become. God alone knows what is in our best interest, what moves we should make in the divine drama that is life. Were humanity to actually listen to God for one day, the world would fundamentally change. God constantly sends prophets to wake us up. Sacred writings that speak to God's voice did not stop with the Bible—or any other manifestation of God in the world. God is constantly active. The free will he has given humanity is the primary reason God eludes us. We choose to not listen or see. Most of us rationalize our disobedience, but in the end, we all make choices. Fortunately God knows how long it takes many of us to come around, so she is patient. Very patient.

Remember in the book of ACTS, Peter was gung ho for God. He had no fear and seemed to be in constant touch with God and what he wanted. Until it came to letting the Gentiles in. That was a roadblock. It wasn't in Peter's mindset to have anyone but Jews in the kingdom. Even filled with the Holy Spirit and the resurrected Christ, Peter missed the point. God had to break through his mind and find his Spirit---he gave Peter a dream. It was through the dream Peter came to see the error of his ways and changed. Mary, Joseph, Paul, and Pilate's wife all had life changing dreams. I suppose one could say they all fabricated the dreams to meet their individual needs. But look at the stories, not one of them gained in the end by following the dream. A mother watched her son die on a cross, a father was ostracized because he clung to his bride who claimed to be a virgin and was pregnant, the star of the Gentile Gospel spends most of his time in prison and Peter is martyred.

God does not give us dreams for fun, they have a purpose. Our job is to see what God is trying to tell us that we are missing in other ways, for God is speaking to us on a variety of levels all the time. In relation to God we need to ask two basic questions with all of our dreams:

1.   What is the pattern? God is patient and persistent. If he wants you to change, he will continue to give you hints until you listen

and change. The images of the dreams may change, but the collective pattern or issue won't.

2.	Where is the novelty? If you make change out of a dollar, the value is the same, but how you see it is different. There are an enormous amount of ways to make a dollar with change, they are novel ways of seeing the same thing. God wants us to see our lives in novel ways. Find something new and unique every day you go to the same job you've had for 20 years. Find something new in your spouse or significant other. All of us are changing, how observant are we of the changes within ourselves and in others? Our dreams are a way of God, our souls, and our psyches trying to get us to see something. Like parables, dreams are symbolic, often straying from rational explanations. Why, of the 6 billion people on the planet, is there no one like you?

God's dreams are primarily concerned with the soul and our relationship with the soul and its maturity. God understands if our soul is mature, our psyches will not be far behind.

In capitalism, we lift high new ideas and the people that create them. New discoveries are made every day. But what about discoveries internally, the ones that matter most to who I am as a person today? Do we raise those up? Do we pay attention to those who help us find ways of discovering who we are? Do we care? By and large, those who discover novel ideas are people who care, people with passion. They have an inner drive to find something. We are all familiar with famous ones like Einstein, Freud, Lincoln, Siddhartha, St. Francis, Picasso, and others. But each of us have remarkable talents, insights, and gifts to share. We tend to undervalue who we are in light of who we perceive others to be. God does not make that mistake, but God does have an expectation that we will do our best to rid ourselves of the blocks that keep us from reaching our potential. Dreams are one avenue within that process and openness to novelty is a necessary feature. If we are unable to let go of what we cling to in search of deeper truths, we will often miss the boat. Don't get us wrong, this is not a call to throw everything away, just a call to be open, to seek, to listen, and to let go of that which gets in the way.

The conductor of an orchestra should know the lines of the instruments by heart. They hear the music in their heads and have a specific tonality they wish to bring out. They put their imprint on the music as it is played. No orchestra plays a piece in exactly the same way twice, it's just not physically possible. For many of us, it all sounds the same, but to a trained ear, they pick out how this instrument or that one is played a bit differently. If everyone in the orchestra were the conductor, the piece would be a nightmare. Each person would want things to sound a bit differently or played at a slightly different pace. All players have given the privilege of determining the final sound to the conductor.

What happens if in the middle of a symphony, a horn player decides he wants to play a blue's piece and just does it? Perhaps a few laugh, but certainly not the majority or the conductor. I think that horn player would be looking for a new job. While musicians need to make a living, they also have a passion for the music and are deeply interested in what each conductor has to say; how their spin on a piece will change things, what they can learn from the conductor about their own instrument.

This is also true with God. We are all players and God is the conductor. Life is the symphony he is attempting to conduct. God has seen the piece of music, she knows every player. She is able to make connections you and I can't even fathom. Our job is to listen and to connect in the ways we are called to. Like the horn player, most of us stray and don't listen, we'd rather be the conductor or play different music. In the end, that is sin. It takes us from the conductor, it frays the relationship and the connection we have to God and to people. The more we understand God, the more we understand ourselves and the more we deeply understand others. Jesus's intuition came from his relationship to God, to the transcendent, to the one who connects with all things. Again, dreams are an inherent and hard wired part of that process. Dreams are woven into the fabric of the universe, they are a language of a world much larger than just our chemical brains.

God then has several functions in the world of dreams. He is more than able to simply create them. She can add to them or shift parts of them so we have a better chance of understanding what they are trying to tell us. The Holy Spirit acts as a translator to the soul of this language we have either forgotten or were never taught. Many world religious traditions teach the young to pay attention to their dreams.

God is writing the symphony even as you read this. Your reading this may be part of the symphony and what you do with your understanding of this impacts yourself and others. The question becomes how many notes will I make God change because I refuse to play what he has asked me to? If I claim to not know what he is asking me to do, then I need to pay more attention to my dreams as a start.

We said God uses symbolic language in our dreams. Numerous books have been written on what symbols mean within a dream. While there may be recurring patterns, the notion that water always means the unconscious takes away from the very act of novelty. Water may be something to fear for some and for others an image of great joy. On a day when I am sitting in a beautiful hot spring on a mountain my mind will have one layer of what it means and on a day when I'm hunkering down in an ice storm quite another. Symbolic language is not based on absolutes, it is based on you. God uses the Collaborative Unconscious as the fundamental resource to forge dreams. He does this because he realizes it is through the systems of the world that we comprehend that he will best meet us. By using images that touch the core of our being, God elicits wonder and a curiosity to understand. To comprehend the meaning of symbols in your life, you need to know yourself and your world. Don't ever let someone else tell you what a dream means. You can certainly get ideas from others, but it is your dream, given to you, not to the other person. In the end you have to accept what the dream is trying to teach you and how you will respond.

God is second by second luring us into a world of connectedness, where we understand who we are and our purpose in the midst of others. God is most concerned about our relationships. How we relate to him, to others, to ourselves, and to the planet, are the key foci of God's work with us.

People will ask why it is that people dream who do not believe? There are many things that impact us whether we believe in God or not. God makes it rain on the just and the unjust. If God's desire is to be in relationship with us, how can that happen if God is not constantly attempting to build those bridges? God's love is infinite. The ability to understand dreams from God is more inherently possible for those who have a relationship with the one creating the dream. . Again, this is not a guarantee, just a potential.

In the end, we most fully determine whether a dream is specifically from God and the Collaborative Unconscious when we view them through the lens of our souls. Those who do not believe in a soul or in God will determine that all dreams are from the Unconscious, memory or the Shadow. We believe they are missing out. They can certainly make rational sense of their dreams, but all this means is that they have rationalized something that isn't. We understand that from their perspective we are doing the same.

THE SOUL AND DREAMS

The soul is part therapist/counselor and part linguist. Because the language of God is so broad, vast, and deep, we often need help understanding what she is telling us. As humans, we can only use the understandings and language we have. We know how things can get lost in translation between earthly languages. The infinite communicating with the finite provides its own challenges.

The answer lies in the attributes of the soul. God uses the language of Transcendence, Holiness, Connectedness, Imagination, and Call to reveal his will and our purpose to us. Because we can't fully live out those two if we are not complete within ourselves, he helps us comprehend our finiteness, our fractured relationships, and those things that bind us as well as those things that make us whole.

These traits act as filters within our minds and brains. They help us narrow down the field of things our dreams are teaching us and give us a way of talking about them in ways that are hard-wired into our being. While each of us may not intellectually have a deep comprehension of what transcendence is, we feel it, we have an intuitive knowledge of its presence in our lives.

Take a look at your dreams. View them through the eyes of these five aspects of the soul and see if they aren't trying to tell you something. Because we have spent so much time talking about those five areas, we will not do so here. A couple of examples may help in seeing what we mean.

Connectedness---A woman had been working and volunteering most of her life. At the age of 60 she retired and decided to pull back. She went to lots of workshops and did several retreats a year to deepen her relationship with God. She meditated daily. In essence she became a hermit. She had a recurring dream where she was lost in a forest, sadly dancing by herself. She kept waiting for someone to join her but none did. This dream had been going on for months. In the most recent version the trees were starting to die. After talking, I suggested she might want to get back to helping others. Within a short time she returned to say the dream had been replaced. She imagined she was in a field dancing in a circle with people, laughing and singing as Picasso painted them (the famous print). She had lost her connection to the world. She had become far too Mystical in her soul and the dream pulled her toward the Temporal end, finding balance.

You could also say this dream was about Holiness or Transcendence. Clearly her meaning system changed as she started being with and for others. Her own identity shifted as she gained the perspective of others. Her Imagination changed as she joined with others in the dance of life. By changing her core purpose, her Call changed as well. All of them are interconnected.

Purpose—A young man came in to see me. He was quite driven in life for all the good reasons. He wanted to take care of his family, be a good employee, and do what was right in life. He was a teacher and felt his profession was a good fit for him. He was frustrated by public education. I asked him at first about what he felt God thought of his teaching in public schools. I was just curious, not making a value statement (since I have been a principal of a public school and loved it). He said he hadn't really thought about it. I then asked him about his dreams. He said the one he remembered most occurred a couple of weeks before.

He was learning to whittle from a very old man. At first his whittling was minimal. He would break sticks and only be able to cut in one direction. The old man at first just gave instruction. He would explain things then let him try it out. The old man was patient but he could tell he was getting frustrated. Then the old man had him put down the knife and they had a conversation. A talk about life, about the sacredness of wood, and about creativity. The conversation seemed endless to him. After that he picked up some wood and started whittling an amazing piece of sculpture. The old man smiled.

Being an educator I asked the young man about his teaching style. He was not unlike many teachers and showed students what to do and let them loose. When they had questions, he'd answer. I asked him what the dream might be saying about his teaching style. What did it say about his current perceived purpose as a teacher and what God might be calling him to? He was silent for quite a while and then smiled. "I get it. It's about relationship, not just about knowledge."

He came back to me several months later and said that dream had changed his life. His purpose now was to connect with students, to build relationships and to use those to teach. Students now sought him out for issues in their lives. Discipline in his classroom was almost non-existent and their interest in the subject matter rose. He felt God called him to teach because of these relationships. He rarely talked about his faith, but did not hesitate when the door was opened. He believed he was changing lives and I had no doubt about it.

I didn't mention his other dreams of which there weren't many. This one dream was so potent to him we focused on it, but we did put it in the context of his other dreams and his perception about himself.

Holiness--- A gentleman came to see me for depression. He was in his 50's and had had a fairly successful career. His children were grown and he reported a good marriage of almost 30 years. He couldn't figure out why he was depressed because all was well in his life. We went through all the basics and nothing popped out. I asked about dreams and he laughed. He said throughout his life he didn't dream much. I corrected him and told him he always dreamed, he just didn't remember them. He went on to say in the past few months he'd been having strange dreams and remembering a few. I asked when his depression had started. He laughed again. "About the same time the dreams started, I mean when I started to remember them." I asked what they were about and he said he had no idea. What follows are two of a series of dreams with the same theme.

There was a large field with a thousand wild horses in it. I (the client) was one of the horses. We all talked. I was drinking out of a lake on the edge of the field and for some reason noticed my reflection. I realized I was just the same as every other horse. While we talked a bit differently, we all looked exactly the same. This became a concern to me. I started at first walking through the herd, then more frantically running, driving myself nuts. Then I stopped suddenly. My eyes found a horse of a different color. One out of a thousand horses was different, how could that be? I walked over to the horse and asked why he was different. The horse simply looked at me and said, "Because I know who I am." That was it.

The second dream was even stranger he said. He was in the country riding his bike. It was a beautiful day with the sun blazing. He stopped on his bicycle and started looking around. He saw a giant tree and felt for some reason like touching it. He got off his bike, walked over and touched the tree. As soon as he did it was like he became the tree. He felt a connection to the earth and the sun, felt his human self communing with his tree self. His rootedness felt amazing to him. He came out of the daze and looked up and saw a hawk sitting in the tree. Instantly he became the hawk and took off, soaring over the earth, seeing things he'd never seen, felt things he'd never felt. He flew higher and higher and as he looked at the sun he became the sun. He understood the unique import of his place in the cosmos in relationship to the earth. Near the earth he saw the moon and became the moon. He saw how he pulled the oceans back and forth, gave creativity to romance, art, and literature. Then he became himself again but felt the moon, sun, hawk, and tree enter him and understand the world through his perspective.

Two remarkable dreams especially for someone who didn't remember dreams. My thought was he was having a self-identity issue. He'd allowed his identity to become solely wrapped up in the world and had lost his sense of sacredness. I asked him the question that the horse had answered: "Who do you say you are?" Everything he said was what could be written in an obituary. There was no soul there, no essence. He started looking at himself through different lenses. At first it was a fight and a struggle, but as he moved from a Terrene perspective to a more Sacred one of himself, his depression lifted. After many months he came in one day laughing. I asked what was so funny. He replied, " Remember that dream I had about the horses, where there was one that was different?" "Yes," I answered. "Well, I had that dream again, this time I was a different color too." He'd found himself in a new way.

Our souls are the internal part of our being that takes the dream or other avenues the Collaborative Unconscious and God might use (visions, lucid dreaming, sudden insight) and relates them to the psyche. At some point, the spiritual must become real and active. Some component of our essence must be the mediator between the transcendent and the psyche. The psyche is bound by the world. It is the realm in which it must survive and thrive. The soul is not bound by the same constraints and yet the soul has no direct effect on the brain, it works through its relationship with the psyche.

Counselors are taught over and over that one of the most important ingredients to successful counseling or therapy is the "therapeutic alliance," the relationship between therapist and client. The counselor can't "make" the client do anything. It is the trust built between the two that enables the counselor to have an impact. There are times when a client may not really believe what they are hearing, but they are willing to try it on for size because they trust the therapist and believe they would not willingly lead them astray.

Our soul's desire is to do the same. The soul wants to make us whole because it is in and through our wholeness the soul finds the most complete relationship with the divine. As was mentioned earlier, just because a person may not believe in the soul, does not mean it doesn't exist. There is no proof one way or the other. The idea of a soul makes many things more easily understood. Just as God wants to be in relationship with us even if we are not interested, so too the soul desires a relationship with our psyches and is perpetually trying to build those bridges. The choice we have is of acknowledgment and listening, of paying attention to our soul.

Perhaps the most difficult part of dreams is determining what part of our being any given dream is relating to. On the one hand, they are all interconnected so it doesn't really matter. Most of us would like to get to the root of our issues rather than skirting them indefinitely. Does this dream speak to my soul, psyche, unconscious, or physical activity and relationships? One might think God would speak directly to the soul. Let's remember that while we are alive on this planet, the soul is embedded in our bodies and minds. The soul can't work outside a context and language they do not understand. The soul is intimately connected to our psyche and is to a large degree dependent on it for growth and maturity—not for its existence. Therefore, some dreams are meant for the soul.

All dreams speak to relationship. They are the essence of who we are as human beings, as God's creatures. It is an unfortunate thing our lives have become so separated from the creators of those things we use in our daily lives. Most of us have no connection to where our food comes from, the houses we live in and what fills them. We lose something in the lack of those relationships. Our families are much more mobile, our jobs not nearly as long-lasting, and the connections to our past more limited than ever before. We are not saying we should retroactively return to those days, but we do know we need to find new ways of building deep relationships in the contexts in which we find ourselves.

Is it a coincidence that many people in prison and many who have severe psychological issues in their lives have few if any deep and meaningful relationships in their lives? Where is the anchor of love, trust, and purpose for them? If their souls have no psyche that has the material on which to mature, what do we expect? This is not an excuse, just a way of understanding. In the end, while each of us makes our own decisions, good or bad, we are responsible for one another. We hold a collective guilt for not watching out for our neighbor, for not building bridges, for not listening to our dreams that are calling us to "be for others."

Working with dreams

This process of working with dreams comes from the work of Robert Johnson (**Innerwork**, Harper and Row, 1986) expanded upon by Steve Bearden, PhD.

In order to work with dreams you need to remember them first. We know for a fact everyone dreams, they are an important part of sleep, REM (rapid eye movement) sleep. Without this type of sleep the brain quickly falls into dis-ease. Many people will claim they do not dream when the reality is they do, they just don't remember them. Why do we not remember dreams? There can be many reasons. One could be that our brain chemistry is not facilitating the bridge between the part that creates the dream and the part that remembers it, they are different parts of the brain. Taking some vitamin B complex has helped some people with this. Another obstacle could be that a person is such a disbeliever in dreams their brain is conditioned to not remember. We don't see things in life we don't want to see, we build mechanisms to protect us. The world of dreams is no different, if we don't want to remember, then most of the time we won't. A third reason why we may not remember dreams is because we don't want to deal with the issues they bring up. Our brains are probably not great filters of types of dreams. They can't filter out the God dreams from the basic memory or event dreams from those that come straight from the unconscious. We either remember dreams or we don't. Some people remember some dreams but not all. No one remembers all dreams which makes the study of them all the more interesting. Why do we remember the ones we do and not others? What are we missing?

If you don't remember your dreams but want to there are a few things you can do. First is to think about taking some vitamin B complex. Second is to ask God to help you remember them. Third is to tell yourself before you go to sleep that you will remember, be open to remembering, no matter what. If you don't at first, be patient. Fourth is to find someone that is open to dream work or does it already and tell them you are hoping to start remembering your dreams. Engaging others in dream work can be very powerful, both in remembering and in processing.

As we have said before, it's important that you not let others tell you what your dreams mean, you are the person with the knowledge to interpret them for your life. Images in dreams mean different things to different people. There is no one size fits all in dream work. Certainly there are patterns and over all a given image may have something to do with a given theme, but not always. Having someone to share your dreams with and to help you process can be very beneficial. Finding someone who has done dream work and helped others is the best. We all fall prey to delusion at times and another voice in the process can ask questions as a check and balance to our own interpretation.

All this being said, let's assume you have a series of dreams written down (always write them down, your memory of them will change over time). Here is the process we suggest.

1. Record your dreams. Start by getting the essence down; the who, what, where, when of the event you see.
2. List the elements. Give details about what you remember. Who were the characters? What was said or done in the dream? Outcomes? What do you remember on the level of the senses? What did you hear, smell, taste, see, or feel?

3. Make associations. Go back and look at those elements. What do they represent to you? What feelings do they illicit? In your waking mind, what do they make you think of? You may have had a meeting with someone who is dead. What did that person represent to you? You may have dreamed you were in a different time, what meaning does that time have for you?
4. Of all these associations which are the most powerful for you? Choose a few to start with or just one if that is what works. You are looking for things that grab your attention, heart, and mind.
5. Once you have these, describe your present life dynamics of each. What is going on in your life where that idea, image, or theme may apply?
6. Collect all those dynamics and see if you can't merge them into a single theme or narrative. When you have that, read it over 5 times.
7. Attempt a grand interpretation of the dream. Now that you have found the components, given them meaning, made some real life associations and found the core themes, what is the dream trying to tell you? What is it saying to your unconscious, your psyche, and/or your soul?
8. Find a way to honor and ground the dream. It's important to honor the wisdom and source of the dream, just as we would a person who gives us insight into something about ourselves. Lighting candles, lifting a prayer of gratitude, sharing, writing or creating something are all ways of doing this, there is no right or wrong way.

This process takes patience and time. The more you do it the easier it becomes to remember your dreams and understand their role in your life. Those dreams that come from the Collaborative Unconscious and God will become increasingly obvious and the work of helping the soul mature will speed up.

GOD AND THE BRAIN

Clearly our souls are connected to the universe on a transcendent level, but they must also be connected to our physical selves, to our brains. We have touched on this briefly before, but here we want to delve further into this mystery. Because there is no "organ" that is the link, as was once believed, the process by and through which the transcendent and the immanent, the sacred and the profane dialogue, must be understood in new ways. Again, let us say we do not believe science will ever be able to understand the transcendent nature of the universe, the tools they use to perceive the world are fundamentally different. There is no physics of the soul, no neurobiological place where our spiritual identities exist. Science will tell you they can "create" religious experiences by toying with certain parts of the brain, that prayer itself is seated in part of the brain. In reality, all they are able to describe is how the world of the spirit becomes known in the physical world. This by no means negates the reality of that world. There are so many questions that science will probably never "prove," even though they will try to make us think they have. Below are but a few questions that are rarely raised.

Where did the beginning come from? Scientists boldly assert the Big Bang theory—note the word theory. Most forget to point out that even if the Big Bang turns out to be fact, they have no idea where the initial ball of matter came from that exploded to create the known universe. Some will tell you the universe contracts and expands over and over again, that we are in the midst of yet another expansion. But science also tells us all things have a beginning and an end. How could the mass that became the universe just pop out of nothing on its own? In the worlds of physics there are no free lunches, matter doesn't just appear. This is certainly not proof of God, we offer none, but it does point out the limitations of science. At some point, they must raise their hands and say they don't know. Scientists hate doing that but they are constantly seeking answers to more deeply understand the universe and we applaud that effort. God's desire is that we put effort into our search for the transcendent universe as well.

One of the great questions being asked is," does God create the brain or does the brain create God?" How we choose to answer that question fundamentally determines how we view life and the lens that brings some things into focus and by definition keeps others out. Evolution—The authors are believers in Evolutionary Theory, but again it is a theory. We do not see a problem being a Christian and believing in evolution, God impacts creation and lures it back to the Creator. The problem with evolution is that there are so many missing links, so many challenges as to where and how consciousness arose within early humans. Anyone who doubts humans are fundamentally different than all other animals have already missed one of the purposes for which we were created. Part of the wonder of being conscious, from very early on in the development of humanity, is the notion of the transcendent. We know from pre-historic times, there was a sense of something greater, something deserving of worship and ritual, something that could impact who and what we were and were becoming. There is no evolutionary necessity for "knowing" God, all other creatures have done fine without the depth of understanding we have about God. It is one of the defining traits of being human. We choose to see the process as Creative Evolution, rather than a separation of Creationism and Evolution, one negating the sacred, the other negating the profane.

DNA—We are all well aware that when a sperm enters a female egg, something new is created. The two cells split over and over and over again. Very soon, cells differentiate into different parts of the human anatomy. Blood and brain cells, enzymes, muscle tissue, nerves, bone, a heart and a liver. But we are not remotely close to understanding how they know that. How is it that two single cells know when and how to differentiate in perfect timing to become what we are? Humans are without question the most complicated creatures on earth, by a manifold magnitude. We are just beginning to understand the depths of life in a simple one-celled bacteria. To give you just a small taste of our complexity, check out the website at :

http://images.google.com/imgres?imgurl=http://www.yeastrc.org/pdr/im ages/go/go_images/1/7/0/0043170.jpg&imgrefurl=http://www.yeastrc.or g/pdr/viewGONode.do%3Facc%3DGO:0043170&usg=__kwtQ07aaWE

WWv16bGyMOgxUpPu0=&h=362&w=832&sz=94&hl=en&start=44&um=1&tbnid=QFFC5DZg5UXQkM:&tbnh=63&tbnw=144&prev=/images%3Fq%3DMetabolic%2Bprocess%26start%3D36%26ndsp%3D18%26um%3D1%26hl%3Den%26sa%3DN   It shows a tree style diagram of the metabolic systems within a yeast cell. That is one fairly simple system and you will see how complicated it is. Multiply that by thousands. Or look at http://www.iubmb-nicholson.org/chart.html. This is a chart of what it takes to create an important chemicals in the human body. Stunning in its complexity.

Why is it easier to say we will figure it out than it is to say it is a mystery that God has created as such? The beauty of the soul is that it accepts mystery while not being afraid of discovering God's creation. Our spiritual identities relish mysteries in life, including the largest mystery of all, God.

As we have mentioned before, scientists know experiments are affected by those doing the experiment. Light acts as a wave or a particle depending on how you want to see it, how you set up the experiment. Our spiritual identities are at some level affected by what we believe we are looking for. We need to be careful when talking about the soul to understand that it isn't science. We have a view that works for us, where we believe we can make the jigsaw pieces fit and some evidence that backs up these ideas. But we do not claim them to be fact any more than those from eastern religious traditions can prove there is no soul or that reincarnation exists. They are belief systems that drive people's lives and beliefs and are very powerful. All of us have slightly different theologies, beliefs about God. We come together around common ground, but as you dig deeply into the nuances of God we have different thoughts or we simply say, "I don't know."

Our brains were created to be curious, to survive, and to be creative. They exist to help us in our temporal lives. Our souls exist to seek and understand the transcendent aspect of our nature and to bring that into our temporal lives. Our souls are constantly asking questions, attempting to get us to open up and seek God. The bible tells us to "seek first the kingdom of God." Far too many believe they have all the answers; that they are right and everyone who disagrees is wrong. Exactly like the Scribes and Pharisees of Jesus's time whom he constantly chastised. We are in a lifelong search for God, to deepen the relationship between who and what we are with God, to find our spiritual identities and then help them mature. Theology is a theory, not a fact.

God gave us brains to use, not to fear. Yes, we were also given free will to choose what to do with those brains. Sometimes we use them for the good, to benefit God's creation, and at other times we use them to damage or destroy God's creation, not always with intent. So how do we use our brains to deepen the relationship with our souls and with God? How do we exercise them? How do we open them to the transcendent power of God's Spirit?

We know life impacts our brains; how we perceive the world and respond to it. What and how we learn changes our physical brains. Eric Kandel who studied sea slugs has shown how small changes in learning and learning curves change brain structure and thus everything about us (Si, K. *et al.* **A neuronal isoform of the Aplysia CPEB has prion-like properties**. *Cell* **115**, 879-891. December 26, 2003). Tie that in with Daniel Siegel's (***The Mindful Brain***, 2007, W. W. Norton and Company) and Newberg's (***How God Changes Your Brain***, 2010, Ballantine Books) research on meditation, prayer and the brain, and we see how the power of those actions can have a profound impact on who we are and on our perceived relationship with the transcendent. Think about this; meaning changes the brain. For most creatures, meaning is to stay alive, to find food and to bear young. To even insinuate that those functions have "meaning" is perhaps a stretch. For humans, that is not enough. We long to find a deeper purpose. Our lives may necessitate a focus on survival, but our internal switches are still wanting and seeking more. Maslow talks about self-actualization as a need of humanity. Heinz Pagels in ***The Cosmic Code*** (Simon and Shuster,1982) tried to make humanity purely physical. He talks about how mathematical alogorithms define who and what we are. What we learn becomes feedback into our brains. These experiences create reactions and response which in turn over time create change. What this doesn't explain are significant changes. Novelty and creativity change our lives with no real tie to the past. The soul is not solely reliant on the world for the input it uses to change us. The transcendent world directly impacts the soul and of course, the soul impacts the brain. Pagels discusses how important context is in the change process. But what happens when the context is outside the world we know? That is one of Jesus's central points, he even tries to enlighten Pilate at his trial. "My kingdom is not of this world." If we are actively part of the spiritual kingdom, we have access to a realm that doesn't show up on any earthly radar screen or scientific instrument.

Dr. Daniel Amen has become well known for his work with brain imaging and enhancing the brain's capabilities. His book, *Healing the Hardware of the Soul* (Free Press, 2002), shows how different parts of the brain are connected to the soul and how we can care for them. In this book we will not go into great detail about the brain, but it is the central point where the soul interacts with who we are as physical humans, so it bears attention.

The brain was created to be in relationship, to be a social entity. Dr. Ornish in his book called *Love and Survival* (Harper Collins, 1998) talks about the necessity of being connected, how important belonging, love, feeling supported, and having purpose are to a healthy life. Look at the brains of children in Romania who were barely touched for the first two years of their lives *(Local Brain Functional Activity Following Early Deprivation:A Study of Postinstitutionalized Romanian Orphans. NeuroImage* **14,** 1290–1301 (2001). They literally have holes in their brains and lack ideas of connection or how to be social. But if all we were created for was to be connected to one another, the vast majority of humans would not seek more. We are literally drawn to the transcendent. Our souls drag us, sometimes kicking and screaming, to seek something larger than ourselves, larger than the world itself.

One is certainly correct in asking about those that feel no pull to the transcendent, for many don't. We all know how our minds can interfere with our connections to anything, in the end we believe what we want to believe. If we have convinced ourselves or been convinced by someone else that there is nothing transcendent we can have a relationship with, then that is probably what we will see, just as light can be seen as a wave or a particle. There may also be specific parts of the brain whose functioning enables those connections more fully.

This notion of the connection between our social natures and our spiritual ones runs deep. It is not a coincidence that A.A.'s success is based on the premise of people gathering around a common need and belief. Churches exist to bring people together around common transcendent themes. Even the family, as dysfunctional as it may be at times, is an important part of life. Our social worlds have a huge impact on who we are. Do this: take some time to look at who you are closest to, your inner circle. What would you say are the key similarities and differences between you and them. Now it's important to be honest with yourself. If you tend to be a critical person, then just admit it, don't pretend that you are otherwise, there is no judgment here. Most of us live in worlds more similar to ours than different. Depressed people tend to hang around other depressed people. Highly active people hang around other active people. This should be no surprise. But ever action and interaction feeds back into our being and reinforces what we have become. Sometimes a jolt is needed. When we are depressed we need to force ourselves to hang out with happy people, as painful as it may be for a while. It takes energy and effort to break our cycles, but everyone has areas of their lives where it needs to be done.

It is very important to remember that our souls by their very creation are attached to the transcendent power of the universe. Our negativity does not come from our souls, but from our human natures. When we build a strong sense of spiritual identity, we have a very deep well of hope that can help get us through difficult times. This happens on several different fronts. First, we become spiritually mature by discovering that transcendent power of hope, love, and grace. That depth is built on experiences and connection.

Because we are influenced by our spiritual identity, we can't help but be lifted up in the midst of despair. Secondly, we do not create this soul in a vacuum; we do it in the midst of some form of fellowship. Our spiritual identities mature as we make ourselves vulnerable to others in the midst of our journey. That vulnerability helps others in their struggles as they see they are not alone. When the community of faith brings together the combined strengths and struggles, everything feeds off of and into the whole. In difficult times, that fellowship is still there. We should not be surprised that Jesus had three or four people he trusted with virtually everything. There was a group of 12 he trusted with much, and increasingly larger communities with which he shared less and less. Sadly, his closest group of friends were not there for him at his time of need. Hopefully we will be there for our closest friends and family and visa versa. Thirdly, remember our souls, when in balance, see the world clearly, it is our brains that distort it. We should not be surprised that in and through prayer and meditation, the parts of our brain that are very active during anxiety and depression, calm down. When we slow down the brain and allow a deeper sense of self to rise up, perspective happens; we get a different sense of what is going on in our lives. Those who have lost all hope have lost touch with this part of their being.

Our brains are very unique and very fragile organs. We know chemical imbalances can lead to depression, anxiety, learning differences, and a wide variety of other conditions, affects, and actions. Just as our souls impact our brains, so too our brains create the environment through which the soul communicates with us and the world. If our brains are dysfunctional, it makes it all the harder (not impossible) for the soul to mature. We all need to do our best to optimize our brains.

There is a fine line at times between psychological dysfunction and an overtly empowered soul. If you read the writings of some of the saints and the mystics, it will sound like someone with psychosis or severe depression. But that is how it is viewed through the human eyes of science. How we describe an experience with the infinite transcendent force of the universe will certainly not be in normal terms. Think about it this way. If all the sudden you were to become a single-celled organism. What do you think you would say; "I felt small." "I moved in a fluid sort of way." Our words come from the world we know, describing a world we do not live in is difficult at best. This is an inherent problem with working with our spiritual identities. Human language can not capture it. Even Jesus was forced to use parables because there was no direct language to express what he knew to be true. Our souls are experienced, not thought. We translate the spiritual and transcendent realm because in this life and in this body we have no alternative. In the spiritual domain there is no need for language, being is enough. In Mark 2:1-12 (which you will learn a great deal about as you read about each of the types), Jesus tells the paralyzed man that his sins are forgiven. At that moment, the man's soul is released. There are no words to express what he is going through. He is fundamentally changed. The same is true for Paul on the road to Damascus. Externally, he is blinded. Internally, he is cleansed.

Dr. David Elkins and others have noted some interesting positive attributes for those working on maturing their souls (***Beyond Religion: A Personal Quest for Building A Spiritual Life Outside the Walls of***

Religion, Quest, 1998). We'll grant this research looked at regular church attenders and non-church goers, but we believe at some level, churchgoers are putting some effort into being part of a fellowship and deepening their faith. These characteristics include: having less stress in general, have a 25-35% lower mortality rate, having more than 3 times likelihood of surviving open heart surgery, spend half as long in the hospital, ten times less likely to smoke, and recover 70% faster from a depressive episode. This does not mean "spiritual" people are immune to the vagaries of life, only a tendency to be more resilient for the reasons mentioned above.

We do need to understand there are exceptions to every idea or rule. There are certainly very healthy and content people who claim to be atheists and who do not believe in or seek a spiritual identity. There are those who claim deep belief who work hard at taking care of their souls who seem to be constantly in trouble—like Job. Mysteries abound at all levels of life. Just as science seeks to answer questions, so to do these authors and many others. Theories rise and fall on the preponderance of evidence available at any point in time. The theory of this book is based on what we feel is the evidence at hand at this time.

Dr. Amen talks about how weak or strong parts of our brains may impact our views of God. Those with a healthy limbic system see God as caring, present, and compassionate while those who have a weak limbic system feel more abandoned by God and are insecure. People with strong Pre-frontal cortexes tend to gravitate to more evangelical and experiential denominations while those with strong anterior cingulates prefer the more theological and liturgical branches. There is no value placed here, neither is good or bad, they are just differences. Would you really like everyone on the planet to be just like you? Do all worship in the same way? Diversity on every level is what keeps us creative. Virtually every human on the planet is capable of living just about anywhere on the planet because we create ecosystems within ecosystems. We can create a cooler climate in the desert if we need to and a warmer one in the arctic. Our brains capacity have helped us adapt. Animals do not have this ability. They migrate, hibernate, are cold blooded, or live in an environment that doesn't change that much. So again, we need not underestimate the relationship of the brain and the soul.

We have chosen to not go into detail about how the different parts of the brain specifically deal with aspects of our spirituality. In the bibliography on the website you will find books that do that, some mentioned in this chapter. The key is to understand that just because the soul is not a physical entity does not mean it does not exist or work in conjunction with our physical bodies and brains.

We have dedicated a chapter to dreams which is one very specific place where God, the Collaborative Unconscious, our souls and our psyches all work together. In that chapter you will see a bit more about the brain.

We hope you are beginning to see the tapestry we are weaving. Everything is connected to everything, everything impacts everything. But there are a few critical areas of life that need attention if we are to grow as a human and as a spiritual being; our bodies, psyches, and souls. God knew these were needed when he said love God with all your heart, mind, and soul. The notion of heart and mind unite body, emotions, and psyches. Some would say the environment is critical, but we would contend you can not truly love your body, psyche or soul and not care for the environment on which they are all dependent. The decreased quality of the environment over the past 100 years has had a direct impact on all aspects of who we are. We know for a fact what we eat has affected us and probably increased many of the health issues we currently face. The increasing pressures on energy resources and water will continue to put pressures on humanity. This is not a doomsday scenario, for we are optimistic about what humans can do and our ability to change, but we can't deny as our environments change we are affected.

Throughout this book you will find pragmatic ways of learning more about your bodies, psyches, and souls as well as ways to help them be the best they can be.

Near the beginning of this chapter we asked the question of whether God creates the brain or the brain creates God. Our answer is that both are right. God created us or at least the process by which we have come into being. Our free will gives us the power to create whatever we want. We can choose to push our personal view onto the world (like people did when they believed the earth was flat) or we can be open and let the universe and God unfold before us. There is no question that each of us creates an image of God, that our images are far from perfect. Anyone who lays claim to know the mind of the infinite needs a lesson in humility. We are on a quest, a never-ending search for wisdom; a wisdom that merges the transcendent and immanent truths of the universe.

STEVE'S OVER ALL THEORY OF THINGS

This work comes from the premise that while the soul and the psyche are different, they influence one another. One of the challenges of this book is to find distinctions between the two. In this chapter we present one way of looking at the two, looking at how five core concepts of both are differentiated. These five are Need, Belief, Contemplation, Action, and Feeling. They are cornerstones for every relationship and activity we go through each and every day of our lives.

NEED

We all have needs. Our needs are at the core of what drives and motivates us. We see them in our psychological, social, and spiritual beings. Our needs are what bring the rest of our being into focus, what feeds the deepening of our being and our relationships, and what moves us forward. Having certain needs not met tends to stifle the overall process, although we do acknowledge that high spiritual needs and values can be met while struggling to meet basic physical ones. Think of Jesus, fasting for forty days, at the peak of malnutrition and probably exhaustion he is spiritually clear. He was tempted as no one ever has been. In the midst of this, his Spirit soared and his spiritual connection to God was amazingly strong. Every fiber of his being screamed out to accept what was being offered to him, his psyche yearned for the strokes being given to his divinity and the needs of his body ached for the nourishment Yet his Spirit was being fed by a higher order that was stronger than the other needs, more connected to the source of all life, transcending the profane in favor of the holy and sacred. This is not to say he didn't want to fill his stomach or that the worldly needs weren't important, but from Christ's perspective, spiritual needs are more important in the long run, in the eternal sense, and they provide a foundation for all other needs.

We will use Maslow's hierarchy of needs as a starting place (***Toward a Psychology of Being***, John Wiley and Sons, 1968). While we may not agree with his theory behind the needs, they provide a solid framework of what needs are and their relative importance in survival and becoming what we are meant to be. Here is a brief list of his hierarchy of needs.

Physiological: Breathing, food, water, sex, sleep, homeostasis

Safety: Security of body, of employment, of resources, of morality, of the family, of health, of Property

Love/Belonging: Friendship, family, sexual intimacy, community

Esteem: Self-esteem, confidence, achievement, respect of others, respect by others

Self-Actualization: Morality, Creativity, spontaneity, problem-solving, lack of prejudice, acceptance of facts

Psyche--- Recent research has shown how important feeling attached and connected in our early years are. If you are concerned as an infant and a child for your safety, if you fear being abandoned, if you are under threat in your own home, your attention will be primarily on staying safe. Our culture seems to be moving more and more towards feelings of insecurity. More crime, more burglar alarms, less trust of neighbors and yet a deeper trust in the ways of humanity than in the ways of the Spirit. Internally, we have vast defensive mechanisms that try to keep our egos and psyches safe. We repress memories, deny or rationalize reality, act out, take our feelings out on people other than those they are meant for, and sometimes regress. There are some more positive forms of defense such as humor, altruism (performing acts of service to cover a deeper pain), sublimation (where we take internal feelings and put them into other things like, writing or music), and introjection (taking an idealized idea and making it part of our being). While all of these are geared towards protecting us in the short run, they can keep us from a deeper sense of self in the long run if not dealt with.

Our safety needs carry over into other areas of life as well, not just our physical and emotional safety. We also include safety of resources, employment, family, property, and the moral basis of what we have come to know. We want to know there is order in the world, that injustice is under control and that the familiar is common.

Life takes energy. The amount of energy each of us has is like a pie. Some pies are larger than others, but all pies are finite. Some of us have a lot of energy, seemingly endless, others struggle to get up in the morning. If all of our energy is focused on keeping our internal and external lives safe, where does the energy come from to deal with the rest of our needs?

We all have a need to belong. This goes into attachment again. We yearn for friendship and intimacy, to be counted as worthy by friends and family. Part of our being needs to be creative, to have a purpose and to fulfill that purpose. Our survival instinct tells us we need to pro-create and bear offspring. Different needs have a different intensity depending on the conditions in which those needs arise.

For some, understanding certain needs is difficult. We take their fulfillment for granted. Many reading this book do not truly understand the need for food, we always have it. Yes, we know that without food we die. Yes, we can choose to fast and physically feel hungry. This is vastly different than starving without the ability to get sustenance.

The challenge is for us to know our needs and how they are filled. What is the difference between a need, a want, a desire, and a dream? Our needs are the crux of what keeps us alive and makes us viable. Most people reading this have their basic needs met and much more. People's needs are different. We all have a need to belong (whether we admit it or not). The degree it takes to fulfill that need is different in every person. Our wants are those things we don't have or need that we believe are important in our lives. We often confuse wants and needs. I really want a milkshake right now, but I don't need one. Most wants are things that are within the scope of getting or achieving. Wants can come from both a rational and emotional level, but most often they are more thought oriented than emotionally oriented. Desire on the other hand is pure emotion. Lust is a desire. Greed is often more based in emotion than reason. We desire things because we believe they will enrich our lives and in the short run it is possible they will. Dreams in this context are those things we fantasize about that in the moment are distant but could become possible. At times they aren't even possible. I dream of traveling to a distant planet. This is well beyond reality but I dream it none the less. Being able to distinguish between the three in our lives and in the lives of others can be helpful in organizing our lives and in putting energy toward the need end of the spectrum.

Soul---Our souls have specific needs as well. Their needs are not all that different, just on a different level. Our psyche's need to feel connected to their primary caregivers, primarily their families, and our souls need to feel connected to their creator, The Creator. We shouldn't be surprised that people who most of us feel should feel very safe often write or speak of feeling angst and fear. The needs of their bodies and psyches are being met, but their souls are not in the safety of the transcendent, they have given significant priority to the mundane rather than to the sacred. On the other side it's interesting that deeply spiritual people don't worry as much about safety, no matter what the situation. They are secure in the eternal sense of the word, their security is not based upon worldly and temporary notions of safety.

The defense mechanisms are much more difficult to isolate in the soul, but they are at work. The central difference is that we can't hide and ignore the world, but we can ignore or avoid God and the transcendent nature of our being. Why you might ask would we hide from the very relationship that would keep us safe? Good question. Let's remember the psyche and the soul are interlocked. If the psyche is the dominant force, the soul has a harder time breaking through. The defense mechanisms of the psyche seep into the soul. We can consciously activate the soul and use it to transform the needs and perceptions of the psyche, but it takes an act of will. We repress spiritual memories, rationalize why we believe what we believe, avoid spiritual fellowship, set ideals that are so far out of reach we can't possibly reach them, play the martyr card, and even use humor to defend us from the painful truth of our choices. Theologies are created to explain hunger, suffering, and pain. They are theologies that exempt us from having to accept much or any responsibility for one another and in the author's opinion, they are an escape from spiritual reality.

The good news about the soul is that it is not dependent on the ways of the world for its growth and existence. Certainly our souls mature more readily, deeply, and quickly when surrounded by a cloud of witnesses that are equally committed, but history is full of people whose souls were radiant, even while beset by the world.

The vast majority of needs come from relationships we have built; in our families, friends, neighborhoods, jobs, churches, and other groups. Our soul's needs are met in the same way, but the most significant relationship is with the Creator who is the ultimate, eternal place of safety, who creates all we need, who beckons us to be in her presence.

We live in an odd spot, having temporal and eternal safety needs, sacred and mundane, transcendent and immanent.

The soul too needs to be attached, attached to God and the transcendent. Like the psyche, without this attachment there is no growth or growth is minimal. The soul needs to belong. It joins with other souls in the Collaborative Unconscious and even on earth with those who are also overtly trying to grow spiritually. The soul yearns to be creative and use its imagination for the betterment of all. The soul has a need to fulfill its purpose, to discover its call and move into the world in action. The soul does not want these things, it needs them. The growth of the soul, its mere survival as a viable entity is dependent upon acting upon these needs.

How is it that we fill our needs? What is the basis through which we move into the world to have our needs met?

BELIEFS

Our needs are met primarily through the beliefs we hold. Each of us is born into a set of values and beliefs. Most of us take them for granted. While you may believe thousands of things, do you know what your core beliefs are? We are writing a book about the soul because we feel many people do not really know what they believe about the soul and this may give them some ideas to contemplate. There are different levels of belief. We have those that are pretty fundamental; the earth is round, the sun will rise tomorrow (even if only for a brief time), and I am alive. These beliefs are based on science and experience over long periods of time. They have been passed down through schooling and relational teaching over generations.

Then there are beliefs about relationships and other things that are time specific. We believe our parents love us the best they can, we believe my shelter will be there tomorrow and that when I plant seeds, they will sprout and grow. Why would you plant them if you didn't think they would grow? All of these beliefs make sense and yet we know the belief is not always well founded. We do not know when a tornado or fire may strike, we do not know years ahead of time when a relationship may become strained to the point of breaking and we don't know which seeds will sprout and which ones won't. We still believe. To go through life not having belief is to take away all hope, to give into a world that doesn't exist. Severe angst, depression, and anxiety are often exacerbated or created by lack of beliefs or by the fact that the world around them is not acting within their belief system and they have yet to figure out a way to cope with that incongruence.

There are beliefs about the transcendent, about God or what exists outside this plane of existence. Obviously there is no "proof" to any of these beliefs, they are acts of faith. People can talk about having gone to heaven or talking with the dead, the light at the end of the tunnel and visions, but in the end, we choose to believe them as acts of faith, they are unique to an individual's experience. Jesus could have been resurrected in front of Pilate, shown himself to the masses, but he chose not to. Christ wants people to believe through faith, not through proof. The proof for Christ is what follows the faith on the inside of a person and how that is reflected on the outside. The interesting thing about faith, is that when you believe in something through faith, it shows up in your life. It is not possible to be a person of truly deep and mature faith and be a slime bag. What we believe about the next life and about God shapes who we are and how we act in the world to get our needs met, not to mention helping others get their needs met.

There are people who believe Christ is going to return in a very short time, perhaps within the year. There are those that feel Christ will be returning, but we have quite a bit of time left, and there are those who do not believe he is coming back at all. I'm sure you can see how each belief could impact how someone will live their life a bit differently.

If you do not believe in an eternal soul, your life will be lived differently than for those who do believe in one. If you do not see life as sacred, then morals potentially go out the window.

Our beliefs change over time. They change in relation to the experiences we have, the knowledge acquired, and the relationships we build. Sometimes they change suddenly and significantly as was true with Paul who was a murderer of Christians and overnight became a

Christian and without whom there may not be a church for Gentiles. Paul's case is a bit unique. Most of us are not hit with the baseball bat of God in order to change us, but we are surrounded constantly with ideas that pull us in a wide variety of directions. Knowing what we believe gives us power to say no to what we don't believe. They are what guide us down the path of life and give us a sense of direction. Our actions follow our true beliefs. When we do something outside what we think is our belief we need to look carefully. Actions speak louder than words.

There is a difference between believing because I truly believe and believing because it's what's accepted or current or what everyone else believes. In 2008 we were all given front row seats to the impact of belief and how need turns into greed. The collapse of the economy lies at the feet of all. It's a defense mechanism to blame this person or that. All those who bought homes or consumer goods well beyond their means and need contributed. Those who have an unlimited appetite for power and wealth and who believed those could be acquired to the detriment of others contributed. Those who stood by and decided to let others do all the work contributed. Few are completely innocent. As a culture we had defense mechanisms that kept most from seeing what was coming even though the signs were there well in advance. In the midst of that, was there one person or one faction that accepted any responsibility? Like the garden of Eden, everyone pointed fingers. Until we learn to accept responsibility, nothing will change.

As a culture our greed overcame our need. What is happening increasingly is that our belief system as a culture is changing. In the 50's we trusted our teacher's, priests, doctors, and bankers. As headlines are dominated by individuals that breech that trust, our beliefs change. The few can influence the many. I hope we would all agree that in relation to the number of priests and teachers on the planet, there are very few bad ones and yet we wonder. Our cultural beliefs influence our personal beliefs, both temporal and eternal. Don't you find it amazing that while 80% of Americans claim to be religious and over 70% claim to go to church at least once a month, we no longer can celebrate Christmas as a culture? How does that happen? Because the few have influenced the many, our belief system as a culture is changing and while internally we may believe something different we do not have the energy, vision, or connection to enough others to do something about it.

This isn't meant to be a sermon, but a call to look at your beliefs, to see which ones are important, how have they changed over time and are there any you are willing to make sacrifices for?

Our beliefs determine how we act in the world. We would challenge you to be an observer of yourself for a day. See if you can't find the beliefs that underlie what you do.

When you buy something at a store instead of stealing it, why is that? Is it because you don't want to get caught and go to jail? Is it because by stealing you take away money that is someone else's? Is it because you just think it is wrong or because you were trained that way by your parents? It may be a mix of these or others. You have a unique belief system, they are like fingerprints, no two are identical.

What we believe about the soul and about the transcendent realm impacts us spiritually. This is what the continua are about. They speak to the essence of these ideas. Do you see yourself as unique in God's eyes, as sacred and holy? Do you have a purpose in life? What gives meaning to your life? Where does your purpose come from? What do you believe about yourself? Do you have a relationship with the transcendent? Is it possible to have such a relationship? Do you have a need for connection? What do you believe about relationships? Can you find ways that show you think about God impacts how you deal with life?

When we have needs and we understand the beliefs we work with to get them fulfilled, questions arise. Thinking about the answers to those questions is the next step.

One of the keys to your beliefs is that they are yours, not someone else's. It's fine to read a book or listen to others and take their beliefs on as your own, but own them as yours, know why you believe what you believe.

CONTEMPLATION

From one-celled creatures to humanity, life is run at least in part, by instinct. Primates certainly have some cognition, but in the wild, instinct reigns. Humans have instincts and when put into a corner we tend to revert to them—not a bad thing. The human brain is fundamentally different in our ability to think and contemplate. We are the only creatures that can live (if only for a short time) anywhere on the planet. We control our environment to a greater degree than any other species. Even this fact we take for granted, we don't really contemplate the reality of what that means for us.

To be honest, beliefs are pretty irrelevant unless you think about what they mean for you and how the belief becomes action. You can claim to believe that wearing a seat belt may save your life. If you don't wear them, do you really believe it (or perhaps your belief is that you are invincible or your belief is stronger that you will not get in an accident than wearing a seat belt will save you)? I believe I have the gift of teaching, so what (what is the basis of that belief)? I believe all people are created equal, so what?

The act of contemplation weds our needs and beliefs to our actions. Contemplation takes time and energy to actually make internal connections so that we become a fabric of threads rather than a bunch of separate patches lying on a table. There are times when we discover through contemplation that we really don't believe something we thought we did or that a "need" is actually a desire. The beginning of contemplation is integrity and honesty. Without these it's a waste of time.

What is it we are to contemplate? We are not talking about what shirt to wear, which cereal to have or even which present to buy. True contemplation is for the bigger ticket items, our truest needs at any given moment. Steve R. is a diabetic. Sometimes he doesn't eat enough after taking insulin and his blood sugar plummets. He has a true and deep need for sugar before he goes into insulin shock. He doesn't take a long time of contemplation to fill that need, he grabs (or has someone else grab) any kind of sugar he can find. After the event is over he tries to figure out what happened, why it happened, and what he can do to not have it happen again—that is the contemplation. How do his beliefs about diabetes and how his body functions impact his lifestyle? It's the "so what" question again.

When we become consciously aware of what we believe and what we need, contemplation comes naturally. Sometimes the process takes a second, other times it may takes months. Other than how quickly a need must be fulfilled, there is no time limit.

Our souls contemplate one primary thing; the relationship with God and the transcendent. That is the focus of its attention. We claim to believe in Christ—so what? We claim to believe that Christ is God and died for my sins—so what? We claim to believe we are called to live a life of unconditional love---so what? We hope you see the answers to these few questions have amazing repercussions for our lives if we take them seriously.

Contemplation is an interesting process. We can contemplate without the transcendent influencing our thoughts and outcomes. I don't need God to tell me which jobs to apply for or if I should do community service. On the other hand, if you truly believe God is aware of all that is happening on planet earth and knows you better than you know yourself, wouldn't it make sense to be in dialogue with that being? God knows our needs before we ask.

Our souls must be in relationship with the transcendent in order to mature. Our souls can't grow simply by earthly means because they in the end are not earthly. This connection to the transcendent world ties us not only to God, but to the Collaborative Unconscious; that vast pool of experience that has existed from the beginning of human time.

The soul in contemplation is a paradox. At its best, the soul contemplates by listening. We listen to the voice of the "holy other" in order to further understanding. When we talk, we try to project our worldly ideas onto the transcendent which doesn't play by the same rule book. Love your enemies and bless those who persecute you---does that sound like worldly wisdom? You will find your life by losing it---again, worldly wisdom? To even begin to understand what Jesus meant by those we must enter another way of thinking, another plane of being, another dimension.

The goal of the soul is to be united with God, to have God's will be our will, to submit our lives to the life of God. When you dig through all the needs your soul has, that is what is at the root, the need to be at one with God. We can't leap from A to Z, we do not become perfect overnight, if ever. Contemplation guides us naturally along the path that is right for us, sometimes with small baby steps, other times with quantum leaps as happened with Paul on the road to Damascus (let's remember that after Paul's conversion he went away for an extended period of time to learn what it means to submit to God). On a mental level we can be asking ourselves the question; is this act I am about to do bringing me closer to that union or taking me away from it? With the transcendent there is no standing still, you are either moving toward or away from it.

The act of contemplation is to put ourselves in the middle of the road, to let God and the world confront us head on—no avoidance, no hiding, but our best attempt to be honest. Now let's face facts, none of us is completely honest with ourselves and with others, we all wear masks. Even if we didn't our beliefs are not always accurate, in fact some beliefs are not based on fact as we have said before. Contemplating a faith statement is a bit harder than for a fact of science. Doubts have amazing power. We all live in delusion about ourselves in some aspects. There are things others see in and about me that I do not see, none of us is totally aware. Therefore we need some checks and balances in our contemplative stage.

Christ did not send his disciples out alone, but two by two. He knew they needed each other for support and for correction. We all need a community around us that can hold us accountable for this process—at every stage. What are your needs and beliefs? How are you putting them into action? What are you feeling and thinking? In the best of all worlds we would all have a spiritual director, close friends we share most things with and we trust to kick us when we are out of line or need to be challenged, and/or a therapist to help us with our rough spots (although therapists are great even when things are going well—they help us discover things we may not see). This person who is holding us accountable needs to be acting in our best interest and out of grace and love. Who would make themselves vulnerable to someone who will use that against them or belittle them? We become more vulnerable and grow when we are supported in our weakness. We need different people to support our psychological and our spiritual contemplative moments. In the best situation, we find someone who has been on the journey and has the spiritual depth, breadth, openness, and grace to walk with us as we work on our soul.

Most of those who meditate will tell you it is easier to maintain a discipline with a group than alone. Ascetics banded together to form monasteries and convents because they understood communal prayer, even in silence, is more powerful than going it alone. Do you have someone you share all these things with? Why not? Trust? Internal feelings of inadequacy? Introvert? Don't need them? All of these can and need to be overcome. A basic need of humanity is to belong, to be in relationship, to be held accountable and to hold accountable, to understand and to be understood.

The act of contemplation always ends with action, being is not enough. We must be doers as well. Transformation does not come through thinking about something, but by doing what we are thinking about. Contemplation guides us to the actions we need to do in order to build our psyches and souls, our temporal and eternal natures. As you reflect on this stage of the process in light of the five traits of the soul you can see how being at one end of the spectrum would affect how you do this. People on the Reason end would use their mind while those at the Inspiration end would rely more on intuition. The soul is most helped when both are used.

ACTION

We are born with needs. Our needs are met through action and our actions are determined based primarily on the beliefs we hold. When we come from the womb we already yearn to be touched and fed, we act upon our basic needs. This never changes in life. We are constantly acting, mostly unconsciously, to have our needs met. When we are young, our needs are pretty basic; we need food, shelter, a sense of belonging, to feel safe, and to feel good about ourselves—even though we may not understand what that means. When these needs go unmet, especially in children, our psyches shift and the potential for harm increases. Our souls are put behind the eight ball because the tools the soul needs to move forward are already thwarted.

When we grow older and make decisions for ourselves, we determine how our needs are met and to what degree (this does not negate external realities). Needs somehow turn into desires and often into greeds. Let's be honest for a moment; look around your house and see what things you honestly don't need. Our guess is there are a number. Don't get us wrong; it's not that we are against having things, but it's a matter of priorities, of perspective, of the big picture. We believe it is important to know about yourself. We all have wants, desires, dreams. The challenge is to understand their place in our lives.

Steve Rodgers is a musician; he loves music and his life would be very different without his guitar and piano. I could claim I have a need for them. On the other hand, if I moved somewhere and they were not there, I don't think I'd waste away. I might be sad, I might try to figure something else out, or use sticks to become a drummer on rocks or trees, but in the end, the true music I need is in my head. We'll say more about this later because sometimes, something like music that may or may not be a true need, can fill other people's needs. We are all given gifts, not for ourselves, but to build up others.

Actions come in primarily two forms; for us or for others. In the best of all situations both are done at the same time. When we teach in a school, many needs are being taken care of at the same time. We get paid to teach so we can put a roof over our head, food on the table, and other basic needs are met. We also belong to a group of teachers and to a school with a vision. We feel good about ourselves as we impart knowledge and skills to others. We continually push ourselves to learn more about the subject and in turn that information and the very process of learning helps us develop our own psyche and well-being if we are doing the learning correctly. Those at the other end are having their minds shaped, their ideas challenged and praised, their dreams and hopes bolstered, and the options they will have in the future to meet their needs, broadened. One of the fundamental goals of education is to increase the options for the learner, especially in public schooling through high school. Even when the information may never be used in their life, the process of learning that information forms their brain and impacts other data or ways of thinking and being that will help them in the future. Education simply for the sake of stuffing data into a brain is useless----temporally and spiritually.

Think of life without action. Is it even possible other than in death (and perhaps death leads us to more action not less)? Even when someone sits and meditates, totally clearing their mind of thought, they are acting. Action is like communication, remember that famous quote, " By not communicating, you are communicating." We only have a choice as to how we act, not whether we act. Your actions determine who and what you will become and that choice after the age of 10-13 is basically yours, with rare exceptions. We all love to play the blame game, but in truth you are responsible for who you are and what you do.

In chaos theory we learn about the butterfly effect (see the chapter on Chaos Theory on the website), how seemingly very small changes in a system can have immense consequences. We see how a butterfly flapping its wings in South America or Africa could potentially be the start of a hurricane. You never know what action you take may have significant consequences in your life or in the life of others. Teachers do not know how their teaching will affect their students. Good teachers consistently have students come back years later and tell them they were the ones that made a difference. What we do, think, and say influences us and others. The Bible tells us to bridle the tongue---with good reason.

Some people are called to be world-changers, their actions have obvious impact in a wide arena. Most of us are called to be world changers, one person, one small action at a time. The ripple effect is often not seen or noticed by us or by others. Our actions should not be determined by how much we get paid or by how much we get praised, but rather by how the action moves us forward, fits in with our belief system, and helps meet our needs and those of others.

The vast majority of our actions, of what we "do" are done unconsciously. We don't think about breathing, walking or eating, we simply do them. To be fully attentive and conscious of those would drive us nuts, we wouldn't have time for anything else. Fortunately, our minds and bodies are good at multi-tasking.

Many actions take place outside of contemplation, we don't think about what we are doing. If we did, there would be far fewer car wrecks because we'd be aware of our driving. In the big picture, many of the world's issues would diminish if we all acted out of contemplating our beliefs and needs. The less we do this, the more woes confront us. We have all been touched by people whose only contemplation is about them self and their desires and self-centered dreams. The ripple affect can be enormous.

Actions of our body and psyche are done to take care of our physical and emotional needs and desires. Many of our actions are done to create or maintain relationships that are important to us or that will lead to need fulfillment. Internally, we have a reason for doing what we do. We have learned that certain actions produce certain results or perhaps we have heard or read about why we should do something. Advertising is based on the premise that if they can convince you a certain action will produce a certain effect, you will buy it. This vitamin guarantees no colds, this car will make you young, this diet guarantees you will lose weight---the list is almost infinite. If we take the time to actually sit down and think about it, we know virtually all advertising is false, or at least makes false claims. And yet we buy the products, if we didn't there wouldn't be advertising, they pay money to advertise because it works. All this is to simply say actions based on some thought of our beliefs and needs will benefit us more than actions based on impulse.

Our souls are very active as well. They are constantly engaged in trying to build and maintain a relationship with the transcendent. As we have seen, the soul has needs and must act in order to fulfill those needs. The soul acts in a few key ways. The first is to calm the temporal self; to quiet the mind and body in order to sense and hear the transcendent. This becomes all the more complicated because of how the soul and the rest of our beings are connected. The soul uses the tools of the body and brain to act.

Another way the soul acts is by the use of connections. We talk more about this in the chapter on Connections. Suffice to say here as we have before that we are all connected, that in the grand scheme of things, present and past are one and we have the potential to access it all. This is after all what we believe about God isn't it? That God stands outside of time and knows all? If God knows all and we have access to God, then potentially we have access to everything. Jung talked of this in his work on the Collective Unconscious. This is the work of the soul. This work is accomplished through reflection, meditation, dream work, and other means. All of this work is done through a conscious effort in a certain direction. When the soul acts in accord with the psyche the actions are more beneficial to all.

Beliefs can be dangerous. We have seen many circumstances where belief systems drove individuals and cultures to do bad and evil things. Nazi Germany, tribalism in Africa, cults, slavery, racism, and sexism are all based on belief systems that led and continue to lead to catastrophic actions. Individuals and cultures did not stand up and work through the contemplative stage. Wars to some degree exist because belief systems collide and the action of war is seen as the only way to resolve the problem. Muslim extremists have a belief system that leads them to murder innocent people. Most of the world does not agree with those beliefs, but most of the world is unwilling to do anything about it.

So we have needs that are met through contemplating our beliefs and acting upon the answers we find. As human beings we are created as feeling beings, emotions are at the root of everything and we ignore or avoid them at our peril and to the peril of our souls. Every action we take elicits an emotion.

FEELINGS

There are few absolutes in life and feelings are no different. All of us are unique. We see the world differently and we feel different things at different times and at different levels. Most of us however push emotions down within us. This takes effort, even though it may not be at a conscious level. We do suspect that most readers can think of a time you actually put effort into not emoting. You held your anger or frustration in, you didn't jump up and down in joy and excitement as you might have wanted to. There is nothing wrong with this, we are not meant to just emote all over the place all the time. But we do need to be aware of what is happening within us emotionally and to pay attention. Emotions are incredibly important signals as to what is going on in our bodies, minds, and souls.

Think of a world without emotion, we don't personally find it a pleasant thought. Perhaps hell is a place with lack of feelings. Think of a relationship (of any kind) without any feeling---can you honestly say there is a relationship? Most of us would say the deeper the relationship, the deeper and broader the emotions. It makes sense, doesn't it?

There is a tendency to think of only a few emotions. I am happy, sad, or mad. There are a wide degree of emotions. Go on the web and look up lists of emotions, you will find many you probably haven't thought about but have felt.

Our emotions on one level are kind of like a TV set with rabbit ears (our apologies to those who may not know what those are). We move the rabbit ears to tune into a station, slowly but surely the picture gets clearer and clearer. When we attune to our emotions, our lives start to fit into place, we gain perspective, and have a deeper understanding of who we are and why we do what we do.

Whenever we act, we emote. The emotion may not be a significant seismic event, perhaps a mere blip on the screen. When you bite into a sandwich, somewhere you are feeling "mmmmmmmmm this is good" or "ahhhhhh another tuna sandwich again….". When we walk down the street we may feel wonder at the world about us, we may have fear or concern about our safety or belongings, or we may be thinking about something completely different which in itself has emotion. They are ever present, we just ignore them most of the time.

Certain cultures, generations, and individuals are raised to be overly emotive or to not be emotive at all. The central key is to at least be aware of what is going on in you, whether it comes out or not. Expressing emotions is important but not as critical as knowing what they are.

The challenge is to use our emotions to our benefit. Our feelings act as a guide to the process of becoming fully human. Guilt, shame, embarrassment, success, achievement, and tension all come with emotions. We say we feel guilty, but guilt really isn't a feeling. There are a wide variety of feelings associated with guilt. (Go to that list and see what feelings you have when you feel guilty). They point us to what we are guilty of and raise choices within us. When we avoid our feelings, we avoid using a key resource that is trying to help us move forward in our lives. Remember, there is a difference between being aware of your feelings and spewing them all over the planet.

As you have probably seen already, all of these aspects of life are intertwined. What we feel is some way determined by what we believe and how we think about those beliefs, how we act, and even what we need. We are the totality of all of these. Feelings are a barometer of how the process is moving, when roadblocks arise, and what is taking place within our relationships.

We all have ways of determining if we are getting to where we want to get. Fundraisers sometimes use the thermometer, the temperature rising the closer they get to the goal. Businesses set goals on a variety of levels and assess achievement by how close they get to the goal. The challenge is to find the right goal; not too high or too low.

We have ways of assessing relationships. How often do I want to be with that person? Am I willing to go to a deeper level of commitment, and of course, do I feel good when I am with that person? Feelings are perhaps the best method of finding out where we are in a relationship. If we are not in touch with those emotions we forfeit one of the strongest tools we have to build relationships.

The soul is no different. Our souls feel. The feelings are filtered through our physical bodies and thus verbally are the same. Read the mystics and you will see the feelings they describe are ultimately indescribable, there is a loss of words and even of metaphor for the experience of feeling the emotions of God and of that relationship. One of the ways we know we are in touch with our souls is there is a loss of words, the experience simply "is." Our souls are outside the parameters of the rational. We can't think our way to spiritual maturity, in the end, we must feel our way.

Paul talks about a peace that passes all understanding (Phil 4:7), again, soul talk. Read Job if you want to see some emotion of the soul. Read chapters 16-21 of John through the lens of the emotion of the soul. Read the Song of Solomon to see the depth of God's love and the emotion behind it.

It is fascinating to see that humanity has taken thousands of years to understand the importance and place of emotion in our lives and yet even there how often do you hear or read about emotion as being an imperative aspect of our soul's development?

When we do pay heed to our feelings, we find they take us to a deeper place. We should not cling to them, but feel, listen, and watch them. Our feelings will take us to our deeper needs in a natural process of integration. Our emotions can lift us up and humble us, express our righteous anger and our deepest shame. They are part of who and what we are.

Be aware of these five things in your life. Look at them in relation to the five traits of the soul. When you feel you are stuck somewhere ask yourself in which area you are stuck. Have you misplaced a need with a desire? Are your beliefs in conflict with your actions? What questions aren't you asking and who else are you involving or avoiding in the process of seeking discernment? What are you doing or are you simply not doing? What are your emotions telling you about how you are acting and being acted upon? These aspects can apply to all corners of your life and spiritual journey.

ACTIVITIES FOR SOUL GROWTH

Below is a list of activities you can do to move yourself to the center. As you look down the list see which ones you are comfortable doing. Any and all of these are good for you and for your soul. The ones you are most comfortable doing are probably not the ones you need to be focusing on at this time in your life. Comfort can mean complacency. We all find comfort levels in our lives. If we are not in balance then we need to counterbalance our imbalance. Often times the things we are most uncomfortable doing are the things we should find the discipline to do. Obviously we mean this in a creative way using the list below as one of your resources. We would enjoy hearing from you as to other tools or activities you use to deepen your own spiritual life and to find balance.

Our suggestion is to look at each trait and focus on the end of the spectrum where you aren't. If you are on the Supernal end, focus on the Immanent end and visa versa.

Some of the activities will be broken down by trait, others will be more general. Few give detailed descriptions of exactly what to do. It is our hope that this will get you thinking and then you can do some more research on the internet, books, friends, pastors, or workshops to fill in the details.

READING

SUPERNAL (S)---Science, environmental, psychology----The person on this end of the spectrum tends to avoid learning about the world. If God created the world then God can and is found in Science. Look at the annotated bibliography in the Chaos Theory and the Soul section (found on the website for this edition of the book). Over time on the website you will find lots of suggestions. By reading more scientifically oriented material, this type will be pulled more toward understanding the world God created in a much deeper way. Read the Bible, but read it looking at how Jesus meets the world on its terms and how he meets the needs of those he comes into contact with. Interestingly enough, it is no surprise that for many of us, the more we learn about the complexity of the world, the more we come to see God in it. We stand in awe of the created order.

IMMANENT (I)--- At this end of the continuum people rarely read poetry, literature, or books on spirituality. It doesn't matter where one starts, just start. C.S.Lewis, Richard Foster, Philip Yancy, and Thomas Merton are good authors. Read biographies of the mystics and then some of their writings. You may find them difficult at first, but they will feed that side of your soul that is currently lacking. Ask others what their favorite spiritual books are. It's not so much about how much you read, but about what you are reading and what you are doing with what you read. As you read the Bible, listen to what Jesus and God are telling people and the world, what is the message behind simply meeting their needs or is there one? Was Jesus trying to make a point when he fed the 5000 or was he just feeding? Our reading gives us wisdom that we don't have. It is a sharing of the greater community with and for us. The point is not to just get through a book as quickly as possible but to see how much you can get out of it. Underline, make notes, read it with someone else or with a group and bounce ideas off each other.

SACRED (A)—The Sacred type finds them self in everything because their identity comes from the transcendent where all things are both unique and interconnected. Learning to view them self through the lens of the world will help give breadth to their identity as well as a deeper sense of empathy. Biographies are great for this type, even spiritual ones. We can learn about how to view ourselves in different ways by seeing how others view them self. Just about all non-fiction books can be helpful because they speak from a language that attunes to the world. The goal here is to find literature that moves us from solely getting our ideas about who and what we are as spiritual beings from ourselves and our connection to the transcendent.

TERRENE (T)—Just about anything spiritually oriented is beneficial to the Terrene type. Their identity is grounded in the world's perception of the transcendent. They need to unlock their own view of them self and attach to how God perceives them—not just intellectually but at the level of the heart. Poetry is a great way to move to the center. At first it may seem very awkward and perhaps uninteresting. As with all things, give it time. Try different poets. Rumi is a fantastic spiritual poet. We also encourage the readings of other religious traditions. Sufism and Buddhism speak well to self-discovery.

MYSTICAL (M)—Books about relationships are good, especially about deepening them. Scott Peck's book **The Road Less Travelled** (Touchstone, 1978) is a wonderful classic in this area. Just about any good fiction book that deals with relationships (are there any that don't?) are good. Fiction impacts certain areas of our brain and can introduce us to a wide variety of relationships and what they can look like. The Mystical type tends to have a good relationship with God, but that is their focus. We are created to be in relationship with others---deep and meaningful relationships. Just reading newspapers that engage your spirit with the world can be very helpful. It may be frustrating, but the Mystical type needs to open them self to the realities that surround them on every side and not hide.

TEMPORAL (E)—The Temporal type needs to develop relationships on the spiritual end of things. They need to find God in deep and meaningful ways, understand the Collaborative Unconscious and how it works through their dreams and soul, and find ways of engaging the souls of others in relationships. There are millions of books and articles about building a relationship with God. Our section in the bibliography on dream work would also be a good thing to look at. Books on the Jesus Prayer or Centering Prayer also help deepen the relationship with God and help us connect to everything on a deeper plane. This is true for meditation as well.

INSPIRATION (N)—Creativity is a difficult one to "learn" about through reading. In fact, in the long run, change comes through action, not just reading or thinking. There are lots of books that give ways to engage the creative process in our lives. Many of these have to do with art or writing, but not all. Depending on how we view life, everything is an act of creativity. The Inspiration type can learn to view creativity and imagination outside them self by reading about Astronomy, Biology,

Architecture, Cooking, or a myriad of other disciplines. The idea is to see how creative the world is and where that creativity comes from. What is the creative process?

REASON (R)—The rational person needs to read about intuition and the internal creative process. Aesthetics is a good topic for them because it discusses creativity in a rational way while pulling people to see things in a different way. For the R, poetry is again a good way to be pulled toward the intuitive. There are books solely on developing your intuition. Remember, we are not talking about just social-psychological intuition, but about spiritual intuition, learning to be sensitive to the voice of God and the Collaborative Unconscious in our creativity.

IDEALIST (D)—The Idealist feels the pull of God to act in the world in certain ways. They are not concerned about what the world thinks. The needs of the world are secondary. This type needs to connect with the world with their purpose. God is about balance. God knows the world needs to be in relationship with Him, but also that the world has needs that need to be met---can be met if we act according to the principles that are an innate part of our soul. The D needs to get out and act in the world for the world. It's important for them to be part of a larger purpose. Find an issue that moves you and then read about it, do research. Either find a group to work with around that issue or create one. Your reading should fill you with a drive and desire that is coupled with your internal pull of God to make a difference in the world. Educate yourself on the realities of world hunger, global warming, what is happening to the water supply and the impact of the changing environment.

PRAGMATIST (P)—This type needs to sit and listen to the voice of God as to what they should be doing. Meditation and books on forms of prayer focused on listening are good places to start. Finding spiritual purpose behind what they do is the key. Mother Teresa found meaning in helping the poor, she gave them food and shelter----as well as hope, comfort, and meaning. The book by Rick Warren, **A Purpose Driven Life** (Inspirio, 2003), is a good book about working on both sides of the spectrum but especially about finding this internal purpose.

JOURNAL WRITING

Journal writing is one of those concepts that everyone should do, but few of us actually follow through with. There are many ways of writing a journal and we won't go into detail here. There are many books on the subject and loads of ideas on the internet. The key to journal writing (as well as most activities listed) is discipline. Any amount of journaling is good, but consistent, persistent journaling pays off significantly higher rewards. We all know that if you focus on building a new habit 15 minutes every few days it's not as effective as 15 minutes once or twice a day. Your brain and soul will build the habit of writing. They will get used to the fact of you sitting down with a computer or pen and paper and writing. It will start to trigger things in them automatically. Journal writing in this context needs to be spiritually oriented no matter what soul type you are. For us, this style of journaling is to seek balance. We should do some writing in a way that makes us comfortable and we should also struggle to write in a way that is not as comfortable. Some people are good at just sitting down and writing, others need questions. There are hundreds of questions sprinkled throughout the book that would be good topics to think about and write on.

SUPERNAL (S)—This type should make themselves write as if they were an Immanent type. Try to see the world as it is, not as you want it to be. Write about what you see and feel in the world. Can you identify with any of the pain of the world? Is what you are doing and what is being done to you keeping you from going deeper? What are your creative outlets? What do you feel your purpose is in life for God right now?

IMMANENT (I)-- This type tends to struggle when writing about the interior life. They are more diary formatted. They are best served at the beginning by finding a list of "spiritual" questions to write about each day. The practice is the same no matter what trait or type you are, it's what you write about and the questions you answer that are different. **Spiritual Journaling** by Richard Peace (1995, Richard Peace) is a good book as is **Adventure Inward** by Morton Kelsey (1980, Morton Kelsey). The challenge for the I is to get started, to build the habit and the discipline. Sometimes getting together with others for an accountability factor is a good thing. The focus for the Immanent should be on spiritual things, not on their day to day living other than pushing them self to see the spiritual in the mundane. Once we accept the fact that part of life is indeed spiritual it opens us up to new perceptions of ourselves and the world around us. Write about it!! Where do you see the spiritual around you? How do you see yourself as a spiritual being? How is the soul in your relating to the soul of the world and in others?

SACRED (A)-- Journal writing can be used for anything, it's a remarkably useful tool for those who build the discipline. It is however perhaps most effective in self-discovering our self-identity. We write through our lens and we can point that lens at whatever we want. At the core of Mark's Gospel is Jesus's question: "Who do you say I am?" He knows his own identity and has been sharing it with the disciples throughout the Gospel. Now he wants to know what they think. Part of knowing who God is rests in knowing ourselves. The more you know about yourself the more you will discover about God and the transcendent world. Who are you as a spiritual being? What impact does that identity have on the world? Who is that person in relationship to God? Describe yourself as a unique being but also be looking at how you share that identity with others. How do you present yourself to the world? Would others describe you as a spiritual person? Why not?

TERRENE (T)—The T type finds their spiritual identity from what the world tells them. Learning to distinguish what they get from the world and what they get from inside and from the transcendent is very helpful. Where do ideas come from? Who are you as a spiritual person? How do you still yourself and listen to the voice of God? What are your dreams telling you? What is it that makes you unique, special, and sacred? How does that feel? What keeps that spiritual identity from coming out?

MYSTICAL (M)—Journals are great places to keep track of our connections and relationships. We can watch them change over time. The M type will probably have lots to write about with regard to their relationship with God and with their dreams. More attention needs to be spent on how that relationship impacts other relationships and how they

275

act in the world. How do they perceive their interactions? How does what they do impact the world and other people? What is the basis for those interactions? How deep are they and what keeps them from going deeper? How are you helping the needs of others?

TEMPORAL (E)—This type tends to write about what they do but not how they feel. They miss those more internal connections that are equally important. God wants us to relate soul to soul, not just deed to deed. What keeps you from doing that? Where is the fear? Think about what God wants out of a relationship with you and what might be blocking that. Write about how you see God being active not only in the world, but within you.

INSPIRATION (N)—What do we think about in our "off" time? What are our daydreams? Where do our thoughts and ideas come from? How were you creative today? What role does God play in our creativity? These tend to be the types of things we should write about when working on our N trait. The N is highly spiritually intuitive, They make connections and are a sponge for the creativity of God and the Collaborative Unconscious. Sometimes they ignore the brain God gave them. We have brains for a reason. Use them to think about creativity in the world. How we can inspire others, how we can help others to discover their own creativity and how we can learn from others? What do others bring to our lives in a creative way?

REASON (R)—The more rational spiritual type needs to be challenging their mind and listening to their heart and soul. Journals can actually be a trap for them because they tend to write in linear and logical fashion. They want to make sense of it all and when they find written words to back up what they feel and believe it becomes more solidified. Pushing them self to write in a more creative and intuitive fashion can be hard. One way is to try to view the world through God's eyes, but again there is a temptation to see God as a purely rational being. Writing about things that don't make rational sense is a good way to go for this type. Why would an infinite God hold you as sacred? Why does God care? Look around at creation and find things that don't seem to make sense.

Why the vast diversity of flowers, animals, humans? Can God be creative without being rational in Her creativity?

IDEALIST (D)—Journal writing about why we are here is a great ongoing topic. The D should write about how they can take the voice within and put it into actions that make a difference in people's lives. "God calls me to X, what will that look like in the world?" Why does God call me to that? What is going on inside of me as I make the will of God a reality in my life? What do I feel, how does it affect how I see the world? The D gets their purpose more from their interior and spiritual lives. A journal can be a good way of grounding that purpose to their worldly lives.

PRAGMATIST (P)—The pragmatist is very action oriented. Their journal writing, left to their own devices, will read more like a diary of events. They need to ask a very simple question: Why am I doing what I am doing? Is this what God wants me to do? Why? How do I know? The goal for the P is to find a way of finding purpose internally, through God rather than just through actions and what they world tells you. Combining journal writing and meditation or contemplation can be a powerful combination for this type as they listen to their soul as it reveals its purpose to the rest of you.

TAKE A CLASS

There are lots of fabulous classes in the world. We would encourage you to find one through a community college, a church, temple or a wide variety of other options. Contact with others and learning other points of view is always helpful in making us think and feel. Classes in spirituality or meditation are common and excellent ways of balancing our own journeys. You can also take some on line classes. While the learning may be similar, the experience will not be as powerful, but for some this is the only way they can take a class and it's fine.

SUPERNAL (S)-- The Supernal would be best served taking courses that engage them with the world around them, expose them to what the world is into. Computers, science, psychology, and history are but a few.

In the best of all worlds, take a course that will give you a skill you can use to help others. Perhaps a computer class and help do some computer work or run a website for a group or your church or temple. Take an astronomy class and run a night time workshop in your neighborhood. You can both watch the stars and talk about God. Become a master gardener and share your knowledge and your spirituality as you help others.

IMMANENT (I)-- The Immanent type is best served by taking courses that feed that spiritual side of their being. Perhaps a class on meditation, prayer, or yoga. Comparative religion courses are a great way to expose ourselves to other traditions. The more experiential the course the better for this type. Classes on intuition and dreams are also a good fit.

SACRED (A)—Sociology, psychology, anthropology, comparative religion are all great because they help the A type see the wide variety of experiences people have and how identities are shaped by the world as well as by God.

TERRENE (T) – Most schools will not offer courses that will be helpful here because they are all world based. Find centers of spirituality or classes at religious institutions for this work. Anything that helps develop a relationship between you and the transcendent will be helpful. Meditation courses are very good. A class on spiritual journaling would be great. Going on retreats is perhaps the best way to open this part of your identity to the transcendent.

MYSTICAL (M)—Courses that look at how people relate and help you enter into the lives of those who struggle are best. Psychology, history and sociology are good ones to focus on. Smaller classes within interaction is also a good way to go. The M tends towards not talking a lot and needs to get out of their shell and hear what others are telling them and share their own valuable insights.

TEMPORAL (E)—Unfortunately, this can't be taught in a class other than perhaps a group within a spiritual center or institution. Learning to build relationships with God and the Collaborative Unconscious can't be taught, it has to be experienced. Certainly a good well rounded course on dream work would be useful and interesting. Short term intense retreats are also a great way to catapult you towards the center.

INSPIRATION (N)—Any artistically oriented course would be good here. Learning to pull out of our souls what is creative and do something with it or seeing how others do it is helpful. Even art history classes are good as long as you push the teacher to talk about the spiritual dimension of art. If they deny that, find a new class. Any class that introduces you to creativity in the world are good. Architecture, science and yes, even math, are wonderfully creative things to study.

REASON (R)--- You can't earn or reason your way to heaven or into a relationship with God or the transcendent. At some point you have to let go and just experience. Classes feed this person's way of existing. The only classes that are good for the R are those that are experiential—classes that do art, do yoga, do meditation. There are lots of them around but this type, especially if they are big readers or workshop goers need to move in a different direction for a while.

IDEALIST (D)—We can find God's purpose in life just about anywhere if we focus the lenses of our minds, souls, and hearts on it. The D is so internally driven with regar

d to purpose they often miss how God has, is, and will work in and with the world. The D needs to learn about things outside them self and understand how the world shapes how needs are met and how the spirit is fed. Becoming involved with community service that meets the basic needs of humanity is a wonderful way to meld the purposes of God with the needs of the world.

PRAGMATIST (P) --- The P feels they are constantly doing God's will by the degree of their activity. They find their purpose through their actions. They lean towards the theology of works, that at some level we earn our relationship with God. If they also happen to be an R they know this doesn't work. This type is well served by learning about the needs of others on more spiritual levels. Comparative religion courses,

279

psychology courses, and anthropology courses are good. Psychology may be tricky because the tendency is to think they are discussing spirituality when they aren't—but they are connected. Meditation courses are perhaps the best thing for this type because it slows them down and makes them look inward and connect on a different level.

DREAM WORK

As we said throughout the book, we believe dreams are very important to our well-being and we ignore and avoid them at our peril. We have listed several books in the bibliography on the website and have a large section on dreams in the book. Dreams are important no matter where you are on the continuum of any of the traits. We will include here a repeat of a process to work with dreams based on the work of Robert Johnson. Steve Bearden has tweeked Johnson's scenario.

In order to work with dreams you need to remember them first. We know for a fact everyone dreams, they are an important part of sleep, REM (rapid eye movement) sleep. Without this type of sleep the brain quickly falls into dis-ease. Many people will claim they do not dream when the reality is they do, they just don't remember them.

Why do we not remember dreams? There can be many reasons. One could be that our brain chemistry is not facilitating the bridge between the part that creates the dream and the part that processes it or remembers it, they are different parts of the brain. Taking some vitamin B complex has helped some people with this. Another obstacle could be that a person is such a disbeliever in dreams their brain is conditioned to not remember. We don't see things in life we don't want to see, we build mechanisms to protect us. The world of dreams is no different; if we don't want to remember, then most of the time we won't. A third reason why we may not remember dreams is because we don't want to deal with the issues they bring up. Our brains are probably not great filters of types of dreams. They can't filter out the God dreams from the basic memory or event dreams from those that come straight from the unconscious. We either remember dreams or we don't. Some people remember some dreams but not all. No one remembers all dreams which makes the study of them all the more interesting. Why do we remember the ones we do and not others? What are we missing?

If you don't remember your dreams but want to there are a few things you can do. First is to think about taking some vitamin B complex. Second is to ask God to help you remember them. Third is to tell yourself before you go to sleep that you will remember, be open to remembering, no matter what. If you don't at first, be patient. Fourth is to find someone that is open to dream work or does it already and tell them you are hoping to start remembering your dreams. Engaging others in dream work can be very powerful, both in remembering and in processing.

As we have said before, it's important that you not let others tell you what your dreams mean, you are the person with the knowledge to interpret them for your life. Images in dreams mean different things to different people. There is no one size fits all in dream work. Certainly there are patterns and over all a given image may have something to do with a given theme, but not always. Having someone to share your dreams with and to help you process can be very beneficial. Finding someone who has done dream work and helped others is the best. We all fall prey to delusion at times and another voice in the process can ask questions as a check and balance to our own interpretation.

All this being said, let's assume you have a series of dreams written down (always write them down, your memory of them will change over time). To refresh your memory return to page 240 for the process.

SUPERNAL (S)—If anything, the S will have to struggle to not find spiritual meaning in all dreams. They may get more easily frustrated when times come when they don't remember their dreams. They have little problem accepting that some are from the transcendent realm. Dream work can be a very powerful tool for understanding them self to the S. The S needs to make room for the unconscious which dreams are attempting to illuminate for the benefit of your conscious self. Doing dreamwork with someone who knows about it can pull this type more fully into balance.

IMMANENT (I)-- The Immanent type will struggle with this. It may take them awhile to remember their dreams and then to believe there is spiritual meaning that they comes from God. We encourage you to "act as if" it were true and see what you learn. Challenge your internal doubts and fears, God may surprise you—just as he did Peter and others.

SACRED (A)—Much of dreaming is about self-identity, trying to show us who and what we are; spiritually, psychologically, and in all other ways. When the A type accepts the fact that dreams are a key way God communicates with us, they relax into their dreams and learn from them. Because they are experiential in their spiritual lives dreams can be a struggle for they are not experiential in the same way. They do enjoy ecstatic mystical dreams because they touch a deep internal nerve of experience. Like the disciples at the Transfiguration, they want to live in the experience of the dream rather than the meaning behind it. Dreams exist for our benefit, use them. Understand that part of you is spiritual and part is found in the unconscious part of your physical brain---both are imperative for a balanced life as we were created to be. This type needs to expose them self more fully to the human side of dreaming.

TERRENE (T)—The T will hesitate when looking at dreams. Because most of the imagery comes from their lives they will view them as psychological or meaningless, what we call memory dreams. We would encourage the T's to read John Sanford (**Dreams: God's Forgotten Language,** 1989, Harper Collins), Morton Kelsey or others who give good reasons to pay attention to your dreams. Another way for this type to look at dreams is for them to ask the question; What if they are to be listened to? What if God is trying to tell us something? What if our unconscious is trying to help us grow? Think of what you are missing. Give them a chance to speak to you.

MYSTICAL (M)—Dreams are almost a passion to many M's. Because they are one of the most obvious ways the transcendent manifests itself in our lives, they thrive with dreams. Look at the mystics, all heavy dreamers. Like the A type, they tend to miss some of the meaning within dreams. Those heavily on the M side of the continuum will probably be getting dreams pulling them to the center and they misinterpret the meaning—one of the reasons we encourage people to do dream work either in a group or with someone who has a solid understanding of dreams and their spiritual significance. Fortunately for most M's, the issue is not dreaming or believing they are from God, but discerning which are from God and what their meaning is. Many dreams are about relationships, the core of the ME trait. The M should look and see what their dreams are telling them about both their spiritual and their physical relationships and how the spiritual is trying to be manifest within them.

TEMPORAL (E)—Because the E finds God in the world, they will view dreams as a connection between the spiritual, the unconscious and the world. The key issue for the E is relationships and they view them through what the world tells them about them self and about the world around them. They are more likely to consult a book or other people about what their dreams mean than to look within. Dreams are deeply personal and giving power to someone else to tell you what something means can be dangerous. This becomes increasingly problematic the more symbolic dreams get and the less pragmatic and realistic.

INSPIRATION (N)—This is the type that is most adept at dreaming and using dreams to their benefit. They are intuitive types that find internal answers and understand the creative and imaginative nature of the divine. They understand that this is part of their nature and are more than happy to dive in. They need to be cautious that they don't jump to early conclusions about the meaning of any given dream. The transcendent is very patient and give recurring dreams or the same patterns with a common theme. Learning to sit with a dream(s) is important for this type to learn. Also accepting the fact that they may be wrong in their interpretation is a growing edge.

REASON (R)—Dreams are a mental exercise for this type. They want to make sense of what God or their unconscious is trying to tell them—not always a bad thing. The problem with this strategy is that if everything made sense, we wouldn't need dreams. There are obstacles that keep us from understanding the logic of God and the transcendent. Dreams are a way God circumvents our brains and the roadblocks we put in the way of becoming more whole. Intellectual pursuit of dreams is a good thing as long as there is a balance with a more intuitive stance and an understanding that dreams are not based on rationality.

IDEALIST (D)— The Idealist will find purpose in the dreams. They look at the Bible and see that dreams come with a purpose for the one doing the dreaming and at times for the greater community. The D will look at what a dream is calling them too. Like other types they may miss the mark because they predispose them self to what they want to find. At times they will indeed find what they want, at other times God calls us to ideas and actions outside the range of what we want or expect. Spiritual balance is about being open to the intensity of the transcendent and its power. The beauty of dreams of any kind is that they are trying to guide us to wholeness if we will listen.

PRAGMATIST (P)—The Pragmatist wants to know what to do with their life. They find the answer to that question in their dreams. For them it's about action in the world. Sometimes that is precisely what a dream is---often they are not. God calls us to act in and for the world but God also calls us to other purposes that are more internal and look at the larger picture and the more eternal one. Dreams convey ideas that are often transcendent in nature. Trying to bring them into a practical realm doesn't work well.

ACCOUNTABILITY

Like many activities this one goes for all. We all need to be accountable. Yes, it's great to be accountable to God, but we all avoid God pretty easily. Being accountable for who we are and what we do with others is remarkably effective. It adds a little extra pressure to our discipline. The idea is not to be made to feel guilty when we fail (which we will do from time to time), but to know we aren't in this alone, we have support. We won't need the other(s) to tell us we blew it, we will do a great job of that internally. A few tips on accountability:

1. Find someone or a group that you trust and you know will follow up. Amazing how when we succeed we want to tell the world and when we fail we don't want to tell anyone.

2. Two to four people is great if you are serious about following through on what you want to be held accountable for. Group accountability classes are great.

3. Choose goals that are well within your reach. You can always make them harder. It's important to be successful. Better to shoot to low and be successful than too high and fail. But do push yourself and make it meaningful. Meditating 5 minutes a day is not really meaningful—10 minutes a day would be a good start if you've never done it before.

4. Make sure your goals are measureable.

5. Don't lie to yourself or others. If you succeed you succeed, if you fail you fail. You don't have to prove yourself to anyone, you are trying to grow and admitting failure is part of the process. Perhaps your goal was too high to start with?

6. Maintain a goal at least for a short period of time before adding to it. Building habits takes time, the first time you are successful does not mean it has become habituated within you. If you are learning to meditate, try 10 minutes a day for a week or two, then up to 15. Slow steady growth.

7. Don't have too many things going at once. It's better to work on 1-3 goals well than 5-10 not so well.

8. Ask God to help you.

SUPERNAL (S)—This type needs to be accountable for engaging the world with what they feel inside. Think of it this way; how fair is it to hold the vast treasure you do and not share it? Part of the process is understanding that God wants to help fill many needs, not just spiritual ones and that you are a significant part of the solution. We are called to act out our faith and love. The S will have a hard time being accountable because they feel they are accountable only to them self and to God and that that is enough. It isn't. There is meaning even in the act of accountability. What does it mean that God wants you to be accountable to others?

IMMANENT (I)-- The goals of the Immanent type should be focusing on being accountable for exposure to the spiritual side of life, sharing what is happening inside of your soul, and being present to God and the transcendent through meditation, dream work, and group work. Finding someone or a group to be accountable to that is on the spiritual journey will be an asset as well as a big help. A spiritual director is a must in the long run.

SACRED (A)—Our accountability is tied to how we see ourselves, our identities. The Sacred type gets this from within so we shouldn't be surprised that having someone else hold us accountable is difficult. They believe they know who they are and in the spiritual dimension they may. But we are creatures of the earth, bound to one another in creation. We need to extend our sacred nature to the world and in so doing learn to see ourselves in that vast constellation we call humanity. How can you be held accountable for who and what you are in relation to the world?

TERRENE (T) -- As creations of God and with whom God desires to be in relationship, it's necessary that we are held accountable for building that relationship. God's consequence of our actions is the relationship itself. We either are or are not in relationship with the transcendent—direct relationship. The Terrene type prefers having a relationship with God in and through the world. The relationship is based on doing rather than being. We need to learn to build that direct relationship. Finding someone or a group that is committed to that process and/or understands it is beneficial. Deepening one's prayer and meditation life and learning to listen rather than to speak is another.

MYSTICAL (M)—We are put on this planet to be in relationship, not to be hermits (except in rare circumstances). This connectivity is the breeding ground of positive accountability and depth. We learn how to rely on each other, to exhort and to encourage one another. The M tends to like spiritual relationships, but misses that there are some basic things people need out of relationships. Learning to attune to the needs of others is important and this type may need help both seeing that and changing their lifestyle so they can be more fully present to others.

TEMPORAL (E)—While we want significant relationships in our lives we also need to be in connection with the transcendent, with the one who tries to guide all things. What does a relationship, one on one, with the transcendent even look like? How do you get there? How do you deepen what you have? All of the answers to those questions take action and we need to be accountable for those actions if we want to succeed. You can start by describing what a direct relationship with the transcendent would look like. Do you believe you can have that while in your temporal body?

INSPIRATION (N)---- All of us are created to be creative creatures. Finding those sources of creativity can be tricky and many are shy about showing their creativity or they deny they even have any. To do so is to deny the creative power of God. The Inspiration type finds a wellspring within but struggles to either manifest it or to seek the creativity of the world. Become accountable for both to someone else. Have them challenge you to use your creativity and to find how imagination is rampant in the world. How does this apply and impact the other traits?

REASON (R)—Sometimes we think too much and don't experience enough. Everyone is born with a well spring of creativity within. We attach to that by listening to our souls, by building a relationship with the divine. Our accountability should challenge us to move beyond our minds and put ourselves into the presence of the transcendent to experience. Powerful experiences can shift and transform the mind.

IDEALIST (D)—The Idealist feels the call of God, feels purpose in their lives, they struggle at times to make that call real. They love the idea but actually following through can be tricky. Accountability is perhaps most helpful for this type. It's like Paul who says he doesn't do what he knows he should and does those things he knows he shouldn't. It's important to share what we believe about our Call and then to make a plan with others to put it into action.

PRAGMATIST (P)—Those who have a very pragmatic nature need to look at where that pragmatism comes from. Being practical is fantastic, it's how we get things done in this world. But what is at the root of those actions? Why do we do what we do? What is the purpose and how is that purpose tied to the transcendent? If we don't feel internally a call from God, we need to find one because it is there waiting. Being accountable

287

for that process is critical for this type because they are so enmeshed in "doing" and feel the doing is the purpose. The best way to know is to see how the manifested reality of God is manifested in your actions. How are you making God present in a way those being affected by your actions know?

WORKING WITH A SPIRITUAL DIRECTOR

If you are truly serious about your spiritual life, a spiritual director is a given. Why? As we have mentioned many times, we are not on this journey alone. Think of it this way, if you are studying to be a surgeon, would you prefer learning merely from a book, from a friend, or from someone who has done surgery for a long time and is good at it? We hope the answer is obvious. So much more so when dealing with the most important part of our existence, our souls. You can and hopefully do share your spiritual life with others, but our relationship with the transcendent is unique. Not everyone is in touch with or knows how to foster that relationship. The exercise of spiritual direction is one of pushing us to deeper and deeper levels of freedom with God. It is not working through more world oriented problems, that is for counselors. Spiritual direction focuses a laser on your relationship with God and the transcendent, finds obstacles that get in your way of moving to the center of the five traits we have discussed. Does it have to be someone "trained?" No, but as is true in all fields, training comes in handy. In the best of all worlds, your spiritual director is not your "friend." Friends are great and are wonderful to have to talk about spiritual matters, but when two people become spiritual directors to each other, it changes the dynamic of the relationship and should be avoided if possible. Spiritual directors should be able to see where you are out of balance and work with you on finding that balance. Spiritual directors can hopefully help you with your dream work to some degree since (in our belief) many dreams are spiritual in nature. If after a few sessions you are a)not comfortable sharing with your director b) not feeling persuaded to do something in your spiritual life c) not feeling heard or understood d) disagreeing significantly on theological issues that are important to you or e) not feeling an internal shift in your life, try another one. If the director is offended by that, it's their problem, not yours. Good spiritual directors let go of their egos to serve your soul.

SUPERNAL (S)— The Supernal type will find this work easy. The challenge for the spiritual director will be to help you see that spirituality needs to manifest itself in the world. "They will know you are my disciples by the love you show one another." "They will know you by the fruits you bear." Actions speak louder than words. Our relationship with God is out of balance if there is not both faith and works. The Supernal type will enjoy the spiritual direction process, they are in search for meaning and thrive in the spiritual environment. The spiritual director can be caught in this because some don't understand the essence of balance, that God is found in the world as well as in the heavens. If we are seeking freedom then the S is trapped by a lack of ability to see God at work in and through people, making a difference in their lives on multiple levels, not just the spiritual one. How does the S find meaning in the world? Who do they listen to? What do they read to gain meaning?

IMMANENT (I)-- For the Immanent type, just having a spiritual director will be a leap of faith. They may not have a clue what to say. The spiritual director will see that and will help you start to build a language to talk about it as well as find ways of helping you have more experiences of God. For the Immanent type having a spiritual director may be a ways down the road, you can't do this all at once. Starting just sharing in a group or with a friend who you know is openly spiritual will be a great start. On the other hand, at times it is easier to show our spiritual shyness and work on it in the context of a confidential one on one relationship

SACRED (A)—Spiritual direction is a wonderful way to discover who we are, what is our identity and who are we becoming. Spiritual directors are not therapists, they don't (shouldn't) get into the psychological end of life, but focus their attention on the relationship with God and how that impacts the directees life in the world. The A type gets a significant part of their identity from within. They attune to them self and too God. This sounds fantastic—and is. But we are not alone on this planet. We engage with other spiritual beings and are called to be in relationship.

The director needs to highlight that and ask questions about how they think others see them as spiritual beings.

TERRENE (T)—This type finds their identity more externally, from what the world tells them about them self. They at times accept to quickly what others say without checking it against what they know about them self. Remember the Johari Square, there are things we know about ourselves others don't know and there are things others know about us that we don't see or understand, both are important for balance. This is true spiritually as well. Spiritual direction can help focus more attention on the direct experience of the self and how that self is in relation to God. Encouragement and accountability for journal writing and meditation should certainly be near the top of the list. Each of those will supply a mountain of material to work on.

MYSTICAL (M)—Spiritually, we need to see how we are connected to God, the Collaborative Unconscious, and to the world. The M is comfortable with the transcendent but not so much in the world. Discussing the connection with God is the way into this seeking of balance. What does it look like? Feel like? What does the connection do for us and to us? What are we not free to do? Augustine said, "Love God and do what you will." What keeps you from loving God fully? Doing what you will, fully? In those questions lie the connections to the world.

TEMPORAL (E)—The Temporal person loves their network in the world, they feed off it for many things, including their relationship with God. They have a tendency to not relate directly with God but in and through relationships with others and what they do in the world. Spiritual direction calls them to deepen their direct relationship with the transcendent. They will be encouraged to pray, study, meditate, and worship more. The very nature of relationship as it applies to the spiritual will need to be examined.

INSPIRATION (N) – The spiritual process is a creative one. The Creator wants to keep the creativity going, no more so than in our relationship with Her. Spiritual direction is a good place to see how we use the creative and imaginative energy we have within us, within our souls. The N is creatively intuitive but often lacks the motivation to make those internal ideas real. Direction is a good place to encourage that. Writing, drawing, sculpture, photography, and a myriad of other venues are good fodder for the N to manifest their internal sensibilities.

REASON (R)—The R likes to reason their way to creativity. They use what they see around them as a starting point and transform things into something new. The director should help them listen to the internal voice, to find the deep well of creativity that comes with having a relationship with the transcendent world. Meditation, journal writing, and joining with others as they talk about their own creativity are good areas for the R to use in growth. The R needs to feel free to let go and trust their intuition and imagination.

IDEALIST (D)—Purpose is a key idea in spiritual direction. What is it all about? Am I here for a reason? How do I know? What is keeping me from fulfilling my purpose? As we work through these questions with our director we begin to see lots of other things and layers. We see more clearly the obstacles that keep us from letting go and either more fully living in the world or in the presence of God. We start to distinguish between our purpose and God's purpose. The D sees that they have an idea of God's purpose for them, but see that it isn't coming to fruition and what stands in the way.

PRAGMATIST (P)—The P needs to slow down, the director can help them focus on the spiritual side of life and not get caught up in the "doing" of things all the time. Grace is an important topic for the P. The idea of purpose is not to earn points or to be busy, it's to listen to the Creator and do what the infinite asks of us. The P tends to be trapped on the works side of the works and faith debate. The D is trapped on the faith side, both are needed and reflect each other---balance. Spiritual direction is a lot about balance; being and doing, becoming, transforming.

COMMUNITY SERVICE

SUPERNAL (S)—The S may do community service but as they do it they are looking past the service to the spiritual meaning behind the service. How can I bring hope to this person? Why does God want me to clean up the beach in the long run? There is nothing wrong with this approach but we seek balance. We believe our souls need to understand that God wants this world to be a wonderful place, that we are to take care of what God has given us---to be good stewards. Our stewardship is to care for one another and the planet so we can speak to our actions to others through that understanding. This is a level of meaning that gets to the heart of what the needs of those we are serving are; the physical, emotional, and spiritual needs. For the S it's important to understand the difference before starting. This is not a natural way for them to perceive the service they do. The S tends to be detached from their service, they need to ground them self in the suffering of those they seek to bring hope to and to serve. Look at what blocks you from feeling the pain of others, of empathizing with them.

IMMANENT (I)—The I is normally very active within the community. They do this out of duty and out of a belief that works matter, that love must be an action, not just a thought. For the I it's not so much getting involved as thinking about what the involvement means for them other than just doing what is good and right. Where is God in the acting? What is God's purpose in the activity? How are you an ambassador for God in and through what you do and how does that bring a deeper sense of meaning to your life?

SACRED (A)—Because we are in the world because of God, part of our identity is found in and through the world. The A has no problem internally on a spiritual level knowing who they are, that they are sacred and come from God. They know that spiritually all souls are connected, are loved equally by the Creator and that we are called to serve the one's God loves. Their struggle is making that real. Deep truth and deep faith lead to deep convictions that lead to deep action. Community service is one of the best things for the A to do because it brings them into contact with those who struggle, especially with self-identity.

TERRENE (T)—The T finds them self in service, through loving God in the world and see God's actions in the world. The T needs to understand at a deep level that God is serving them in the world just as they are being served. Our identity comes both from within and without. We are molded in part by what we sense and learn from the world about spirituality but also from our direct experience of the transcendent internally. At some level then service becomes a devotion to our own self-identity which is slowly conforming to the will and ways and image of God.

MYSTICAL (M)—Being connected to the transcendent through our dreams and experiences is a marvelous thing. New horizons are opened and new senses experienced. The M sees and feels thing other's don't. God uses those connections to help us serve the world, she moves us in ways that are mysterious, creates serendipitous opportunities, coincidences are rampant, and building networks of hope in the world and for the world lure us at every corner. The M needs to grab hold of those things God puts in our path.

TEMPORAL (E)—The E is well networked on the earth but is unsure how to use those connections for the benefit of the eternal and transcendent. They listen to what the world tells them about its needs while tending to downplay the internal voice telling them what God needs for the world. They can be righteous, holy, just, and all other things wonderful, it is the reason for the connections that eludes them at times. Service needs to focus more on the eternal aspect of its usefulness even as they take care of the more temporal sides of life.

INSPIRATION (N)—Creativity and imagination can be found anywhere. Serving others is an amazing place to be creative. We are surrounded by the creativity of service. Many of us stand in awe at what people do. Small children raising millions of dollars to dig wells in Africa, even in their death. The seriously handicapped pushing their own physical limits to show what can be done, seniors sacrificing everything they have for those less fortunate are among millions of examples. Saints abound. Finding the creativity within and using it to serve others in very meaningful and practical ways is one of our calls. The N tends to lack the tools or the drive to make real what they dream. Push yourselves, set small goals and reach out to others with your ideas—reach out to those who know how to make creative ideas real. God's desire is for us to be successful. Move forward towards the final goal of perfection step by step.

REASON (R)—The R is filled with wonderful ideas of what to do and they are very active in doing them. At times they are too active, they get lost in the activity of being creative and lose sight of what it is all about. Why am I doing this? Who is it I am really serving? Why? How can I listen to my soul and find yet an even more creative way of doing this that brings the soul into the mix. How much service that you do directly involves the soul? It's not enough to think it will be impacted, our imagination yearns for us to use it to inspire the imagination of others.

IDEALIST (D)—The D listens to the will of God and feel they know it, even though they struggle to make it known in what they do. They find purpose inside, from the transcendent. They move to service through this spiritual sense of what they are called to do. To find balance they need to see that God wants, perhaps expects us, to serve the world in his name. We are to clothe, feed, visit, and heal the world in what we do, not just in what we think or pray. Meeting the world on their level is the key to the D finding balance in their lives.

PRAGMATIST (P)—In trying to serve the world as we are called to do, the P misses the more eternal point of what it is all about. There is a difference between serving people and serving God's children, God's beloved, God's most prized possession. Who is it we are called to serve? Who are they really? Just hungry people? Just the lonely? They are God's creations that for some reason have been separated from the deep and abiding love of God at times. And of course there are many times when those in deepest temporal need are the most spiritual. Wow. Who is serving whom? Can we allow those in need to serve us as we serve them? What a blessing.

PHYSICAL EXERCISE

Our bodies are perhaps the greatest example of God's creative power. You can't help but learn about the human body and not be in awe of its complexity. We are told that the body is the temple of God. Discover it and take care of it. The S sees the body as where the spirit lives, but it is much more than that. Our bodies are the vehicle God uses to help others. This is not to say God is limited by our bodies, obviously people with significant health issues do remarkable things. It does say we need to do what we can with and for our bodies. They are the vehicle in this life of our soul. There is a connection between our bodies and our souls. The S often fails to bear witness to that fact. Listen to your body. Find ways of exercising it within the parameters of your life. Yoga is a very good and spiritual way to help our bodies, to listen to them and to find that balance we seek. We can't really escape our bodies except in death, they are an integral part of who we are and for many provide a significant piece of our self-identity. They can also determine how we fulfill our purpose in life.

The vast majority of people get too little exercise for the temple of God. Exercise is the number one thing one can do for anxiety and depression. We think that because our souls are spiritual they don't need exercise and ultimately they don't. But our souls exist in our physical bodies and are directly tied to them. Our souls need bodies that are nourished to the degree possible. Some of us have ailments or handicaps that keep us from doing much exercise. The challenge here is to push yourself to go a bit further than you are at present. This is not a call to all be ironmen or women, but to do the best you can to take care of the house of your soul.

The reality may be that your body was created and purposed to simply be a home for your soul while on earth. We tend to think that the body is the priority and the soul secondary, perhaps it is the other way around?

Our bodies are the vehicles that connect us with the world that we are called to learn from and serve. Your senses do not exist without your body. Your soul needs the senses to process the spiritual.

GARDENING

What a wonderful way of literally grounding ourselves. Read about what is happening with your garden, dig deep and be in awe of the mystery of God in the earth. God uses photosynthesis and cellular structures to feed the earth. The intricate web of life is remarkable, learn about it in the midst of a potted plant or a garden. Share the wealth of your garden with others. Take time to let your senses attune to the world of your garden. Pay attention to the sights, smells, tastes, sounds, and touch sensations that surround you. Every second we are bombarded by God's creation and yet many of us block it out. Take time to focus on the little things, the intricacies of God's vast creation.

Some live in places where gardening is not possible. Have some indoor plants, rent space at a pea patch, convince your church or place of worship to have a garden, join a gardening club, help your neighbors with their garden, have some outdoor pots on your deck. There are lots of ways to get in touch with the earth in a physical way.

The idea here is to get beyond looking and get into contact with the earth on a more sensorial level. We are learning more and more about how the entire planet is interconnected, about how when we affect one part of the giant web we affect it all. All we have to do is look around and see the rise in cancer, autism, mental illness, addiction, and learning difficulties to know we are out of touch with our environments. Making those connections in small ways will help us find deeper meaning in our lives, help us understand who and what we are, boost our imaginations and give us a deeper sense of stewardship and purpose. Will having a potted plant solve the ills of the world? Of course not, but being connected to the world helps us gain perspective and more deeply grounds us to that which can help us as we cope with the struggles in our lives and in the world.

CRAFTS

Again, getting our hands engaged with more worldly things brings us more in tune with what God is doing in and through the world He created. We are given creative abilities from God. Perhaps this is one place you haven't tried your talent. Perhaps you feel you have no artistic or creative ability. Give it a try. Don't underestimate yourself or God's power. We are not after creating the next major piece of art here. We simply want to expose ourselves to how we can find meaning in and through what we and others create. Crafts often bring great joy to others—nothing wrong with that. Origami, shadow boxes, drawing, painting, models, holiday crafts, are but a few. The internet is filled with great craft ideas. Especially for the Supernal and the Mystical types, it's important to do this venture with others. While you are making them, have a conversation about what this all means to them. Why do crafts? What does it do for me and for others?

What would happen at your place of worship or with a group of friends if you put in the bulletin, "Spiritual Crafts Group---Come and make crafts to deepen your spirituality, to discover new things about your soul and your relationship with God." That would get some attention.

The lenses we wear have a profound impact on what we see and how we see life. Making a quilt can be a solo process or a group one. It can be simply stitching and putting pieces together or it can be a spiritual edifice of meaning and significance. Why do we do what we do? What is this saying to others? Whom does my "craft" serve? For what purpose? How does doing my craft bring me into deeper connection with others and with the transcendent? How can I reshape what I do to bring God more fully into the process? What does my making the craft say about who I am and how I perceive myself? Where is God in the process? What are the different levels of meaning in what I do and in what I have created? Is this a way of looking at crafts you have not thought of before? Try it out.

BUILD SOMETHING

The listings below work for many of the other areas including gardening, hobbies, and crafts.

Hands on work is always good for those on this end of the transcendent spectrum. Habitat for Humanity, a soup kitchen, or some kind of hobby will put you in touch with God's creative order in new ways. If you are doing something with others, talk with them about why they are doing it. Listen to the reasoning of others. You will learn something if your eyes, ears, and heart are open.

SUPERNAL (S)— Our meaning in large part comes from what we glean from our senses in response to the world around us. The S finds meaning in response to this world from inside. They appreciate a house or a garden or a building and see what God has done in and through human activity. Now it's time for the S to deepen the meeting by actually making those things. There is something about becoming physically connected to that which is being created. We become proud of what we have done and made. Depth of meaning comes when we understand how God is part of the entire process; from the creating of the materials used to the power of God to create the human brain and provide it with creativity.

IMMANENT (I)—The I's enjoy building, many Habitat for Humanity people are "I's." We can see the idea of balance when we ask them why they are doing it. Listen closely to the answers and see which traits they lean too. An "I" will say, "I love serving God by helping others. I know that the family in this house will appreciate it and perhaps find God by seeing what we are doing out of love for God." Nothing wrong with those responses. But why else might we build a house? What does it say about us as creations of God? How does it connect us to the world? If no one knew we were building the house how would the meaning change?

298

SACRED (A)—We are surrounded by things in the world we can use as metaphors for our lives. There are few better than building something. The tools we need, the resources we harness, the internal vision and skill, the process of watching something become what we envision, the surprises along the path of growth, the joy of achievement and the despair or frustration at not having something go quite as expected are all part of the building something and growing into ourselves. Find yourself in what you build, build the bridge between the sacred and the profane, the transcendent and the immanent. This notion of building is not just of structures but can be mechanical like working on a car. Some of us are engaged in "building" as our livelihood, how do we see that process in the context of our spiritual lives? Do we lose a sense of spiritual purpose when it becomes our career?

TERRENE (T)—The reverse is true of the Terrene. They find them self in what they build but don't make the connection to their sacred identity within that process. It's like the alchemists who focused on creating gold rather than on using alchemy as a process for refining their inner lives. A building is a building, it will last awhile and disappear. This is not to minimalize our efforts in that creation, but to say the process of building can become part of who we are, shape how we see ourselves and connect us to the transcendent that created everything we use to build, including ourselves. How do we find the sacred in what we put together?

MYSTICAL (M)—There are few better ways to connect with the world than through creating something tangible. Crafts, hobbies, food, or building something are all ways to make physical connections through our spiritual being. The Mystical type likes to make connections to things from the inside out, the E (Temporal) from the outside in. We need to have the lines of communication going both ways, feeding each other. The M needs to get their hands dirty, get their body sore from work, engage with others in the process of building something, painting something, cooking something. More mystically oriented people need to do their work in community rather than alone since solitude is a natural state of being for them. It's preferable to build something that will last a while. It's also best to build something on a level you don't normally do. If you are a carpenter, making a house probably isn't that beneficial.

Build and find the connections to what you build, see how many levels you can get into it—the lives it will touch over generations or hours, the impact on others, what it brings to all who experience it.

TEMPORAL (E)—The E feels the connectedness of them self to what they create. The E needs to make the connection on a different plane, the spiritual one. Who is it that created all the things you use to create something new? What are the deeper connections being made? Who are you creating for? Things made do not last forever, what is it that does that is embedded in the building of something? What relationships have deepened in the building process?

INSPIRATION (N)—All building is in the end a creative process. We all learn by trial and error, listening to others, and by making mistakes. The process of transforming ourselves outside and in is a creative process. The N trusts their intuition in this process, they accept the mystery inherent in the process, especially that part which deals with the transcendent. Sharing those insights and ideas is important to bring the N into balance. One of the key spiritual issues for the N is keeping things in. It's ok to share even mystery. Others may not understand, that isn't your problem. In the building of a building the N helps others find a larger reason for doing what they are doing. They have the ability to bring a peacefulness and joy to the process---even in pouring rain.

REASON (R)—The R likes to think through the process of building. They want their creativity to fit in with what is around them, what makes sense. Their connection to the spiritual is through the mind, they think about the spiritual rather than experience it. Creativity is both a mental and an experiential process. The R needs to let go and trust their intuition and reach out to the transcendent to enhance the power of their mind. Many of us get trapped by the boundaries our minds set for us. R's should push through that boundary and enter the world of mystery and spontaneity. One of the best things for an R to do in the building process is to slow down, pay attention to the little things, let your body feel what is going on, not just think about it. Become more fully aware of what is going on around you and use all your senses.

IDEALIST (D)—Why do we build? Rarely do people think about building for God or for God's purposes, but all things work for the common good. We all need shelter, workplaces, places to meet and exercise, and places to get well. Under each of those are spiritual reasons why we build. Our shelter protects the temple of God and creates a haven of safety. Our work environments help us live out the purposes for which we were created and offer a sanctuary for relationships. Coffee shops, churches and temples, and a variety of other places afford us the chance to connect with the transcendent bringing all it offers into the world. Ask yourself what the purpose is behind what you are building or doing. Ground the building in the reality in which it is located.

PRAGMATIST (P)—The P understands the context but at times misses some of what was just discussed. They need to look inside and listen to the larger picture about what this is about. What can this creation do for others and the world, even in small ways? The P can get so busy doing and counting they lose sight of the larger purpose. We tend to think of our home as a building and to some degree it is. We also hear that home is where the heart is. You can be physically homeless and spiritually very much at home. What does that mean---to be spiritually at home?

GET A HOBBY

Hobbies do a lot for us. They tend to be hands on which grounds us to the earth. Often we find others who enjoy the same hobby. It's good to build relationship, share ideas, and eventually meaning in those relationships. What does this hobby mean to you and to them? Explore the hobby at a deeper level, push yourself to understand why you are interested in this—where did it come from? The mind of the Supernal is not prone to cogitating and thinking about the big questions in life, they accept what is. The truth is that there often are answers to our questions. Listen to the challenges of others, be open to learning, to not knowing everything or to being wrong about something. The idea of being a life-long learner applies to the spiritual world as well. Use the concepts above in the building section and apply them here as well.

EXPOSE YOURSELF TO A DIFFERENT CULTURE

All types that are serious about their spirituality are on a search some of which is internal search for meaning. But their internal life had to come from somewhere, usually their childhood or a mountaintop experience. They are more prone to trust meaning that comes from within than from without. The problem with that frame of reference is that we miss remarkable opportunities. Many of the Scribes and Pharisees were like that. They had a world view and didn't really want to see or even be exposed to other viewpoints. Reading about, listening too, or experiencing other avenues of finding meaning does not mean we have to accept them. By exposing ourselves we not only learn from other religious traditions and cultures but our own sense of who we are deepens. We find we must fit our puzzle piece into the larger picture and make some meaningful sense of it all. Go to different churches or temples. Meditate with a wide variety of traditions. Look around for festivals of different religious traditions. Steve R. learned to pray by studying with a Zen Community. He did not sacrifice his faith, but found he could be with them while maintaining the integrity of his faith. The key point is to understand that I as an individual do not have all the answers, to feel that way is to be spiritually egotistical.

Our exposure to other cultures stretches our minds and challenges our assumptions, many of which are false. We learn to start thinking more for ourselves and not just accepting the prejudices of others. As we push our internal self our souls connect with the universality of all souls, we make connections that bring us together rather than tear us apart. Our pains and range of emotions are the same the world over. Our purposes in life are the same and while the context of meaning may change the root of meaning does not.

In exploring other cultures we find we have much more in common than what separates us.

TRAVEL

If you can afford it, there is probably no better antidote for the imbalance of the S than travel—especially if it is with another person or a group of people. The point of travel in this context at least is exposure to the breadth and depth of God's created order. It's one thing to read about a culture or to visit a festival in your own country. Going to the homeland of the culture and seeing it first hand is by far the best. Being on foreign ground tends to have an impact on us. Barriers come down, we see things in new ways as well as to perhaps appreciate our own. Meaning shifts as we see how others live and view reality. Tour groups are fine, but ensure you mingle with the indigenous population. Seeing sights is one thing, relating to those who live there brings far more spiritual growth and depth. Ask them about their faith, how they view the world, and from where do they get their meaning. While traveling, write a blog or a journal to reflect on what you are seeing, hearing, feeling, smelling, and touching. What is your spirit telling you about all you are experiencing?

There has been a great deal of speculation about the travels of Jesus. We know that he went to Egypt in his infancy to escape death and that he showed up at the temple in Israel at age 11. 27 years of Jesus' life are essentially missing. Lots of legends exist as to what happened. Some say he went to Persia or Asia, others say he spent a great deal of time with the Essenes, a more mystical Jewish group. There are certainly parts of Jesus's teachings that could lead one to see that he at least learned from other traditions.

Not everyone has the opportunity to travel, but if you do, grab it. There is perhaps no better way to see the world than to experience it personally—up close. The key in light of our discussion is to use your travel to see how other people perceive spiritual reality. Different cultures bring different rituals and belief systems to their lives. Even Christians around the world worship differently and have a different perspective on what God brings to life than you do, no matter where you live. When we start to feel we have all truth, we are in trouble. When we start to judge other people, including other Christians, it's time to get perspective because there is only one judge.

SOCIALIZE

Get involved clubs, groups around a similar hobby---The point of socializing is to find grounding in the world, to learn with and through others. It's more than just going bowling, it's figuring out what bowling means for others. How can any given activity become a new source of meaning for our lives? Are there metaphors we can use within that activity? What does the activity do for others---internally and externally? What are your relationships based on? Can you broaden those parameters?

Socializing can impact all traits. Just ask yourself how being more social could impact the Mystical or the Temporal types? What influence might it have on discovering your spiritual purpose in life? How might the way you socialize or who you socialize with change if your spirituality becomes a higher priority in your life?

WORSHIP

Worship is an important part of a spiritual life and discipline. We are called to worship by God. The form does not matter, it's the intent and discipline of purpose that we should care about. We believe we are called to worship both individually and corporately. While we are called to worship the Creator, having the experience be meaningful to us helps the process and intentionality. Here are a few suggestions on what to look for, ask yourself, and feel during worship.

Private Worship

1. Form—Sometimes consistency is important, having the same ritualistic tone each time you sit down to worship God. Other times it's good to change things up because we get in a rut and lose sight of what it is we are doing and who we are worshipping. One of the features of worship is that we have no distractions. We put God at the top of the priority chain during worship, not sharing God with other things. It's a matter of focus and of quality, not quantity.

2. Worship is about expressing ourselves, our gratitude, and our awe to the One who created us and loves us unconditionally. Muslims have 99 words they use to express their feelings towards Allah, how many do you have for God?
3. Private worship is unique to you, a time when you express yourself in ways that are deeply meaningful to you.
4. This may include reading (to yourself or out loud), singing, praying or any other means that let God know how you feel and think. While God does not need this, God wants to know what is going on within our souls, minds, and hearts from our perspective.

Corporate Worship:

1. Find a community of faith where you feel comfortable, where you find meaning in their worship, and where at the end of worship you feel you have expressed your soul, mind, and heart to God with others.
2. There is no "proper" form of worship. Some enjoy more ritualistic forms, others don't. The beauty of God is that His world is vast, not narrow. Don't judge others and how they worship just because it's not what brings meaning to your life. All are welcome at God's table.
3. Pay attention to the words being said and sung. Feel them in your heart, listen to them with your mind, don't just let them roll through you because you've heard them a thousand times. The Lord's Prayer should be meaningful every time to you say it, If it isn't, then stop and ask why or stop saying it for a while. If our worship and prayer is not that meaningful to us, imagine how it comes across to God.
4. Look into why you worship corporately, have a discussion with others about it. Why do we do what we do? Are there things that would make it more meaningful to us and to God? It might be interesting at your place of worship to have a public discussion about why we do what we do.
5. What role do the sacraments play in your corporate worship. What do I personally get from a Baptism, Marriage, Burial,

Annointing, Confession, Confirmation, Ordination, or Communion? How does our corporate body use those to truly worship God as a body?

6. How do I view myself in the midst of this corporate worship? Am I engaged or am I just letting others do the worship and I am simply by myself in the midst of others?

SUPERNAL (S)-- The Supernal type tends to be more in their own world during worship. They may not even sing or join in corporate prayer. Their minds may wander during sermons. It is more a private form of worship in a corporate setting. Communion for them is often a pivotal part of the service, rich with meaning. They need to learn to be an active part of corporate worship. They have no problem with individual worship and are often very good and disciplined at it. Even there however the Supernal type needs to be diligent to ensure they don't fall into a rut. Creativity in worship is important. Looking at the meaning within the context of worship is important for them to assess.

IMMANENT (I)—The I finds meaning in the midst of the worshipping community. They bond with others to worship the "holy other." In one sense they are more Jewish in their approach to worship in that it is corporate. They are filled with God's presence in the midst of others. They enjoy music that is joyful. Psalm 150 brings smiles to their faces. They like pragmatic sermons that give them solutions to issues in their lives and in the lives of those they touch. Communion is something they respond to but more because it was how they were raised or because we are called to do it by Jesus as a community. There is little deep felt connection within that ritual. The Immanent type needs to learn to worship from within, to feel the meaning the Spirit gives them just through the act of worshipping. They need to meet the Spirit face to face rather than just through the faces of others.

SACRED (A)—Truth be told, it is in and through the pure act of worship that we finally meet who we are and what we are meant to be. Part of pure worship is the letting down of all masks and being pure before God. Pretensions and opinions are gone. We worship with who we are, not with whom we wish to be. God would rather be honored by a sinner who admits to his sin than by someone pretending to be pure who isn't. The A knows they are sacred from within. They understand their attachment to God. They need to find a way of connecting that part of them self with the side that is more attached to the world. God knows both sides. God does not fear being worshipped by your shadow. The Sacred type finds they are enmeshed in all forms of worship. Worship speaks to them because deep worship comes from a deep place within.

TERRENE (T)—The T comes to worship with a sense of who they are that they get primarily from the world and the church. Preachers tell them who they are and often they believe it. This type needs to acknowledge those external voices but listen more intently to the one's within, to the voice of their soul and to the voice of God. They are unique and need to find that sense of uniqueness within them self and be proud of it, just as God is. Worship is an amazing time to be surrounded by the spiritual. The T should find a way of worshipping with others on the outside while finding a deeper sense of who they are on the inside. In the end, you are responsible for who you are, for who you present yourself to God as, not the community. "Know the truth and it will set you free." (John 8:32) That statement is true when talking about yourself. In and through worship we come to see the truth about ourselves and when we accept it, we are set free through the grace and power of the transcendent.

MYSTICAL (M)—The Mystical type loves worship. It is there they may feel most connected to both the world and the transcendent. They feed off the symbolic nature of the rituals and the degree to which they feel connected to the people they are worshipping with. While this is all well and good, the M needs to learn how to connect to the people walking in the doors. The ultimate purpose of being spiritual is to bring that connection into the world, to merge the immanent and the transcendent. What is best for the M is to get engaged in helping with worship; join the choir, be a reader, usher, greeter, or help with communion. Finding ways of getting out of the more internal expressions of worship and into some of the externals would help them find the balance they need.

TEMPORAL (E)—The E type thrives in large corporate and contemporary worship. They feed off the collective energy, the passion in singing, and the very thought that there are so many other "like-minded" people around. They are grounded not so much in the liturgy of worship as in the communal nature of it. Baptisms, marriages, and communion tend to be powerful for this type because of their communal nature. In many traditions during the baptism and marriage ceremonies the community is asked if they are willing to do their best to support those being baptized or married during their journey. The resounding "we will" is a manifestation of how the community connects. The Temporal type needs to look internally for more depth to their worship experience. Worship is not just about connecting with the community to reach out to God but also how you and your connection to the transcendent function. The E relies on others for worship. They would be helped by learning how to rely more on them self. Every person has all the necessary ingredients within them self to worship God fully—even in the midst of a corporate setting. Being with a large group of people all wrapped in silence can be a powerful experience.

INSPIRATION (N)—Worship is a creative event. We are called to reach out to God with our imaginations and to create internal and external space for the transcendent. Cathedrals are one remarkable show of that creativity. Some would say they are ostentatious. It is difficult to enter a beautiful church and not be inspired and pulled to some place other than the world. Stained glass beckons our souls. From the simplest New England church to Chartres Cathedral in France, architecture lures us to another dimension. Our souls pull us to internally be creative as well. God would be bored if everyone worshipped her in the same way. God loves variety. We need to allow our internal selves to explode with the power of the transcendent at work within our souls and brains. Ideas in and of themselves are a creative event. We create by singing, dancing, being artistic, being helpful to others, writing, sharing, parenting, learning, working, and in virtually everything we do in life. Our creativity and imagination are only stopped by our ability to act upon them and this tends to be where the N gets stuck. Their internal creativity is strong. Acting upon those ideas and intuitions, especially the spiritual ones is difficult. The N needs to find some accountability to externalize the internal experiences they are having. In the end, life itself is an act of worship, of giving who and what we are and are becoming over to God as a gift. Asking "what impact does worship have on my life?" is an important question for the N. What does it mean? Why is it important in my life? What are the most powerful parts of worship and why?

REASON (R)-- In worship the R tends to fixate on words. They want worship to make sense and much of it does. Their desire is to have theology and worship unite, which at times they do. Their creativity is a choreographed event rather than just an experienced one. Worship, like so many things for the R, is a jigsaw puzzle. Putting the pieces together into a uniform whole is what brings them satisfaction. They get frustrated when the pieces don't align. Songs that don't seem to fit, sermons that don't follow biblical lessons, prayers that seem rote and out of touch with the reality they see around them are all ways they might struggle with corporate worship. Their private worship tends to be more linear and programmed. There is nothing wrong with this other than the fact you are missing out on half of the worship experience. The R needs to work on simply being present in worship, not analyzing it. Learning how to let the mind go for a while and just worship with the heart and soul is an important step for this type. Are there irrational parts of worship? How do you worship internally?

IDEALIST (D)— The focus here is on what we see the purpose of worship to be. The D sees corporate and private worship as the central place to draw believers together around a common creed. We worship with those who we hope have similar ideas and purposes. Often churches or temples will have a common project they work on together which they lift in prayer both corporately and privately. The D sees this as a communal reaching out to God. Worship is part of the purpose for which we were created. Our worship is at the core of our hopefulness. We come to worship to be inspired not dragged down, raised on the shoulders of others in our despair, not trampled on by the masses. The D enjoys worship because it is a center of hope and that is at the core of their purpose in life. The Idealist needs to find ways of expressing that purpose in worship. They tend to be more attracted to sermons of a purely spiritual nature rather than a practical one or one that hits the issues of the day head on. They believe church is not a place for politics or for bringing people down with numbing statistics about the woes of the world—and they are right. But worship is about connecting the dots and seeing how our time of worship can inspire, encourage and perhaps exhort us into becoming better people who take hope into the world. Balance is what should be sought. The Quakers have a tradition of silence in worship and waiting for God to speak in and through us. Silence can be a profound thing in our lives, both corporately and privately—as long as we are listening and responding to what we hear that pulls us deeper into God's world. Here is a hint: If you agree with everything you think God is asking of you, you are probably listening to yourself and not to God. Biblically most people had issues at first with what God asked of them. God's purposes change as the needs of the world change. Are you in a worshipful frame of mind to both listen and act upon those changes?

PRAGMATIST (P)—On the other side is the Pragmatist. They enjoy political sermons, commissioning rituals and other things that manifest the work of God's people in the world. For them the purpose of worship is to engage God in the work. God does not want us just to work for the sake of work, but to bring hope and freedom through the work. The P can become frustrated when worship exists simply for the sake of worship. They view worship as a collective act of forging a purpose and a plan to enact that purpose. We pray about what we are doing, we sing to build hope and energy to carry out the purposes of the transcendent. We do communion because it reminds us of the sacrifice Christ made for the world that frees us to make our own sacrifices. While God certainly wants us to be active in the world, God also calls us to be apart from the world, to engage in the simple act of worship in response to the one who created us. Think of how we act out of gratitude for things people do for us. Sometimes we give them a gift or a card of thanks. Other times we simply say thank you—it's enough. Is there anything you can possibly do to equal what God has given us? Worship is a response of gratitude out of a sense of humility and perspective about our place in the universe. The P needs to let go of a need to always be doing and just be.

SHARE THIS BOOK WITH SOMEONE OR START A GROUP

Groups are a great way to grow on any level. While this book would be a good one for discussions and growth there are many others that are fabulous. Check out the bibliography for a few ideas. Group work does several things for us. First, we are not called to be on this journey alone, but with others. Sharing what is going on inside is imperative. For some it is easy and for others difficult. Groups help us see that others struggle, that we are not as unique in the world as we might think, give us new perspectives on things, and challenge our views. Push yourself to either find a group or start one. In the context of this book the over-riding idea of the group should be finding and working on your soul. Just having a group talk about the issues of meaning, identity, relationships, creativity, and purpose could fill up months of time. You could also do one or more of the activities listed each session and see how people respond. Because each of us has a unique soul, how we deal with those activities will be different. You can also have people work on one thing for a week and come back and report on how it went—have everyone keep a journal—a spiritual journal.

POLITICAL ENGAGEMENT

In short, politics. It need not be a dirty word. Like it or not a significant part of our lives is in the end, run by politics. We avoid it to our and other people's peril. Yes, it can be an ugly part of reality, but it is what we have. There is perhaps no better place than in the political arena to have your meaning system pushed, prodded and challenged. Everybody involved in politics has an opinion and a sense of meaning. They are engaged because their meaning system is being systematically challenged or they wish to challenge someone else's. How and where we find meaning in life impacts our political views in large ways. Get to know your local and regional politicians and their aides. When you have a political discussion with someone ask what it means to them, why are they so passionate about something. Find out what you are passionate about. Getting in touch with the political process also introduces us to

311

people. We build networks, make friends, hear other viewpoints, learn to voice what we think and feel, and are pushed out of our comfort zone.

SUPERNAL-- The Supernal type needs to simply get engaged at any level. Rise above the pettiness of it all. Get to know your local and regional politicians and their aides. When you have a political discussion with someone ask what it means to them, why are they so passionate about that issue. Find out what you are passionate about. Getting in touch with the political process also introduces us to people. We build networks, make friends, hear other viewpoints, learn to voice what we think and feel, and are pushed out of our comfort zone. Find meaning within the political process.

IMMANENT--The Immanent type may already be engaged in political arenas. For them the challenge is to not get overly attached to the issue or candidate, but to hold people accountable to the core purpose and meaning behind the candidate or issue. If we had a significant number of people doing this we wouldn't have negative campaigning or lies or spin. We would simply have honest and bold discussions about the issues. Spirituality brings a higher sense of ethics+ and purpose to the world of politics. We need a politics of soul. The Immanent needs to work on how discussions are framed. At times it may come down to "winning" using immoral means or "losing" and being moral. Which is right?

SACRED—We tend to become an issue based in part on our perceptions of ourselves. The A type understands internally the sacredness of all things. Their more spiritual perspective on who they are as a person at times will get in the way of putting their soul into the world. The sacred type needs to find holiness in the midst of politics. This journey will produce great frustration because this is the antithesis of how the world works. The A needs to bear witness to their beliefs in the public arena. Speaking externally to what we feel and know internally is an important part of maturing.

TERRENE—The Terrene finds their identity more in and through the world. They spiritually identify with the struggles that people go through and may at times find their own spirituality mired in the cultural morass of the world. A depth of spiritual well-being gives us a well of wisdom, peace, energy and grace the world does not know that keeps us afloat. The T needs to take care not to over identify with others, either psychologically or spiritually, to do so is to set oneself up. Before the E dives into a more politically oriented issue they should take time to look inside and see what the motivation is. Is this what God is calling me to? Is there something I am bringing to the people I will be working with or serving that is bigger than just the issue or candidate? How much am I committing to this and how much of that will feed my spiritual soul?

MYSTICAL—The M finds it more difficult to connect to the world in the political arena. Their connections are to the transcendent and while the transcendent may be calling them to get more involved and reach out, they are not prone to do so. One of the issues for the M is that they are able to see the big picture and most political issues are very narrow, often hurting as many people as they help. The M understands at a very deep level how much God truly loves all humans and shows no partiality on a spiritual level. God's focus is more on helping us get our eternal natures in order. We are called to take care of our temporal order. Think about this: If the world were all spiritually mature, do you think we would have the problems we do? It is our lack of spiritual focus and maturity that gets us in trouble---even as we claim to be mature. Our bars are set very low.

TEMPORAL-- The E's head spins in the political world. They are constantly connecting the dots, seeing how God is active in the world and trying to engage the world in God's activity, albeit in an indirect way. The further they go towards the E end of the spectrum the more they see things from the world's view and not from God's. Politics and networking become ends in themselves rather than means to a just end that is in God's purpose. They are brilliant rationalizers and can spin just about anything. The E needs to spend time alone with God and the transcendent. They need to build a deeper sense of connection apart from what the world offers. This may seem like an odd concept at first but given time and effort the fruits will be plentiful. This is not a forsaking the world, just an intention to gain perspective.

INSPIRATION—If ever there was a needed type in the political arena this is it. Politics lacks all sense of creativity. The N breathes imagination, has a multitude of ideas that come from being transcendentally aware. The N thinks out of the box and their ideas tend to bring hope to the world and inspire others to do the same. They can also be very stubborn. They will listen to others ideas but believe they are right. Politics is more often than not a world of compromise and this is where the N needs to work. It is the very art of compromise that will bring them to the middle, to balance. Push yourself to find ways of getting your ideas into the public.

REASON—The R both loves and hates the political world. They love it because things should make sense, because the underlying motivations of spirituality should be reflected in what we want for people and how we conduct ourselves with each other. The problem is they don't. Greed and a lack of civility rule the day in modern American politics as well as in many other countries. Reason wants to make sense of all this in a spiritual context but sadly the only reason is sin. Now and then some creative mind finds a way to use the system to actually do something of benefit to everyone, but it is rare. The R looks to the world more for its creativity is limited by what we know. God's has no limits.

IDEALIST—The Idealist is a big picture person who dreams of utopias. They understand how important politics is and want it to bring the best to the world. They are often frustrated when time after time the political world falls short when to them it seems so easy. The D has difficulty seeing the world through other people's lenses. They are optimists and harbingers of hope. This type needs to work on grounding them self in the reality of politics; to get involved in a practical way and listen to the hearts and minds of those around them. The D wants to bring the transcendent into the world, that is their purpose. Doing that through the realm of politics can be difficult, but the truth is that many decisions that affect all of our lives start there so if we have concern for the world it is to that world we must go.

PRAGMATIST—The Pragmatist likes to get things done. They have a vision of what the transcendent wants based on the concepts of caring for your neighbor, treating all people with respect and love, and fighting for the oppressed. Their purpose is to change things. This type works well in the day to day world of politics; seeking compromises, building coalitions, and asking the right people the right questions. The issue for the P is that they see life through the political lens and miss out on the deeper purposes to which they are called. It is not a matter of just changing laws, but of changing lives. Politicians need their lives changed as well; they hurt, sin, and dream. The P would be well served by hanging around daydreamers and those who think well outside the box. When the P gets involved, they should push them self to get behind the politic and represent the underlying spiritual needs of those being affected.

FIND A VERY DIFFERENT TYPE THAN YOU

They say opposites attract, find out. Look for someone who isn't into the spiritual at all. Find out what makes them tick, how do they find meaning in life? This doesn't mean you need to become like them, it just offers a different perspective that will help pull you in a new direction that will broaden the base of meaning in your life. When is the last time you had an open conversation about meaning with someone? Have a conversation with someone from a different religion and see what they have to offer you and you have to offer them. This is not a conversation about conversion, but of understanding. Find someone at the opposite end of the scale from you on any one of the traits or on all of them. If you are an Idealist, find a Pragmatist. Listen and learn from each other. Focus your conversation on the idea of purpose. We have a tendency to hang out with people more like us than different from us. Growth and depth come more from being pushed and encouraged than from being comfortable.

Learning how to put ourselves into the shoes and souls of others has a great impact on our own development. When we become so self-centered that our way is the only way or the right way, we lose sight of the infinite nature of God's world. This is not to say we can't have deeply founded opinions and beliefs. It's a matter of learning to view the world with someone else's lens, to understand I am not the center of the universe. This is an especially important notion when we find ourselves reacting to something someone does or says. Again, it's not a call to become like them, just to understand them. Would you rather have someone try to impact and have an effect on your through the means of love or of fear? Fear has been the strategy of far too many religious followers for millennia. A faith born out of fear breeds fear and is that the kind of faith we want? Does God want us to live in fear? The Old Testament notion of fearing God has more to do with awe and respect than with fear as most of us conceive it—although having some fear doesn't hurt.

Soul types on the more Immanent end of the spectra tend to have a harder time listening and attuning to the views of others. Many people do not like talking about religion because it often ends in arguments. If we truly listen and respect others, no arguments take place. We all need to be heard and when we feel heard we tend not to argue. Watch an argument sometime. Watch how the listening stops as the pace and level of voices go up. If we are seeking, we will find the truth and God is very patient, much more so than we are.

PRAYER

There are a wide variety of forms of prayer and meditation and at times the distinction between the two is blurred. Perhaps the easiest (far from perfect) way of seeing the difference is that prayer is a form of petitioning the transcendent, asking God for something. Meditation is more a reflecting or contemplating of the transcendent or a stilling of the mind and soul to allow the transcendent greater access to our souls and minds. Different soul types are attracted to different forms of prayer. Broadening those styles can help each type and trait find balance.

It is a bit odd to think of praying in and through each trait of our soul because our soul is a whole and all the traits work together. As we focus on one style of prayer we start to move one or more traits to the balance we seek.

IMMANENT-- The Immanent type looks to find meaning in the midst of prayer. Prayer becomes more of a storytelling time to God. It is an expression of their life and a yearning to understand. There is a beckoning in the midst of mystery. Their prayers tend to be more supplication on behalf of the world. They call out to God and to fellow believers to be the conduits for God's power and grace in the brokenness of the world. At times the I type needs to let go and simply find meaning in God, the world will not have answers. The answer they seek may not even be found in their relationship with God, but if they turn to God in prayer, they will find that God suffers with them. Letting go means being present----period. No words are needed to be with the one who knows everything already.

SUPERNAL—The Supernal type feels the presence of God in the midst of prayer. They have a tendency to focus on the eternal in the midst of the temporal. When people suffer they pray for the eternal world without suffering. They pray for hope and yet at times forget that they may be the very hope they are praying for. God has given us as the answer to many prayers. We are the conduit for God's grace and power. We are the conduit for love and hope. We are the vehicle for God's movement on earth. The S type needs to pray for them self that they can find meaning in and through the relationships they have with others and the work God is presently doing to feed the internal and external needs of people. The prayers of the S focus on the dreams of a better tomorrow while those of the I are on the pains of today. We need both.

TERRENE—The Terrene prays for them self in the world. They focus on their sinfulness and lack of obedience to God's will and purpose for their lives. Because their spiritual identity is attached to how spirituality is viewed in the world, their prayers mirror the cultural values and struggles of the world—how could it be otherwise? They struggle with ancient prayers that find no grounding in their lives. They want to understand and be understood. Many of their prayers about them self revolve around changes they need to make and yet what they lack is the change that takes place inside. They should be still and listen to the still small voice of God. They should learn to pray more from the heart than the head.

317

SACRED—The Sacred type prays from the heart. Their being longs to be in the presence of God. They ache for mystical experiences and relish the writings of the mystics who have found a deep sense of them self within their hearts and souls as apart from the world. The focus is on the grace of God and the remarkable unconditional love God gives us. But who we are is dependent on the world around us. As hard as the mystics tried, it always came back to human images and language. While we can experience God through prayer and our identities are in part found in that experience, we do need to live in reality. We are here with purpose. God wants us to discover who that person is in the world and to raise up in prayer our short comings, questions, doubts, and fears. We all have them. To find the balance of owning up to who and what we are as well as listening to God to see what we can become is the balance we seek.

TEMPORAL—The Temporal prays we find the connectedness between us that is where hope lies. There is very little difference between the very rich and the very poor, perhaps simply a matter of luck. Our commonality with all people as creatures of God is what makes us care for one another. If we don't believe that, why should we care? The temporal understands the connection between parenting, crime, mental illness, the environment, war, diet, and how they all impact each other in the web of life. They pray for that web. This type needs to pray for a connection to the transcendent, to God and the Collaborative Unconscious. This connection not only brings a peace that passes human understanding, but also gives wisdom and a deeper sense of ordering our lives than the world can give with its limited knowledge and ego-centric way of doing things.

MYSTICAL—The Mystical prays that we can find the connectedness with God, that is where the hope for the world lies. They understand on a spiritual level that we are all connected, even as we try to differentiate ourselves. Nationalism is contrary to a mystical understanding of life. This type feels the connectedness in their prayer. They center on that internal relationship. What they tend to fail to do is to carry those connections to the world that God created. They need to ask to be shown the connectedness within the world. God is constantly trying to make connections in the world, to guide us to those who need God's help and yet we are at times so full of ourselves we don't feel or hear that voice calling us into the world, into relationship with others, even strangers. The M needs to open them self to the movement of God in the world.

REASON— The reasonable person prays in and through reason, no less so on the spiritual level. Remember, here we are looking at creativity and imagination. But for the R, logic rules the day. They are more likely to focus on things they can engage in or see a real answer to. They will probably not pray for "peace on earth," because they know it won't happen. Peace in one country or another is a more likely prayer. They are concrete in their prayers and believe because they understand that we are the conduits of God's power to answer prayers, prayers need to engage their own level of activity to the largest degree possible. The R needs to let go and realize that God does not work entirely on our plane of existence. God does the impossible on a regular basis. Prayer should be at the same time both something we can do something about as well as pushing our faith to its limits, an act of inspiration. Many of us love hearing people who pray well out loud, they inspire us and move us.

INSPIRATION—This type is more an orator of prayer in a wonderful way. Words flow from them and beckon God to remarkable depths. We know that we are called to pray through faith and that with faith the impossible can be achieved. Perhaps it is more a matter of understanding the level of our faith. If we truly believe that if we have faith of a mustard seed we can move mountains, then the faith of humanity is excruciatingly small. In life and in prayer, success breeds success. It is no surprise that when we see miracles in front of our eyes, our faith grows. The N inspires us and is inspired by what they believe can happen in and through prayer. The challenge is for them to balance the vision with the reality. What are things I can pray for that God can use me in an active way to bring forth? How willing are you to become involved with what you are praying for? If you pray for peace are you willing to do things that bring peace. If you pray for a healing are you willing to go and lay hands on that person? Prayer is a sign of what we claim we believe. Are we willing to act on what we claim?

PRAGMATIST—The Pragmatist asks what the purpose of prayer is. For them praying is not only a duty, but a way of communicating; both with God and with ourselves. It's a way of putting forth what we feel is needed in the worldview we have. If we are true to purpose, we pray for those things that fall in line for the purposes for which God has called us. Attention is paid to discovering their purpose in life on a practical level. Should I do this or that? The P tends to focus prayer more on the who, when, where, and what of life. To balance their prayer life the P needs to enter the world of God and let God do the praying. Perhaps the best way of doing this is through Centering Prayer which may be more meditating than praying, but it allows the voice of God to fill our minds and takes our need to speak out of the picture. Ultimately, if God knows what we need before we ask, then just being present is prayer.

IDEALIST—The Idealist enjoys being present, of envisioning a world full of the hope of God and that is what they pray for. They are more engaged and interested in what we may become than on what we are. Because their purpose, spiritual purpose, is more tied to bringing hope to the world they are not so interested in day to day concerns. God wants both. Yes, God knows what we want before we ask, but do we? God is interested in what we say and how we say it. What are our priorities? How are we actively engaged in the prayers we ask? How are we bringing hope to the world if hope is the purpose? The D needs to find ways of praying that will pull them into the prayer on an active level. Just thinking about hope does not create hope, but having hope as a deep well spring within gives us the strength and wisdom to move forward.

MEDITATION

Meditation has many forms and functions. Its essence is about reflecting upon something, emptying one's mind, or simply relaxing. The Bible calls us to meditate on the Word day and night. Meditation takes the mind and focuses it on something in particular—without distraction. Most of us struggle with meditation because we are easily distracted and have an attention span of a gnat. The deepest forms of meditation move from reflection to merely being. We no longer think, we just are. Our minds take a break from active thought and relax on a very conscious level. This is not falling asleep. There is no right or wrong way to meditate. In fact, many meditation instructors will tell you not to judge the time you have in meditation; it is what it is. Meditation is a discipline and takes effort to establish and maintain a habit. Meditation has been proven to be a powerful tool to develop mindfulness and it has a positive impact on body, soul, and mind.

The core of meditation is discipline. You will see below that each trait is attracted to different things. It would seem that we need to have multiple forms of meditation to meet all those needs. Any form you choose will benefit all traits of the soul. The traits feed off of each other and help to balance each other out. Once you build a discipline in one tradition it may be helpful or interesting to try a few others knowing you can always return to the one you know works best for you. You can also use different styles of meditation depending on what your needs are at the time.

The best way to meditate is to learn as part of a group. You will have questions and struggles and the support of the group can be very helpful in starting a discipline. You are trying to build a habit and habits take time to build. Be patient with yourself and give it time. I would suggest a minimum of 20 minutes a day for 30 days. Your life will change.

IMMANENT—The Immanent type will be attracted to forms of meditation that reflect on things that have meaning in their lives. They tend to be active thinkers so letting go will not be easy. Contemplation is the form they prefer because they can spend time reflecting on what they feel is important. The problem with this as the sole form of meditation is that it can cut the transcendent out of the process. Do we really believe we have all the answers? The Immanent type needs to let go of human notions of meaning, even spiritual ones and directly experience God. They need to shut down the thinking process and simply listen, although it's not as simple as it sounds. You can learn from other religious traditions without forsaking your own or allowing evil to take over your brain which is the concern of some. Steve Rodgers meditated with a Zen community for two years while in seminary. They taught him how to silence the mind while no losing sight of his own faith, just made it stronger. Zen, Vipassana, mantric styles of meditation and Centering Prayer are all potential forms to look up or find a group to join.

SUPERNAL—On the other side are the Supernal types. They thrive on listening and gaining meaning from within. This is fabulous but we were given brains for a reason---to use them. Some who use forms of meditation to silence the mind say they use their brains almost 24 hours a day so they aren't worried about that. We would have no contention with that if the brain is being used to focus on God and the transcendent. If you are asking questions of meaning and seeking what the world has to say about it on a spiritual level, that's fine. Many of us put our "spiritual time" into a condensed space. We don't live our spirituality out 24/7. The S type does feel the spiritual internally more than the I type but they are not as adept at seeing God in and through the world. More contemplative forms of meditation are the best balance. Lectio Divina and the Cloud of Unknowing are perhaps the two most famous Christian forms of contemplation or at least a way of contemplating. The four core stages are to read, meditate, pray, contemplate. Find something to read that isn't long. To meditate in this form is to intellectually think about what you have just read without holding firm to your beliefs, allowing the transcendent to enter the intellect. When a person prays in this style of contemplation they are having a conversation with God about the passage—knowing full well who should be doing most of the listening. The final stage, contemplation, is to be wrapped in the passage where the Holy Spirit speaks in, to, and through our souls. The key to this being an effective strategy for the S is to have some attention paid to what the passage means for them in the world, not just internally.

TERRENE—The style of meditation that comes the most easily for us has a direct relation to how we perceive ourselves as an individual, our self-identity. The Terrene person finds their identity in and through how God is found in the world. They listen to the voices of others and find God there. This type will meditate most comfortably in a group or with direction. Stilling the mind takes great inner concentration and discipline, something the T lacks. The T enjoys thinking (contemplating) how to make the world a better place, how to bring God's power to change the created order. If the Terrene wants to use their mind then they would be well served to use it to find God within. Who are you as a creature of God? What does it mean to be sacred and holy? Our minds are naturally wrapped up with ourselves. To let go and let God is a useful thing for this type to do. Any forms of meditation that show you how to let go of the mind and relax into the presence of God would be ideal. Again, Centering Prayer, Vipassana (Insight Meditation) and Zen are good ones.

SACRED—The Sacred type finds their identity within, they rely more on how they see them self than on how the world sees them. They trust that the sense of the transcendent they feel is real—and it may be. As the mystics tells us, we are very prone to self-delusion on the spiritual front. Look at people throughout history who believed and convinced others that they had "the truth" about God. Self-confidence and a strong faith can be an immense asset or liability if its faith in the wrong thing. When the A type is truly centered all is well. You know this by what they do with their beliefs and how they speak of them self. There is a strong sense of humility with integrity. There is no boasting other than in God. There is an urgency in them to help others find that inner well spring of hope and depth in the transcendent. This type loves Centering Prayer and letting go of them self into a more mystical union with God and the Collaborative Unconscious. But God puts us here to be in relationship with others, to learn from others and to minister to others on all levels. A bit of intellectual contemplation would serve this type well and expand their own sense of them self. In a wonderful way, yoga is a great way to achieve this as well as Tai Chi.

TEMPORAL—We all need to make connections in life, we are social and spiritual creations. Some people make spiritual connections on the temporal plane. They like talking about spirituality with others, they network to enhance theirs and others spiritual connectivity. They like meditating with others because it boosts that sense of togetherness. The E would like the story of Mark 2 that we used because of all the characters and the relationships they all bring to the forefront. The E needs to also connect internally and directly with God, not just through God's actions in the world. Centering Prayer would be the best style for this type. It calls forth their heart and soul and fills their being with the presence of God. A direct experience of God is a powerful thing and reorients our souls quickly. If this type wants to do more reflection and contemplation, they would be well suited to look at their dreams as spiritual messages from the transcendent and see what they are saying.

MYSTICAL-- The Mystical type finds it easier to sit and feel the presence of God. Relaxing into the Spirit comes more naturally. They embrace the mystical nature of our being. They have found a mystical and mysterious way of connecting to others through the Spirit. They tend to be good spiritual empaths. The challenge for them is to bring that connection into the real world. Again, a more contemplative form of meditation that calls on them to find God in the world would be beneficial. Using the methodology we used with Mark could be a useful tool. Learning how to put them self into the lives of others would help them discover connections in the world. Of all the traits, this is usually the one that doesn't really need to meditate more, they need to act more. The M will find Yoga and/or Tai Chi very useful.

REASON—When it comes to creativity the R loves to meditate in a contemplative way. They can think them self into oblivion and be convinced they are on the right track. Because they give the mind so much power, they are often not very good listeners. They feel God gave them a brain, a good brain, therefore they should trust their brain. There is nothing wrong with thinking, but not listening to the one who created your brain is a mistake. When the R can't stop thinking, they would be well served by challenging their views, to see what others might have to say about them, to look into the validity of other perspectives. Thinking we have all the answers is very dangerous. Remember that truth is not a what, but a who. Our imagination runs wild in meditation and contemplation. Because we have put at bay all other thoughts and are focused on some central thought we can spin it in a wide variety of ways. The R should find ways of letting creativity come in from direct experience, not just from reason. Let go of the mind for a while, it will be there when you return. Insight Meditation, Centering Prayer, and Mantric styles are all good for this type.

INSPIRATION—If you read the mystics you can't help but be inspired, and perhaps confused. They exude imagination and creativity. They are so overwhelmed with the divine presence of God they are at a loss for words. Their brains can't begin to express what they think and feel. They use metaphors and even those are left wanting. All one has to do is open your senses to experience the profound and infinite creativity of God. The N type gets this at their core. What they lack is the ability to transfer that wonder into the world. They are on the mountain top wanting to build tents to stay there---hermits do. But God calls most of us to be in the world, to come down from the mountaintop. What is in the N's best interest is to meditate on those things that show the creativity God has given us. Humanity is remarkably imaginative, both in positive and destructive ways. Awareness of both is critical. More contemplative forms of meditation that bring the spiritual into the temporal are helpful here. Looking for ways of expressing the internal and mystical feelings is also a good practice for the N. Poetry, art, music, and dance are all good forms for the N.

PRAGMATIST—The Pragmatist is pulled by the purposes they see in the world. When they meditate or contemplate their minds are looking at how God is working in the world, connections being made and how what they do can impact what the bible and their community calls them to. Purpose is about activity and the P likes doing more than being. They are more prone to do yoga than sit still and yet that is what they need—"Be still and know that I am God." (Psalm 46:10). In stillness, when the mind is quieted we can hear the still small voice of God and meld that with the purposes for which we feel called. God gives us purpose directly as well as through agencies of the world. The core for the P is to learn to just "be." Centering Prayer and Insight Meditation are wonderful ways to enter into this style of meditation.

IDEALIST- The Idealist enjoys feeling the call within. They like to sit and be present to the transcendent. The D has a clarity about purpose that finds its home deep inside their hearts. At times this clarity lacks a connection to the world, a world God calls us to serve in his name. Sometimes our inner sense of God is accurate and sometimes it is more about our deepest desires. Telling the difference can be tricky. We need community as a checks and balance. We need our minds to ask questions and look at the big picture. We need the bible and other sacred writings to temper our spirits. All of these are contemplative in nature at this level. It's the process of deep inner reflection that guides us through the maze of purpose.

All people who are on the journey to God have some similar purposes. We are all called to love one another as Christ loved us. We are all called to bring hope to the world. We are all called to feed the hungry, clothe the naked, and visit widows, orphans, and prisoners. What that looks like in each individual's life may be radically different. If we are truly seeking with humble and open minds, hearts, and souls, we will find both the Pragmatic and the Idealistic purpose to which we are called.

RETREATS

If you want to jump start your spiritual life or meditation practice, or you feel stuck and need something to help you move to the next level, there is probably no better way than to go on a retreat. Retreats are not vacations, they are more than just getting away from the hustle and bustle of life. Retreats are a conscious structuring of one's life to move us. If you want to be statistical about it, you should go for a minimum of three days. A one day retreat is better than none, but there is something about the end of the second day and the beginning of the third. Our minds let go of the world and are more able to focus on the work at hand, we adjust to new surroundings and the purpose for which we went on retreat. Many people find a 4-7 day retreat the best and the most reasonable when thinking about costs and time constraints. Let's talk about the who, what, why, where, and when of a retreat.

WHO: Anyone and everyone. That was easy. There is no person for whom a retreat would not be of immense value if they give them self to that time. Being dragged into a retreat can work but is usually not effective. The retreats we are focusing on here are best for those over 16.

WHAT: There are many types of retreats. You can go on a guided retreat where someone else tells you what to do; how to meditate, what to contemplate on and how to use your time. You can set up your own retreat plan and just go somewhere and be with yourself and the transcendent. We would suggest guided retreats to start. If you go to a monastery or convent they will often set you up with a spiritual director while you are there. Plan ahead, but be open to change as the Spirit moves you. God may have something else in store for you.

The primary goals of going on a retreat usually fall into one of two camps; to learn about something or to find something. You may have shame in your life and want to dig more deeply into it and find God's grace. You may want to learn how to meditate so you go on a week or weekend retreat to learn a specific style. There may be one of the traits of the soul that you want to seek a deeper understanding of and how it works in your life. On retreat we both seek and are found.

When you are thinking of going on a retreat there are some serious questions to ask yourself that will directly impact the degree to which the retreat will be effective. Am I willing to really leave the world for a period of time? No phones, computers, tablets, and perhaps no books. The idea of a retreat is to get away to be with God—without distractions. In the bible most significant changes came into people's lives when in the midst of a "desert" experience. In our world a retreat can be such a period of time. In the wilderness it is you and God or you and a group of people whose purpose is the same and who are seeking the transcendent in the midst of that experience.

What we are trying to do on retreat is to open new doors, new pathways to understanding our soul. Merely putting yourself in the middle of the path is the biggest step. A three day retreat once a year would be a fantastic discipline.

Retreats help break through log jams in our minds, hearts, and souls. When we are true to the retreat, phenomenal things can happen. We go through life saying we give ourselves to God, but in reality, when is the last time you gave three days of your time to merely "be" with

God? We are easily distracted in our lives from a pure and distinct focus on God. On retreat we come to grips with the core of what keeps us from going deeper. At those times we make a decision to become distracted or to push through it. If you don't want to know God and the transcendent in a deeper way, don't go on a retreat.

WHY: The what and the why in this case are not so different. We go on retreat to learn and to change, to discover and to build upon what and who we are. We go because we know there is more to do and to learn about ourselves and about the spiritual world around us. We go because there is a block. We go to discover the power of others who are on the same quest. We go because we have become too enmeshed with the world and need some perspective. There are a million reasons to go on retreat and very few not to. If it is a priority then we can find the time.

WHERE: You can go on retreat anywhere. It's a matter of finding a place you can be still and not distracted. There are sources on the internet for guided retreats. Look for monasteries, convents, or temples. Retreat and conference centers often offer retreats. Ask your pastor if they have one they know of.

YOGA

Yoga has been around for thousands of years. Bringing together the body, mind, and spirit is the overall goal of yoga. It helps with breathing, posture, concentration, and alignment with the transcendent. There are four main branches of Yoga: Jhana, Bhakti, Karma, and Raja. We are concerned here with the different types of Raja yoga which have a more physical path, the type most of us think of when we hear the word yoga. It's important to understand that doing "yoga" is not the same as being a Hindu or Buddhist. We can learn tools from many traditions while remaining true to our own. We have listed a few of the many basic styles of Raja Yoga.

Hatha – Hatha ("ha" meaning Sun and "tha" meaning moon) yoga is the umbrella style of most forms of yoga. The majority of classes in the west are of a Hatha style. It is generally a softer form of yoga. Various poses are used to stretch, relax, strengthen, and develop different parts of the body. Breathing techniques are used as are meditation techniques. The goal is to bring the mind and body together and to help energy flow more smoothly within. It was started in the 15th century in India but various forms of yoga have existed for much longer than that.

Ananda—This style of yoga melds meditation and posing. The physical movement and breathing helps unite body, mind, and soul. Increasing internal energy and conscious awareness are two of its goals. It is a mild form of yoga.

Bikram—This style yoga uses 26 different poses and is done in a room that is 95-105 degrees. The heat makes flexibility easier and encourages sweating which cleanses the body. The heat and poses help internal organs as well.

Anusara—The term means "flowing with grace." It is a recent form of yoga that uses 5 core poses and integrates the heart with the body. It is a relaxed form of yoga and the poses become more than just positions, they become an expression of grace.

Vinyasa—The term means "breath-synchronized movement." It is sometimes called flow yoga. The instructor will direct students to move from pose to pose in sync with inhalations and exhalations. Vinyasa is a broad based style that includes both fast and slow paced movements. Many forms of yoga use the breath as a core piece of their practice.

FASTING

Fasting is a way of cleansing our bodies, minds, and souls. Technically, whenever you don't eat a meal you are fasting. If you are looking for spiritual awakening and depth, one meal doesn't usually do it. Most people can do a three day fast and it is in that third day many find the depth of spirituality we yearn for. Early in the fast you are just aware of your hunger because you aren't used to not eating. Fasting is a discipline in all religious traditions and was at the start of Jesus' ministry. One of the keys is to use the fast for deepening your spiritual life. If you fast but work or play all the time, the value is lost. Combining a fast and a retreat is more often than not a phenomenal event. There are many books on fasting.

NATURE

How often do we take time to appreciate the world around us? Many of us see design and creativity simply in what humans do. What about the creativity of a spider's web, or the fall colors on trees, or the vast array of the color green? We are surrounded by imagination and creativity. How does that creativity inform and impact our lives? How much do we take for granted? Take some time to appreciate all of the creativity that surrounds you. Open your senses and consciously take note of what you see, hear, feel, taste, and smell. What do those experiences do to you and for you? What meaning do they bring to your lives? Great journal writing material. Each day write about at least one sensorial experience.

POETRY

Poetry is a wonderful way to loosen the mind from the confines of overly rational thinking. Poetry is filled with metaphor and symbolism that stretches us and seems to directly attach itself to the soul. The very nature of poetry beckons the transcendent

GLOSSARY

Below we have listed short definitions for some of the key terms we have been using throughout this book. By and large our definitions are in line with basic understandings of the terms. There are some nuances since the very definition of these words is changing.

ARCHETYPE--- Archetypes are innate, universal prototypes for ideas and may be used to interpret observations. A group of memories and interpretations associated with an archetype is a complex, e.g. a mother complex associated with the mother archetype. For some, the shadow and persona are archetypes them self.

The psyche receives input from the brain and the soul and through the aspects mentioned puts everything into context that makes sense to it. The psyche feeds on what it knows. Paranoia is a prime example of this. If you start down the road of thinking you are being followed, what you hear, see, think, and feel will all feed that delusion. Dis-ease builds upon dis-ease. We become trapped in our own cyclical thinking. Addiction works the same way. We discover creative ways of rationalizing our behaviors, even as they drag us down.

Archetypes are important because they help us discover directions we are going in life, what basic needs we have and how those are showing up in our Personas.

Carl Jung's main archetypes are: the Self, Animus, Anima, Shadow, and Persona. The Child and the Trickster are two other common archetypes.

CALL—This is one of the five core traits of the soul whose ends of the spectrum are Pragmatist and Idealist. Our Call in this book relates to what the transcendent would have us do in the world. It is the essence of our intended purpose by the Creator. This is not to say people can't find a purpose in life and be unbelievers. We believe we are all created with both immanent and transcendent purposes. They are not always the same. The Call speaks to this transcendent purpose which impacts how we view ourselves and how we gather meaning from the world.

COLLABORATIVE UNCONSCIOUS--- This is the collection of all ideas, experiences, and thoughts that have ever existed. It is like a giant data base of humanity on the transcendent level. The soul can use this resource to learn and grow. It is the material God uses to help us mature. We find it in our dreams, in thoughts that come from nowhere, in meditation, and in how we interpret life around us. The degree to which we allow this connection to become part of us is dependent on us. It can be fostered.

CONNECTION—This is one of the five core traits of the soul whose ends are Mystical and Temporal. These connections are at the root of all relationships. How we relate to one another and to God and the Collaborative Unconscious impacts all things. We are created to be social beings, making connections for our survival and well-being. We can choose to be disconnected, but in so doing we disconnect from the very things we are given to mature.

EGO--- The Ego acts according to the reality principle; i.e. it seeks to please the id's drive in realistic ways that will benefit in the long term rather than bringing grief. "The ego is not sharply separated from the id; its lower portion merges into it.... But the repressed merges into the id as well, and is merely a part of it. The repressed is only cut off sharply from the ego by the resistances of repression; it can communicate with the ego through the id." (Sigmund Freud, 1923)

The Ego comprises that organized part of the personality structure that includes defensive, perceptual, intellectual-cognitive, and executive functions. Conscious awareness resides in the ego, although not all of the operations of the ego are conscious. The ego separates what is real. It helps us to organize our thoughts and make sense of them and the world around us.

According to Freud, "..The ego is that part of the id which has been modified by the direct influence of the external world ... The ego represents what may be called reason and common sense, in contrast to the id, which contains the passions ... in its relation to the id it is like a man on horseback, who has to hold in check the superior strength of the horse; with this difference, that the rider tries to do so with his own strength, while the ego uses borrowed forces [Freud, *The Ego and the Id* (1923)] ."

In Freud's theory, the ego mediates among the id, the super-ego and the external world. Its task is to find a balance between primitive drives and reality (the Ego devoid of morality at this level) while satisfying the id and super-ego. Its main concern is with the individual's safety and allows some of the id's desires to be expressed, but only when consequences of these actions are marginal. Ego defense mechanisms are often used by the ego when id behavior conflicts with reality and either society's morals, norms, and taboos or the individual's expectations as a result of the internalization of these morals, norms, and their taboos.

HOLINESS---Holiness is one of the five core traits of the soul. Its ends are Sacred and Terrene. Holiness has to do with the formation of our self-identity as a spiritual being. To be holy is to understand the sacred nature of who we are, our uniqueness in the created order. In life we try to bring together our souls and our psyches. One should be a reflection of the other, working in unison. How we perceive ourselves as spiritual beings impacts how we view and exist in the world.

ID-- The Id comprises the unorganized part of the personality structure that contains the basic drives. The Id acts as according to the 'pleasure principle' and is responsible for our basic drives such as food, water, sex, and basic impulses. It is amoral and selfish, ruled by the pleasure–pain principle; it is without a sense of time, completely illogical, primarily sexual, infantile in its emotional development, and is not able to take "no" for an answer. It is regarded as the reservoir of the libido or "instinctive drive to create," seeking to avoid pain or unpleasure aroused by increases in instinctual tension. There is a constant tension between the Id and the Ego as well as the soul.

IDEALIST (D)—This is the transcendent end of the Call continuum. The other end is the Pragmatist. The idealist views the world through the eyes of the transcendent, seeing more of what can be than what is, more of the ideal than the real. This is on a spiritual level. At the extreme they may lose a sense of reality, but they can be spiritually ideal and in their lives, very real. The idealist sees their calling to spread the message of hope and to fill people's spiritual needs.

IMAGINATION—This is one of the five core traits of the soul. The two ends of the spectrum are Inspiration and Reason. Imagination looks at how we creatively look at the world. Do we bring into our imagination just what we receive from our senses and minds or do we attach to the creativity of the transcendent? All people are creative to varying degrees and in varying areas. This view of creativity and imagination is not fixed on the creative arts but on life itself as a creative endeavor. On the one hand we use our minds to produce something creative and on the other we lean on more intuitive methods. The Collaborative Unconscious plays a significant role with transcendent imagination.

IMMANENCE (I)—This is one of the ends of the Transcendence continuum. It finds meaning in and through the world. This type uses the language of the world comfortably to explain things. They look for how God is found in the world. The humanness of Jesus is very important to them for this is the epitome of God in the world.

INSPIRATION (N)—This is the transcendent end of the Imagination continuum. One of the key aspects of this is intuition. Their creativity comes from within. By attaching to the Collaborative Unconscious, this type funnels the creative energy of all that has existed as well as that of God.
Their creativity comes more from finding ways of being creative that attract people to the more transcendent dimension than to specifically just fulfilling a task or achieving a goal which is the more Reasoned approach.

MYSTICAL (M)—Mystical refers to those things more wrapped in mystery than in rational understanding. In this book it refers mostly to one end of the Connections continuum—the more transcendent end. Because our relationships with God and the Collaborative Unconscious can't be fully understood it has an air of mystery, one which this type readily accepts.

PERSONA-- A persona, is a social role or a character played by an actor. This is an Italian word that derives from the Latin for "mask" or "character", derived from the Etruscan word "phersu", with the same meaning. Popular etymology derives the word from Latin "per" meaning "through" and "sonare" meaning "to sound", meaning something in the vein of "that through which the actor speaks", i.e. a mask (early Greek actors wore masks). For this book it is that mask we wear in our day to day lives that changes with context.

PRAGMATIST (P)—This is one end of the Call continuum. The pragmatist is practical in nature. They believe that actions speak louder than words and that we were put on this planet for a reason; to care for one another. The commandment to love as we are loved is to be lived out fully in this life. Their call from God is to change the world, one step at a time, one loving act at a time. Their faith is that God is in the midst of the work.

PSYCHE-- While we would cease to exist were it not for the brain and bodily functioning, our psyches are what makes us tick. There is no place in the brain where the psyche lives, it is embedded in all the brain. We know that certain parts deal with more cognitive functions and others with more emotional. Our psyches have conscious, subconscious, and unconscious parts. Our psyches provide context, a neural network, and the ability to connect the dots. We view the psyche as that part of our nature that is at the core of our personality on an immanent level. It is who we are in the world.

Just as the soul has its traits or parts, so too the psyche. We have egos, shadows, personas, and a variety of archetypal formularies that create the person we are. There have been many books written about each of these and you can find some suggestions on the website. Freud sees the psyche as composed of the Id, Super-ego, and ego.

REASON (R)—This is one end of the Imagination continuum. This type relies on the world and God in the world for its creativity. They are very sense oriented and mentally prone. They like their creativity to make sense and to fit into an overall pattern of how they view the world. For them, the brain is the greatest creative tool on the planet.

SACRED (A)—This is one end of the Holiness continuum. As this type looks at who they think they are, they are attached to the transcendent and see them self primarily as spiritual beings on a way stop on earth. They accept their sacredness and struggle at times with their worldliness. Their identities are found in the spiritual world even though it is often hard to describe.

SHADOW-- In Jungian psychology, the shadow or "shadow aspect" is a part of the unconscious mind consisting of repressed weaknesses, shortcomings, and instincts. It is one of the three most recognizable archetypes, the others being the anima and animus and the persona. "Everyone carries a shadow," Jung wrote, "and the less it is embodied in the individual's conscious life, the blacker and denser it is." It may be (in part) one's link to more primitive animal instincts, which are superseded during early childhood by the conscious mind.

According to Jung, the shadow, in being instinctive and irrational, is prone to project: turning a personal inferiority into a perceived moral deficiency in someone else. Jung writes that if these projections are unrecognized "The projection-making factor (the Shadow archetype) then has a free hand and can realize its object--if it has one-- or bring about some other situation characteristic of its power." These projections insulate and cripple individuals by forming an ever thicker fog of illusion between the ego and the real world.

Jung also believed that "in spite of its function as a reservoir for human darkness—or perhaps because of this—the shadow is the seat of creativity."

SOUL—Our souls are the eternal aspect of our nature. It is that part of our being that is in the end transcendent. The soul starts like our brains with little, but can mature to perfection in this life or the next. We do not presume to lay claim to when souls are created or arrive in our bodies. For this book it's simply important to know that while we are alive there are things we can do to help our souls mature. The soul is a distinct and spiritual entity that crosses the boundary to the transcendent world that the brain can't.

SUBCONSCIOUS—For this book, the subconscious is that level of consciousness which is aware of but not focusing on something. Breathing, walking, the complexity of the world about us and even emotions can be in this arena. They are not conscious because we are not paying direct and explicit attention to them. They are not unconscious because we can become fully aware of them at any time we choose to focus on them.

SUPEREGO-- The Super-ego aims for perfection. It comprises that organized part of the personality structure, mainly but not entirely unconscious, that includes the individual's ego ideals, spiritual goals, and the psychic agency (commonly called 'conscience') that criticizes and prohibits his or her drives, fantasies, feelings, and actions.

" The Super-ego can be thought of as a type of conscience that punishes misbehavior with feelings of guilt. For example: having extra-marital affairs. "

The Super-ego works in contradiction to the Id. The Super-ego strives to act in a socially appropriate manner, whereas the id just wants instant self-gratification. The Super-ego controls our sense of right and wrong and guilt. It helps us fit into society by getting us to act in socially acceptable ways.

SUPERNAL (S)—This is one end of the Transcendence continuum. As we seek meaning in the world there are a variety of places from which we glean meaning. This type finds meaning from the transcendent domain. While we are living in the world, there is an undertone of spirituality infusing all things. It is the story behind the story. It is asking deeper questions about what something means and more often than not is not obvious.

TEMPORAL U (E)—This is one end of the Connections continuum. This end finds its relationships in and through the world. It views God's actions as being in and for the world more than being overtly and explicitly spiritual. Their relationships that they view as spiritual tend to be viewed through more worldly and practical terms. Not only are the relationships themselves temporal as opposed to eternal, but relationships come and go. There is a tendency to have less attachment to them.

TERRENE (T)---This is one end of the Holiness continuum. People at this end find their identity in the world. For them, holiness is about being part of the created order that they can sense. They were put here for a reason and part of that is to be a good steward of what God has given them. They are well grounded in the world even as they may attempt to transform it. But this transformation is again in more worldly rather than spiritual terms.

TRANSCENDENCE—This is one of the five core traits and focuses on how the person finds meaning in their lives. The ends of the spectrum are Supernal and Immanent. The soul is a transcendent entity, that part of our nature that attaches to the spiritual. The transcendent endows all things with spiritual meaning, but not all can see or find that meaning. Transcendent meaning is that which is beyond the world, at times without language. As with all continua we seek balance. Because we are in the world, we need to understand the world on its terms as well as on the terms of God.

Made in the USA
Columbia, SC
25 September 2017